D1450391

INSIDE AND OUT

INSIDE AND OUT

Hostage to Iran, Hostage to Myself

by
RICHARD QUEEN

with
Patricia Hass

G. P. Putnam's Sons
New York

Library of Congress Cataloging in Publication Data

Queen, Richard, date.
  Inside and out.

    1. Iran Hostage Crisis, 1979–1981—Personal
narratives. 2. Queen, Richard. I. Hass,
Patricia Cecil. II. Title.
E183.8'I55Q43   1981   955'.054   81-12134
ISBN 0-399-12645-7   AACR2

Printed in the United States of America

For the eight servicemen who died in the aborted rescue attempt:

Air Force Captain Richard Bakke

Marine Sergeant John Davis Harvey

Marine Corporal George N. Holms, Jr.

Marine Staff Sergeant Dewey L. Johnson

Air Force Technical Sergeant Joel C. Mayo

Air Force Captain Lynn D. McIntosh

Air Force Captain Charles T. McMillan III

Air Force Captain Hal Lewis

ACKNOWLEDGMENTS

I would like to thank Patricia Harrison, Jeanne Jagelski, Linda Krinn, and Barbara Vogt for their help in the preparation of this manuscript. I want to thank Ellis Amburn, my editor at Putnam's, for his special insights, and Gypsy da Silva for her talented copyediting. For her sage counsel and support my gratitude to my literary agent, Lorna Brown, is immense. And finally I welcome this opportunity for a special thank you to the Executive Director, Bureau of Near East and South Asian Affairs, Sheldon Krys, for his enormous contribution to my safe return from Iran and reintegration with American life, and for his continuing help, support and friendship.

INSIDE AND OUT

Chapter 1

I entered the 138th class of the United States Foreign Service on October 10, 1978, in Washington. Twenty-six people started with me, and I think we were all enthusiastic about representing our country in other parts of the world. Even when, in the second or third week of our training course, we got a pretty dismal list of posts to choose from, our excitement level stayed high.

First-year officers usually don't get the best selection. The Assignments Office offered a few small African posts, but none in Europe or Asia, except for Bombay. All the rest were in the Middle East and Central America. My first choice was Beirut, Lebanon, and my second was Isfahan, a beautiful Iranian city about 200 miles south of Teheran. I got Isfahan.

After the five-week introductory course, I took a two-week area studies course on the Middle East—basic information about the culture and history of the entire region, from Pakistan to Morocco. After that, I tackled Farsi, the Iranian language. Farsi is one of the languages (along with others such as Arabic, Russian and Japanese) that the State Department rates as "hard" for Americans to learn. I can't say that I enjoyed the six-hour-a-day, twenty-four-week course, but I gave it my best.

"If you think this is tough," said the instructor, "just be glad you're not trying to learn Arabic."

With that comforting advice in my head, I took the exam and passed it. That night when I looked in the mirror, I was looking at Richard Queen, vice-consul assigned to Iran.

The next day I began a five-week consul training course. This covered everything from what services the American embassy provides to Americans overseas, from recommending legal help if they're in trouble, to visiting them in jail (if the legal help was ineffective), to handling nonimmigrant and immigrant visas.

I was to be assigned to nonimmigrant visas. This meant that in a ten-minute interview, conducted in Farsi, I would have to determine if the person applying intended to return to Iran—as he or she was bound to do under the nonimmigrant visa terms—or disappear in the United States and never come back. Although I learned the various rules and regulations regarding visas very quickly, there was no way a course could prepare me for the bizarre visa chaos I would encounter in Iran.

In February 1979, while I was still training in Washington, revolutionaries stormed the American embassy in Teheran, the Iranian capital, and I thought my assignment might be canceled. Instead, the State Department closed its consulate in Isfahan and told me I would go to Teheran. I was more disappointed than worried; I had thought a smaller post like Isfahan would be exciting—closer to the real countryside. Teheran would be a big city with a huge embassy. Even so, Teheran was already called a separation post. This meant that officers assigned to Teheran would have to leave their spouses and families behind. In fact, people returning from the embassy after the February seizure reported a situation ranging from bad to worse.

Because the Foreign Service badly needed people to go to Teheran as vice-consuls, they allowed Cora Lijek, Mark Lijek's wife, and Kathy Stafford, Joe Stafford's wife, to accompany Mark and Joe. It was agreed that they would work in the consulate, which meant that they were required to take all of the rigorous consulate training and the Farsi course as well. Since I wasn't married, the family ban did not affect me. I was told I could bring in 80 kilos (176 pounds) of baggage and no car.

Some of my excitement faded, reviving only when I took my last course—a one-day seminar on dealing with terrorism. I took it with the three other people from my Foreign Service class also assigned to Teheran: Mark Lijek, Joe Stafford and Don Cooke. Sitting in the comfortable, secure confines of a building in Arlington, Virginia, we watched a film called "Hostage Survival"—what to do if you became a hostage. I did not think I would ever have to use the information; after all, I was a brand-new, low-ranking foreign service officer, not James Bond. In spite of the fact that I was not a likely target, I watched and paid attention.

The basic message was: If captured try to get your captors to recognize you as an individual, not just a faceless number. Do not pretend to agree with your captors'

13

views—they will see through this. Don't panic. Maintain a regimen of exercise for body and mind. Do not compromise yourself or your country. Maintain your dignity and honor. The film ended on a quasi-positive note: Remember, although death is a possibility, the longer you're held hostage, the greater your chances of not being killed and eventually being released.

I clearly remember thinking as I watched that something like that would never happen to me.

I spent the Fourth of July in New York State with my parents and took a tour of the Immigration and Naturalization Service office to familiarize myself with its operations. Then I flew to London for five days of vacation, taking in museums, visiting friends and touring the city. I boarded the plane to Teheran and silently said goodbye to London. I didn't know at the time that I was also saying goodbye to my calm, orderly, civilized world. A world I wasn't going to return to for a long time.

I landed at Teheran's Mehrabad Airport. It was the evening of July 11, 1979.

Steve Lauterbach, the administrative officer who had been in the class ahead of mine, met me. Steve, quiet, slight of build, in his late twenties, greeted me with a big smile and a handshake. "You've got an experience ahead of you," he said, laughing. "It's called Iranian traffic."

I got into the car and immediately we shot into a rush of cars careering in all directions. A cacophony of honking horns and screeching tires filled the air. I watched as one car blocked by several others executed a U-turn onto the sidewalk, made a sharp right and disappeared around a corner.

Steve smiled and shrugged. "You'll get used to it."

We whizzed by row after row of partially finished office and apartment buildings begun under the Shah and abandoned by the new regime. Huge machinery and building cranes sat unused and rusting. Later I would learn that the rusting crane was commonly referred to by my colleagues as the national bird of Iran.

The embassy driver turned the car sharply, thereby avoiding a possible five-car collision, as Steve continued to interpret what I was seeing. "Did you notice the building two blocks back with the roof caved in? It's been that way for months. Nothing ever gets fixed around here."

We were on our way to visit one of my Iranian Farsi instructors from Washington. Her niece was getting married, and we were invited to the reception. When Steve and I pulled up in front of the building in which the reception was being held, she ran out and greeted us warmly. Although I was really tired and feeling the effects of jet lag, I joined in the party with as much enthusiasm as I could muster. After several plates of rice and lamb, washed down by a couple of Cokes, I felt much better. I would get used to the Islamic ban on alcoholic beverages at Iranian functions. Looking around at the friendly, smiling faces, I thought maybe Teheran was not going to be such a hardship post after all.

Eventually I landed at my new apartment. It seemed luxurious after the cramped university rooms I had known. It had two bedrooms and was nicely furnished. Only Americans who worked at the embassy lived in the building. I really didn't need a car to get to work as the embassy compound was only two blocks away.

The next morning at the embassy, I met Cy Richardson,

acting officer in charge of the consulate, the other Americans at the consulate, and the fifteen or twenty local employees.

The first day I recovered from jet lag and adjusted to the different food, which had given me a mild case of diarrhea. Generally, new personnel take it easy at first—I knew I would be there for a long time, and people advised me to take things slowly.

The embassy compound was nicknamed Fort Apache. On February 14, a mob had stormed the embassy and held close to 100 Americans hostage. The Iranian government intervened, and the hostages were quickly released. When I arrived, the embassy was still "protected" by a group of assorted riffraff from the streets, a ragamuffin revolutionary guard unit headed by a corrupt bully named Mashala. Attempts to get rid of the "guards," who spent most of their time sleeping or horsing around, had failed. In fact, as members of the revolutionary guard, they constituted a separate army that constantly challenged or ignored the police and the regular army as well as other revolutionary guard units. In their Iranian camouflage fatigues, they looked very scruffy patrolling the compound, led by a man who wheeled and dealed in alcohol and "favors," keeping the embassy "protected." It was a study in organized chaos, but it was what we had to live with.

It was next to impossible for the dozen or so U.S. marines assigned to embassy duty in Teheran to watch the whole compound, which covered 27 acres. They guarded the most important buildings, staying inside them when on duty.

By the time I arrived at the embassy, Mashala's men were "on duty" at the main gate, which they occupied.

They rarely wandered through the rest of the compound.

For security reasons, we were advised not to wander around the city late at night if it could be avoided and to stay away from the poor sections of Teheran, where the sight of an American face could cause an unpleasant incident. If we wanted to visit the Iranian countryside, we were to inform the embassy beforehand.

The first thing I noticed in Teheran—quickly got used to—was the sight of people wearing military fatigues everywhere and occasionally carrying weapons. The standard weapon was a G-3, a semiautomatic West German rifle. There were shots almost every night, most of them, I'm sure, accidental. Once I heard the sound of submachine gun fire at night, which was a little unnerving, especially since very few of the revolutionary guards doing the firing knew anything about weapons. They always seemed surprised at the cause and effect of a finger squeezing the trigger of a loaded gun. Was this what the Old West was like? I wondered. It's nothing, people would say, you should have heard it a few months ago. Soon the occasional sound of rifle shots became part of the normal city sounds for me.

In any case, going out at night in a car could be risky. Revolutionary guards, who hid in ditches along the roadside to avoid being shot at by Leftist groups, frequently set up roadblocks at night. As your car passed, the guards would either shout "stop" in Farsi or, if they felt like it, just open fire. It wasn't wise to drive around too much anyway, because to drive in Teheran was to feel yourself in bedlam.

Part of the reason for the craziness of Iranian traffic was that the police had no power to enforce any regulations. In

other words, it was virtually legal for Iranians to ignore red
lights and stop signs, to drive in the wrong lane without a
second thought. The primary form of public transportation
was a taxi-bus, a car that picked people up at designated
spots.

Teheran had grown explosively in the past decade—it
literally shot out in all directions. Tadjrish, in the north,
was the rich area, and it was the coolest part of the city.
The Elburz Mountains, up whose flanks the Tadjrish area
had spread, were snowcapped from fall to late spring. The
drop in altitude as you went from north to south was
remarkable—sometimes it would snow in northern Teheran
when it was only raining in the center of the city.

The houses in the north I thought of as Iranian baroque.
Here were the gaudy homes of the nouveaux riches. One I
visited startled me so much my hostess asked me as I
walked in the door if something was wrong.

"Heat," I mumbled, inanely. "It's hot out there and cool
in here."

She nodded at this astute analysis of the weather and led
me farther inside. All of the walls, including the entrance
area, were papered in a violent purple taffeta made in Yazd.
Gold lamé draperies hung fat and full from each window.
The couch, which sat on a bright, multicolored lavender
shag rug, was covered in the same satin wall stuff but shot
with gold threads. I thought of the people in the south of
the city crowded in slum conditions—the revolutionary
guards and their guns, the Iranians clamoring to leave the
country—and I wondered what the lifespan of those gold
lamé draperies was going to be.

The embassy compound, built just after World War II,
originally stood in the suburbs. Now it was located in the

center of town . . . a town that lacked a twentieth-century sewage system. Drainage ditches, called *jubes,* ran along the sides of the streets, and when it rained, incredible filth floated down—dead animals and garbage. Often the *jubes* overflowed and the stink was horrendous. The real nightmare, however, was the number of people who had only the *jubes* as a source of water—to drink, to cook with, and to wash in.

When I arrived in Teheran, the consulate was located in an old, run-down building within the embassy compound. The previous consulate building, several blocks away, had been closed after the storming of the embassy in February 1979. Dick Morefield, who had served in Caracas, was the troubleshooter assigned as consul general at that time. Morefield was a quiet, unassuming man who managed to accomplish things efficiently and effectively without a lot of horn blowing.

The head of the consulate would not ordinarily socialize with staff after hours. But conditions at Fort Apache made the stiff, formal approach to embassy life impossible. Because of this atmosphere there were not rigid distinctions between ranks, and we often met at Dick Morefield's apartment for an evening of beer and conversation. Morefield frequently spent his free time quilting. He was very accessible, and his calm approach provided the right touch in this crazy city. Later he was moved into a house. I don't think he wanted to leave our apartment building, but for a consul general, a house was certainly more fitting.

Morefield went to head the new Consular Section. It was moved to a new, larger building, the former Caravanserai, the compound restaurant. The restaurant was moved to another building.

Bruce Laingen, the new Chargé d'Affaires, or head of the embassy, arrived in August. The United States was not allowed to name an ambassador to Iran after William Sullivan left the post.

When I started work, consular operations were slow. They had closed down after the storming of the embassy in February and though reopened, were still kept to a minimum—only fifteen or twenty student-visa applicants were interviewed each day. There were still American services, and they were still processing some immigrant visas, although that was horribly backlogged.

I was to act as a nonimmigrant interviewing officer. Iranians would come in with I-20 forms, which were certificates saying they had been accepted by a school in the United States, mostly in Southern California and Texas. Often the Iranians wouldn't know anything about the schools, and some of the I-20s themselves seemed to us to be questionable.

Before I could issue a visa, I had to determine whether the applicant intended to return to Iran. Many Iranians who applied for nonimmigrant visas had no intention of coming back, and I had to decide during the interview who was lying and who was telling the truth. I would listen to the applicant, look at his grades and various other documents, and try to guess what the person intended to do in the United States.

I'd hear incredible stories told with absolutely straight faces, occasionally accompanied by tears. In the beginning it was difficult to take. When you turned down the applicant, the results would periodically be curses and threats directed at you, your family, your country. Occasionally, when that failed to change anything, the applicant would subtly try to make a deal, which involved a bribe. There were enough hints that if I were to give the right hint in return, a bribe would be offered. Eventually, I became accustomed to the whole process, but I never liked being subjected to their advances.

The application form, written in English, asked basic questions—why the applicant wanted to go to the United States, his (her) age, and so forth. After more normal consular operations resumed in September, a thriving shady business went on outside the compound. For a fee, someone would provide information on which vice-consuls were tough and which were lenient. For five hundred rials (about five dollars) the prospective applicant was told whether to go to the third or fifth window from the left. When Dick Morefield got wise to the scheme, he had us move to different windows after lunch. The tipsters escalated their efforts, naming specific vice-consuls to avoid.

Student visas were popular because it was difficult to get into the very few Iranian universities. There weren't places for all the people who wanted to attend. A degree was their ticket to a good life. I really found interviewing these students awful. One of the first I talked to was a stunning girl, but there was no way I could let her through. Her grades were grim, she couldn't speak English, and her connections with Iran were very weak (this was an important criterion—weak ties meant the person very possibly would not return). I wavered because she cried. The consular training had not told me about this part. An Iranian employee watched me intently to see if I would give in. "I'm sorry," I said. "Improve your English and come back. I'll review the case." She left crying.

Once a man I turned down muttered he was going to kill me when I stepped outside. One of the Iranian guards at the embassy overheard this and told me. A friend of the applicant let him know that I had been informed of the threat, and he ran back and apologized, afraid he had lost any future chance for a visa.

Women wore chadors, the long black, head-to-toe veils, demonstrating that they were true Moslems and therefore would return to Iran. They'd say "I'm Moslem, I have to return. I can't stay in the U.S." Even very wealthy women would dress in the traditional garb for the interview, their diamond and gold jewelry sometimes visible beneath the cloth. I know the Americans mystified the Iranians because we would not play the "baksheesh" game—a form of bribing that was part of Iranian life. It was also very upsetting to them not to be able to bargain. To have to make it or lose it on one interview was a very alien concept. I understand that people were willing to pay as much as $1,000 for a visa. I was also stopped on the street by strangers asking if I could help them get a visa. After a while it seemed to me that the whole country was conniving to go to the United States. I began to hesitate before telling anyone that I worked at the embassy; if they found out I was at the consulate, they'd redouble their efforts to get a visa from me.

I had promised my parents I'd try to write once a week and I set aside one evening each week to do it. I'd address a letter to my parents in upstate New York and photocopy it for Alex, my brother, who is an artist in Chicago.

August 27

Dear Mom, Dad and Alex:

Nothing truly extraordinary occurred this week, no bombings or shootings around the Embassy. The new Consulate building is supposed to open in two weeks, after Labor Day, but the date could be easily changed. I don't relish working in it. It will be a madhouse when we open up for full consular services. Currently the consular section is officially closed. We process only immigrant visas and handle about fifty student visas. Then there is of course American services. I work in the student visa section. When the new Consulate opens and we begin normal consular operations the number of applicants is expected to be well in the thousands!

The new building is a cross between a prison and a bank. And it has been specifically designed for Iran. There are no real windows facing the outside street where the Iranians will be lined up—if it is possible to line them up—but that is a problem for the local authorities. The walls are massive and the few small windows overlooking the street have massive bullet-proof glass. The Iranians will be let in individually—first through an electronically controlled steel door to an antechamber where they will be seated. Then a guard will open another electronic door allowing the applicant to enter another antechamber where they will be rechecked— before a Marine guard opens another electronically controlled steel door to the waiting room.

The consular officers will sit in little booths behind bullet-proof glass, just like in a bank, and when the applicant is called to a booth, will speak to the person through small microphones.

The interviews are planned to be very short, and then the officer must decide to accept or reject the applicant. If the applicant refuses to accept the verdict and leave, we each have a button to summon a guard to escort the person out a one-way revolving turnstile like they have in the subway. The whole process is designed to be as efficient and as mechanical as possible, but I fear what effects it will have on me and the rest of the interviewers. But it will eliminate all the haggling, which is so annoying and time-consuming.

The new setup could also cause some problems with our relations with Iran, especially since we will no longer be accepting anything like the number of applicants we used to accept before. Already the rejection rate for student visas has gone up dramatically since I have arrived and I might add I have certainly helped that process along. After about two to three weeks on the job, I began to lose my compassion for most of the rejected applicants' pleas—because so many of their pleas are just lies.

Very rarely will a rejected applicant just accept the verdict like a man and leave. They have to beg and plead. But I have become steeled to this. The new Consulate will of course make it very difficult if not impossible for a rejected applicant to do much. I hope the process will not dehumanize me too much. So far I have successfully separated the job from my after-job life but the old consulate where I work now is nothing compared to the new one. We each have our own little office and deal with the applicants individually across a desk.

Sometimes it becomes very difficult to get rid of a rejected applicant.

I am going to more little parties now—actually they are really casual gatherings rather than parties. Several times a week I get together with some girls from the Austrian Embassy and we play tennis, swim, etc., at the American Embassy. They in turn have invited me to their gatherings where I inevitably eat myself sick with excellent Austrian food. It is a tremendous boon to my morale to have become part of this group.

Love,
Richard

The visa business took an exciting turn when we found out about a visa fraud operation. An American citizen of Iranian descent came to get a visa for his thirteen-year-old nephew; the nephew was rejected. When the man, upset, left the consulate he was approached by an Iranian who offered to get the nephew "another chance for $1,000." The plan was to remove the rejected application from the files and return it to the uncle.

The guy came back to the compound and talked to me. Dick Morefield didn't believe it was possible—how could anyone get in the compound files? He told me to follow up on it anyway. I told the man to find out what he could. Two days later he returned with the actual rejected application in his possession. He said he paid the $1,000 and the head of the ring refused to give him the original application but offered him a photocopy instead.

"I grabbed the original from his hands and told him I had four armed friends in the car and if you cause me trouble I'll come after you."

He offered to give us the name of the employee stealing in exchange for his nephew's visa. We agreed and he told us how it worked: the Iranian employee was connected to a ring in Teheran, which would request that a certain name be pulled from the files. The employee would remove the rejected application, stuff it into his pocket and leave the embassy with it. This meant the applicant could apply again as if it were the first time.

Dick Morefield and I talked to Al Golacinski, the regional security officer, who took over the investigation at that time. The nephew got his visa, and we got rid of one enterprising employee.

The day before the new consulate was scheduled to open, it was hit with a rocket grenade. Although the consulate windows facing the street were bricked over, the Iranians had managed to fire the grenade through one of the very small side windows. The attacker also fired a concussion grenade into the compound before taking off. Later, several groups claimed responsibility for the attack.

I felt that this was just one more incident to add to the crazy quilt of "Life in Teheran." After all, the consulate was secure, windows bricked over on the street side, bars on the windows facing the compound side, electronically controlled doors. Rocket grenades, rifle fire, and writing on the compound walls and demonstrations galore all came with the territory. Now I had joined the ranks of those who shrugged and said, "You should have heard it two months ago—this is nothing."

This grenade-smashed window was quickly repaired by bricking it in. The consulate opened two weeks late, and the one condition for opening at all was official Iranian protection for the embassy compound. The Iranian Foreign Ministry, eager to have the consulate open, agreed, and soon, policemen in their blue uniforms guarded the compound. We should have been suspicious that so many Foreign Ministry people were getting visas. We used their eagerness to have us resume regular consular operations as a means of leverage for more embassy protection.

When I talked to the "police," I discovered many of them were revolutionary guards. They were very unhappy in their police uniforms, preferring instead their revolutionary guard attire. Most of all, they didn't like pretending to be police in order to please the Americans. I got to know several of them and was most appreciative that they did not ask me for visas. Instead, we talked about my family, where I lived in the United States, and what the U.S. was like. They told me about their villages or the cities. They didn't try to propagandize me. They knew I wasn't interested.

Since the revolution and the banning of alcohol, a black market dealing primarily in booze was in full swing. The considerable American supply was stored in a warehouse on the compound. I believe hundreds of black marketeers spent sleepless nights scheming about how they could get their hands on this supply and be rich for life.

One of the revolutionary guards introduced me to his friend, who I assumed was also a guard. He visited my

27

apartment and cast an appraising eye over my bar supply. Then he picked up several bottles and sniffed them. I offered him a Coke, though I did have about forty bottles of assorted alcohol—vodka, bourbon, gin. (The Iranian government allowed employees of the American embassy to keep their alcoholic beverages in their homes.)

"Good," he said, approvingly. "This is the best. How much?" I said it wasn't for sale. Then he left. The next day I saw him outside my building. He introduced me to a man dressed in a European suit, collar open, a silk scarf tied around his neck. He was leaning casually against a shiny new Mercedes.

"You have a fortune in alcohol in your apartment," he said, in a tone that suggested I had just won the Irish Sweepstakes. "If you could sell me alcohol from the compound, we both get very rich."

"No, that's impossible. It's illegal," I told him.

He shrugged and shook his head. Another crazy American to deal with. "You don't understand. We are not talking about legalities. We are talking about a lot of money. A Mercedes is not illegal. Do you have something against Mercedes?"

"Thanks anyway," I said and walked away. I must admit I did compute in my head what my forty bottles would bring on the black market—$2,000!

The city teemed with black marketeers, dubious transactions, people out to make a fast buck. Some did very well. I had little contact with the black market because I was an embassy employee and that was, obviously, against the regulations.

When the new consulate opened, we worked long, difficult hours. I arrived at 7:30, and we opened a half hour later. On the first day mobs of Iranians appeared and milled around outside. We had to close the consulate because of the confusion. When the Iranian police got the people into lines the next day, we reopened.

A marine would visually check the applicants through his glass, and press a buzzer which would open up an electronic door leading to the rooms where the interviews took place. It was tedious for the marines and tedious for us to interview the Iranians. The marines dealt with the monotony by checking the good-looking women applicants as they went through the lines—there were quite a few good-looking Iranian women who didn't wear chadors and who smiled. When a marine spotted a beautiful smile, or better yet, made friendly eye contact with a lovely Iranian girl, he jokingly notified us that we were to treat her well—one light note in otherwise grueling days. The lines for visas grew and grew and we couldn't keep up.

People were frantic to leave the country: Iranian businessmen who thrived under the Shah and now feared for their lives; students, their universities shut down, their education at a standstill and no jobs available in their country; minorities—Jews and Armenian Christians and Bahais who knew religious freedom was not going to be part of the new regime's platform; the Westernized Iranians who did not want to give up the twentieth century and return to the veils and ways of the fourteenth.

One Iranian newspaper speculated that a visa applicant could expect to come up for an interview a year and a half after filing his request. At first, people lined up—but eventually, they very effectively organized themselves into groups of fifty rather than waiting so long in line. Generally that system worked very well. To look at the throngs gathered day in and day out you'd think that some sort of permanent bazaar was going on. Vendors hawked fruit drinks and Pepsis; small groups crouched around portable barbecues cooking chunks of lightly spiced lamb; the air was perfumed with the smell of marjoram and rosemary. Others played backgammon or cards to wile away the time, some slept, oblivious to the carnival smells and sounds. Entrepreneurs offered to fill out visa forms for "only 500 rials," even though we had signs posted everywhere telling exactly how to do it; they also sold space in the line for those too elegant to wait it out.

We were swamped; it became a disheartening and hopeless task. I realized I would never see the end of the line—my only goal was surviving from 8:00 to 5:00.

After work, I fell into bed, needing a nap and shower to revive. I tried to write to my parents and brother Alex.

Sept. 29, 1979

Dear Mom, Dad and Alex:

The lines for visas are as hopelessly long as ever
and still growing. The last estimate is that there are
500 groups of fifty people each awaiting their turn.
We process about three groups a day. I know with
all the police inefficiency and probably corruption,
there are many freeloaders getting in who cut in the
line.

I have just finished the first four books of the
"Hornblower" series but the local bookstore doesn't
have book five so I am stuck. I also just finished
Gore Vidal's *1876,* a well written book and bitingly
sarcastic but I am tired of his constant mocking of
American values, history and heroes. I had to
struggle through the middle part of the book, not

because it was badly written but because I couldn't put up with his sarcasm of America.

The problem is, the more I stay here the more rabidly patriotic I become. It is difficult after listening to Iranians, especially the government and that reactionary fanatic Ayatollah attack the U.S., to become anything but a wild-eyed patriot.

The Ardelan building where I lived was close to the compound for safety. A modern apartment building, small by Western standards (only two apartments on each floor), it sat snug on Ardelan street and had seven stories. At the top was a penthouse apartment where an embassy administrative officer, Gary Lee, lived. Sometimes I ate dinner up there. Gary bought a little grill, and each of us prepared a dish. I was experimenting with my cooking and took this opportunity to try out new recipes on my always hungry fellow workers. One of my specialties was stuffed eggplant, with fresh vegetables bought from the Iran Super, a large supermarket with some Western food a few blocks away, or fresh produce bought from the small local vendors who lined every street.

We always had hamburgers or steaks. Don Cooke brought the beer. It was great fun, like a fraternity. We talked and listened to the shortwave radio or Gary's tape deck. We named our little group the Ardelan Key Klub— no rules, no dues, just good food, drinking and conversation. Members were Gary Lee, Don Cooke, Bruce German, Dick Morefield, Mark and Cora Lijek, Commander Don Sharer, plus whoever wanted to stop by.

I felt quite secure in my apartment at the Ardelan, in spite of warnings I'd had from Al Golacinski. But one evening when I answered the phone, expecting to hear what I was supposed to contribute to our group dinner, my "Hello" was met by a muffled voice.

"Khomeini. Khomeini. Khomeini."

Then the phone went dead. Twenty minutes later it rang again.

"Death to the Shah."

Silence.

The next evening when I answered the phone, there was just breathing from the other end. Was someone checking to see if I was home? I wasn't sure if I should be concerned or just annoyed.

The third night, "Khomeini. Khomeini. Khomeini." was back. That was it! This was getting to be more than a nuisance. I went upstairs to Don Sharer and borrowed his small air horn. That would certainly put an end to the crank calls. I placed the horn by the phone and waited, but the phone didn't ring again. For several evenings I waited with the air horn, but I didn't receive another strange call.

It was ill advised to date Iranian women; in fact it just was not safe to be seen with one. Once, one of the staff forgot to bring home medicine from the hospital after he had been sick. A nurse was assigned by the hospital to bring it to him at the compound. When she tried to come into the apartment complex, one of the revolutionary guards outside stopped her, shoving his gun in the male staffer's stomach when he came to fetch the medicine. A marine, Dave Walker, knocked the gun out of the guard's hand and escorted the nurse into the embassy compound, staying with her until it was safe for her to leave the area. I knew that kind of thing would happen if I dated Iranian women—or worse, they would ask for visas. So, women working at the other embassies became the center of my social life.

Karen, a woman with shiny dark hair and a warm smile, was on the Austrian embassy staff and was the kind of girl I liked to date. She was cheerful, intelligent and fun to be with. I sure wouldn't want to go out with someone who chewed gum and watched the soaps all day, but I try to avoid, as well, a bossy, overbearing female. Karen invited me to small parties at her place several times. She was also an excellent cook—a bonus.

Karen liked to have parties and dinners at her house in northern Teheran, and I went out there, at least for a while. On weekends we played tennis in the embassy compound. She was fun to be with but honestly a terrible tennis player. After her third ball went sailing high over the tennis court fence, I suggested as diplomatically as possible that lessons might be a good idea.

"Why, yes, Richard," she laughed. "On one condition—you let me teach you the waltz. My feet on the dance floor are in as much danger as your head on the tennis court."

She also asked me to teach her to drive in exchange for skiing lessons. I couldn't believe I agreed, considering the traffic situation in Teheran.

"No problem," she said. "You can close your eyes while I'm driving."

One night when Mark Lijek and I were returning from a party at her house, three revolutionary guards stopped us at a roadblock. This happened fairly often in the evenings.

An Iranian who spoke English interrogated us. He was not the typical, scruffy revolutionary guard; he seemed like a leader of the Khomite (a committee made up of revolutionary guards; there were many Khomites, all vying with one another). He wore a well-pressed Iranian Army uniform and spit-shined boots, and, unlike the other guards, who didn't wear hats, a helmet.

"What are you doing here?" he asked. We showed him our embassy IDs. He was strangely familiar with our routine, where we lived on Ardelan Street, what the compound was like.

"Get back in the car and follow me," he said, taking off ahead of us. We were led up a side street to Khomite headquarters. Mark parked too close to a jube, and as we got out of the car I miscalculated and stepped into the drainage ditch.

"You have been drinking," he said to me, "and disobeying the laws of the Islamic Republic." I didn't feel it worthwhile to say I had only had two beers and was hardly drunk.

He took us inside as though we were a prize and, as he started questioning us, twenty or thirty well-armed guards gathered around. He lectured us for twenty minutes about our corrupt ways and continued his questions. Another guard started talking to me in poor English, telling me he had traveled for two months in the United States where people called him "raghead" and "camel jockey." I told him those were names generally applied to Arabs, not Persians—then he became doubly insulted that he had been mistaken for an Arab. I decided to get off the subject while I could.

Then things took a curious turn. Our original interrogator asked us what we did in the embassy. When Mark said he worked in the consulate, the whole tone of the questions changed. The interrogator said he was interested in touring America.

"Maybe you can get visas for me and my family? I will give you my name and address and will call you soon," he said, scribbling the information on a piece of paper.

We left quickly and I wondered how many Iranians shared his loyalty to the new regime. After that I was more careful about driving at night, but when one of the defense attaché sergeants gave a party inviting people from our embassy, other embassies and a few Iranian women, we went.

Like many of the men in the embassy marine detachment, he lived in an apartment building across the street from the Ardelan. The party wasn't noisy, although some people had been drinking. Suddenly, there was a commotion. The door swung open and a revolutionary guard armed with a .45-caliber pistol walked in. A couple of his men, armed with submachine guns, waited outside. We all got very, very quiet. In belligerent Farsi, he asked where the Iranian women were. The few that were at the party were hiding in the bedrooms, but he grabbed one young woman and pushed her toward the door.

"I am not Iranian," she yelled, in excellent English.

Two of the marines and one RCMP from the Canadian embassy began to move toward him menacingly; a few Farsi-speaking guests tried to calm him down. After a few tense moments, he backed down and went outside. Helene, who worked at the Norwegian embassy and spoke excellent Farsi, followed him into the hallway explaining in Farsi: "There are no Iranians here; we are all foreigners. There is nothing wrong." She was talking to the revolutionary guard when Mashala appeared and ordered the revolutionary guard to leave.

Mashala was a notorious, roly-poly, unkempt character whose intervention at the party demonstrated again the chaos of Khomeini's Teheran. When the American embassy had been overrun in February 1979, groups of Iranians responsible for the attack were forced to leave. Three groups lingered, one led by Mashala, who was rumored to have been Khomeini's jailer when he was imprisoned under the Shah. He supposedly had a letter from Khomeini which, in Teheran, gave him license to do almost anything. He was heavily involved in the black market and definitely a force to be reckoned with.

When I arrived in Teheran, Mashala's was the only group of attackers left. He and his brothers and several followers had run the others off. It was degrading to see this greasy, gross character around the compound, followed everywhere by his armed goons, especially when we heard that the radical elements thought he was in the employ of the United States. We couldn't get rid of him, but he provided a measure of protection in lawless Teheran. Once, before I came, Mashala's men climbed the compound walls during a major demonstration and stopped demonstrators from coming inside the compound.

We also heard that Mashala had stolen all the vodka—the most popular drink in Iran—from the embassy liquor store and sold it at an enormous profit.

Mashala also promised Iranians visas, took their passports, and brought them to the consulate; he became extremely upset when the consular officers refused to stamp visas on the passports. He stood with his submachine gun in the consulate, impressing everyone. Mashala had women, eager to leave the country, climbing all over him when he told them he would mention their names to his "friends" in the embassy. He got no results, but he still got his "favors." Some months later we were told that he was executed.

After the intruders withdrew, Mashala apologized in Farsi for the inconvenience, but the party broke up shortly thereafter.

That was my first and virtually my last large party. Bruce Laingen forbade any big get-togethers outside the compound walls. Parties were already very few and far between, so this directive did not come as a great blow. Fortunately I prefer small, informal gatherings, which continued at the Ardelan Key Klub.

I also am an avid reader. There was a large and well-stocked English-language bookstore about three blocks from the embassy, right next to the Iran Super. I bought piles of paperback books including Dashiell Hammett's works, the Dune trilogy, the Hornblower series, and a couple of Thomas Hardy novels, along with my hardcover history books.

Occasionally I'd eat with friends at one of Teheran's restaurants, some of which kept beer hidden for their Western customers. But now, almost always, I cooked with the people in my building. The diplomatic community was finding itself in very hostile territory and we stuck together.

My weekends were quiet. I don't like hot weather, and Teheran in the summer is as hot and dry as Salt Lake City. I did take a one-day trip with some colleagues to a resort in the Elburz Mountains, where we went hiking, but that was the only time I got out of the city. It stayed hot in Teheran from late spring until the end of fall. There was no rain.

Since it was summer, for exercise I preferred swimming to walking. There were three pools in the embassy compound; the two smaller ones were filled. We swam in the afternoon, or played tennis in the evening.

The highlight of the weekend for me, an avid softball player, was the softball game. Later, as the weather got cooler, I'd wander outside near the compound and shop at some of the stores. Before I left for Teheran, my father had given me a book about Persian rugs—a subtle hint about what he wanted me to bring him. I looked at Persian rugs and bought some books about them. Finally, I decided to try my luck at the rug-merchant shops congregated on Ferdosi Street, six blocks away from the embassy. I wanted a rug for my parents for Christmas and maybe a couple for myself. I noticed a lovely pale blue one that was priced at $1,000.

"You can have it for $500," said the merchant, "if you throw in a bottle of scotch."

The rug was beautiful, but I decided it was too much trouble to negotiate with the dealer, who had his heart set on that bottle of scotch. Instead, I bought a large tablecloth and some enameled, paillette-covered boxes at the government-run handicraft store next to the compound. I must have disappointed the merchant because when he told me the price of the tablecloth, I paid what he asked and didn't bargain. The price seemed fair and haggling over a few dollars was the last thing I wanted to do.

The bazaar was a very important part of the Iranian economy, but because it was located near the poorer section of the city—where the hard-core Khomeini supporters plotted and schemed—I visited it only once. A lot of wheeling and dealing went on from sunup to sunset. You could buy a bird in a cage—"Very good, will sing anything you want"—as well as rugs, silver, jewelry, food and even, I'm sure, guns and ammunition. The bargainers at the bazaar understood the ritual of bargaining and raised it to a fine art. Bargaining, with all the orchestrated feints and ploys, was an art I never really mastered.

On Fridays, the marines showed movies in the basement of the compound warehouse, called the Mushroom Inn. It was a perfect place for movies (and a perfect place to grow mushrooms), windowless and dark. On Saturdays we saw movies in the ambassador's residence where the chargé lived. Other nights I'd return to the Ardelan, get a cold beer and settle in for a solitaire game of "War Between the States." This was a complicated war game that took hours, even days to play, with a rule book that took almost as long to read. I was a confirmed war gamer—although it was sometimes a problem getting anyone else to play. Mark Lijek was the only other person in the building who played.

The atmosphere in the compound was informal and I enjoyed the camaraderie, but it was difficult to get to know embassy employees because of the constant turnover. Men came without their wives and families for temporary duty of forty-five to ninety days. I was one of the few permanent staffers assigned to Teheran for a year and a half. My small group of friends included Don Cooke, a geology major of about twenty-five who constantly wore blue jeans (we called him the "rock jock"); Mark Lijek and Joe Stafford and their wives; Dick Morefield; Joe Hall, an army warrant officer; and Gary Lee, the easygoing organizer of the Ardelan Key Klub.

Early one Sunday morning (Sunday in Iran is a work day;

Friday and Saturday are holidays) I woke up to hear Don Cooke banging on my door.

"Hey, Queen, don't bother getting up. The marines don't want us showing up on the compound today. One of the Central Khomites is trying to arrest Mashala again. There's some shooting going on and they don't want us walking into the cross fire."

Since I didn't particularly want to walk into the cross fire either, I turned over and went back to sleep. Later I found out that Mashala had been captured, beaten and shoved onto a bus. We never saw him again. Eventually, he was released from prison and vowed to blow up the compound.

One day, about a month later, we were all called in for a security briefing. Al Golacinski, the regional security officer, said tersely, "We've just been notified that the Shah is definitely going to the U.S. We are expecting trouble."

Trouble, we were told, could mean anything from a replay of the February 14 incident, when the embassy was overrun, to mobs of Iranians demonstrating outside the compound.

"Don't go to the bazaar; stay near the compound. Stay away from the poor sections. Lie low," said Golacinski.

Walkie-talkies were distributed so we could keep in touch with the marine guard on duty in the compound. If something happened, he'd know about it first. We couldn't take the walkie-talkies in the streets though. Mine was the old-fashioned kind, so huge that if the Iranians saw me with it they'd say, "This guy must be a spy; look at what he's carrying."

If something happened, we were to rendezvous at the British embassy, a few blocks away. As an extra precaution, the marines prepared to spend the weekend of October 26 in the chancery, fully armed. The compound remained quiet, and we went back to work the next Sunday hoping it would stay that way.

Sunday morning, on the way to the compound from the Ardelan apartments I met one of the embassy employees who lived in the apartment building across the street. As we walked we discussed the chaotic situation in Teheran and the deep hostility the Iranians felt toward Americans.

"You should have been here last Valentine's day," he laughed. "Old Fort Apache was really bombarded on that day; about two weeks after Khomeini returned from exile and took over the country. We started to hear some shooting—it sounded like it was coming from a block or two away from the compound. At first, it wasn't much and we figured the Iranians are at it again—celebrating the Ayatollah's return—the true Imam restored. Then it gets louder and we hear the chanting: 'Death to the Shah,' 'Death to the Carter,' 'U S leave Iran,' followed by submachine gun fire. I look out the window and see hundreds of Iranians in camouflage suits crashing through the compound gate. They're screaming and firing their guns all over the place; especially at the chancery.

"They looked crazed—that same unnerving look Khomeini has—dark, piercing, demonic almost. We knew they were out for blood but our hands were tied. Our orders were 'no shooting, tear gas only.' We waited for the police to come and break this thing up—it was getting very ugly—but no one came. Calls were going back and forth from the embassy to the government that we were under siege and to get men down here immediately. In the meantime the staff started destroying the coding machines and burning documents.

41

"Still no police.

"We were overrun in minutes. They came screaming through the doors yelling and waving their guns, shooting them in the air. The Iranian employees tried to leave, they were terrified. But the guerrillas stopped them—pushed them against the wall and told them, and us, that if we moved they'd blow our heads off.

"Still no police.

"By now they were herding us into a room, pushing and shoving, jabbing the guns in our backs. 'Move and you die,' they said, over and over. They looked eager to shoot us. It was an incredible scene, Americans herded like animals into a room in their own embassy. Suddenly, outside there's more shooting. The group holding us starts talking in Farsi, very excitedly. They look worried.

"The police have finally arrived and are shooting it out with the guerrillas. The shooting subsides and the police storm into the embassy. They spend the next hour trying to convince the group holding us hostage to release us.

"'No!' the leader shouts, his body shaking he's so angry. He does not lower his gun but keeps it aimed at the ambassador. The police finally get through to him. The magic word is 'Khomeini' and his name is mentioned several times. The guerrilla lowers his gun and storms out with the police and the rest of his men. Turns out they were Marxist guerrillas—members of the Fedayeen—an underground group to the left of almost everybody."

In the February 14 takeover, one local employee was killed and one marine was badly wounded. And in fact, it was not the police but the Central Khomite that rescued the Americans at the embassy from the guerrillas.

"After that happened," the guy continued, "everyone,

staffers, families, wives left Teheran by the planeload. We were reduced to thirty-five people, but now that you guys are here, we're up to seventy."

"What are the chances of that happening again?" I asked.

"No way. Khomeini controls everything here, and he's not about to take on the U.S. He may spout the slogans and call us names; probably will allow a couple of demonstrations but something like February 14 will never happen again." He laughed, "How could it? The Foreign Ministry wants the embassy to be kept open and running so half of the government can get visas and get out of this crazy place."

I agreed. What had happened on February 14 was past history and certainly nothing to be concerned about now. Later that day, I took advantage of the calm and wrote to my family.

October 27

Dear Mom, Dad & Alex:

The day the Shah was supposed to arrive in America, all the Americans were quietly called in for a special security briefing. We had no idea what it was about until the meeting actually began. Then the chief security officer explained the situation and the possible retaliations upon the Embassy. Everyone was in a rather jovial but somewhat apprehensive mood.

But actually very little happened. The demonstrations were insignificantly small. So small that when one march passed while we were playing tennis we hardly noticed—the compound is surrounded by a high wall so we can't see them and they can't see us. There were all the usual slogans painted on the compound walls about Americans Go Home and Death to the Carter but we don't even bother to wash those off anymore.

We didn't even cancel the Halloween party two nights ago at the Chargé's residence. It was another fine party with around 250 people from the U.S. and other foreign communities in Teheran—full of dancing, eating and talking. The Chargé is a very informal, down-to-earth midwesterner. He is also an excellent person and just the one to head a post like this. There is no one here who doesn't believe him to be a first-rate Chargé and individual. I am indeed fortunate to have someone like him for my first tour.

Love,
Richard

P.S. If you don't start sending me more letters I will be forced to stop writing my weekly letter. Right now all I have been receiving in the mail these past few weeks are advertisement brochures and they aren't enough for my morale.

I had no way of knowing that this was going to be the last letter I would write to anyone for awhile and that I would learn what "morale" really meant.

Chapter 2

On Sunday morning, November 4, Dick Morefield told us to pull the files on rejected Iranian applicants, pick out the fraud cases and the people we turned down within the past year, and put them into the just-installed computer system that connected consulates around the world. This meant that when applicants rejected in Teheran went to an American consulate in another country and applied again, that consulate would have a record of the Teheran decision. This system, in use in most of the larger American consulates, has helped enormously to enforce our immigration laws.

Joe and Kathy Stafford, Cora Lijek and I began the project. Kathy was very easygoing and pleasant to work with; she complemented Joe's personality, which ranged from serious to very serious. Cora, part Japanese, petite, with dark, shining black hair, began the sorting. I groaned;

it was boring work that would take days. Marine Sergeant Jim Lopez was on duty that day. He brought us a drawing that mocked all the "Yanqui Go Home" signs plastered across what seemed like every standing wall in Teheran. In Jim's drawing there were little signs posted that said "Yankees have gone home—no more visas."

Around nine or nine-thirty, Sergeant Lopez heard a sketchy message on his walkie-talkie. There was a demonstration brewing outside. There had been a number of demonstrations the past week since the Shah's arrival in the United States; this was probably just another refrain of the same old tune. We continued working. Al Golacinski came into our building and told us that the trouble was growing. We were to stop working and wait for further instructions.

"Keep calm. Things will be straightened out shortly. I'm going back to the chancery to find out exactly what's happening," he said, and left. A few minutes later we heard from Dick Morefield.

"Well," he said, shaking his head, "it looks like we have guests again. They've broken into the compound and they're right outside the chancery. Stop work and we'll go upstairs."

Joe Stafford, Cora, Kathy, Bob Ode, who was helping an American citizen at the time, and I quickly followed Morefield. What next? I wondered. Was Fort Apache under siege again? Of course, the police or the Iranian government would stop this nonsense soon and escort the troublemakers out of the compound. In the meantime we were all getting a break from the visa project.

"Stay away from the windows," warned Morefield. They only faced the inside of the compound, but I got near one and saw some Iranians in fatigue jackets, jeans and sneakers milling around the courtyard. They didn't look very menacing. I didn't see any guns; one of them carried what looked like a croquet mallet and another was brandishing a broken board. One was holding nonchucks. They wore pictures of Khomeini, covered with cellophane, attached to their army field jackets.

Sergeant Lopez stayed in contact with Al Golacinski in the chancery. He had orders, as is usual in these cases, that there would be no shooting. Lopez was ready if the order came through. A Mexican–American who grew up in Globe, Arizona, he was very proud to be a marine and very serious about being a good one. He had a shotgun and wore the summer marine uniform—blue trousers and a khaki shirt, over which he was wearing the flack jacket used only in emergencies.

An hour later, Golacinski called him on the walkie-talkie. Lopez let out a stream of angry Spanish. "They've broken into the chancery," he told us.

"They can't get in here," I said. "The doors are too heavy and they're electronically locked. And they won't be able to get in the grilled windows facing the courtyard."

Just then we heard the sound of breaking glass in the second-floor bathroom. Iranians had climbed up and smashed the window—the one without bars.

Lopez moved quickly. He popped a tear gas container as an Iranian was climbing through the window and then rolled it right under the window. It was enough tear gas to last a lifetime. The Iranians retreated. Lopez slammed the bathroom door before the gas could seep into the room.

"Mark," I said, "hand me a coat hanger and we'll try to

wire the door shut in case they try this route again. There's no way to barricade it."

"Get under the desks," said Lopez. "They'll be back."

Suddenly the lights went out and one of the Iranian women employees screamed. Our power had been turned off.

"We better get busy and destroy the visa plates," said Dick Morefield. "I know this brouhaha will be over in a few hours and it will take us a full six weeks to start operations up again if we destroy the plates but . . ." I certainly didn't want those plates available to the mob outside, and I didn't mind the thought that we wouldn't be able to resume the normal visa operations for six weeks—a nice long break.

Morefield smashed the plates and put the pieces in an envelope. Was this really happening? I wondered. We were all a little uneasy but it was an uneasiness tinged by excitement. This is what we had come to expect from Teheran—the unexpected.

After about an hour, word came from the chancery that the basement had fallen to the militants and the first floor was about to fall, also that the police seemed to be making no effort to come in. That seemed odd. I knew they were out there and it was time for them to make their appearance. For the first time I felt something was not quite right, but I dismissed it quickly and volunteered to go with Sergeant Lopez to check security on our first floor. We had done this once before but we wanted to check again. On the way up, I grabbed my pipe, some tobacco and my briefcase from my visa room interviewing window.

We held out for two hours; then Lopez, in contact with someone at the chancery, reported that the Iranians—we didn't know how many—were climbing on the consulate roof. They were trying to burn it down. It was raining.

"Fools," said Lopez chuckling. "They're trying to start a fire on the roof—in the rain." He picked up the walkie-talkie to contact Golacinski again, held it to his ear for a moment, and then clipped it to his belt.

"Al doesn't answer," said Lopez. "The Iranians have taken the chancery and they're on our walkie-talkies."

"It's time to leave the consulate," said Dick Morefield quietly.

Our basic contingency plan was the same—we were to meet at the British embassy, five blocks away. Because uniformed marines were not supposed to go out on the streets, lest they inflame the populace—already pretty inflamed from the sound of things—we tore the stripes off Lopez's pants and removed his marine belt. I gave him mine. It was a feeble attempt to disguise him.

"At this point," said Lopez wearily, "I don't care who I inflame."

We removed some fiberglass panels on the ceiling and hid his gun. I took my pipe, tobacco, a lighter and briefcase. Morefield put the envelope with the visa plate remnants in his pocket. Lopez took his radio. I took a flashlight.

Morefield asked me to go downstairs with one of the Iranian employees. The electronic locks were out, but the doors luckily opened from the inside. Two doors opened onto the street—one a sliding metal garage-type door. When I opened it I saw three or four Iranians in police uniforms standing outside. I recognized the one in charge. I couldn't tell which, if any, were real police. I didn't know what to expect but I greeted them in Farsi. It was clear that the leader wasn't connected with the militants.

"We're leaving the building now," I said.

"Fine," he answered, waving us on.

The Iranian employee ran to tell the others they could leave. I knew they were not happy about this demonstration; it interrupted their work and jeopardized their jobs. As everyone calmly filed out, a couple of the guards checked their IDs. In addition to the Iranian employees trying to leave the building, there were a few Iranians who were caught in the consulate while applying for visas. Several American employees and one American applying for American services were among those who left also. I watched them get into their cars and drive off.

When the last people got out of the consulate, Morefield shut the sliding door and locked it. Morefield, Ode, Lee, Cooke, Sergeant Lopez, and I walked away from the compound. We were a few steps away when I heard the guard question one of the Iranians who had left the consulate when we did. The guard seemed to be giving him a hard time. I ran back and asked what was the trouble.

"His papers," said the guard. "What are they?"

"Visa documents," I told him. "Everything is in order. He was applying for an immigrant visa when the demonstrations began."

"Okay," said the guard, "go on."

The man, perspiration beading on his forehead, thanked me profusely, if hurriedly, and ran out of the compound. I hurried to catch up with the others. A half a block from the compound, a jeep pulled up with two revolutionary guards inside. They stopped us and tried to grab Lopez's walkie-talkie, but he slammed it to the ground. The case was shattered, the batteries rolled out. Then they took my flashlight.

"We're leaving the compound. I've got to have my flashlight back; the power's out," I urged.

They examined it slowly; Morefield and the group had already left. "C'mon," I said, "it's only a flashlight."

"Hurry up, for God's sake, Richard," called Morefield, turning around. They handed the flashlight back to me, and I took off to catch up with the others.

We were now a block and a half away from the American embassy. The Swedish and Austrian embassies stood on the street to the left. We debated whether to go there. We didn't realize that Joe and Kathy, Mark and Cora and another consular officer, Bob Anders, had gone down the street to the left and reached the Canadian embassy, slightly ahead of us.

"I know the Austrian embassy is closed on Sunday," I said. "I'm not sure about the Swedish."

"Let's just go to my house," said Morefield. He had just moved. It sounded like a good idea. We could spend the day drinking beer, playing cards, waiting this thing out. We turned right.

An Iranian in a checkered sport jacket, his white shirt opened to reveal several gold chains nesting on his chest, pulled up beside us in a bright red sports car.

"Would you like a ride?" he asked.

I looked at the small car and realized it wouldn't hold all of us. "Thanks anyway, but we'll be alright."

We set off, still walking, toward Dick Morefield's house.

Two blocks from the compound, within a few minutes of Dick Morefield's house, I looked back and saw a group of

51

eight or nine militants chasing us and shouting angrily in Farsi. The group on the consulate roof must have spotted us leaving and shouted down for the rest to get us.

They were getting closer and closer, but we continued to walk, neither slackening nor increasing our pace. I could hear their sneakered feet hitting the pavement, getting closer.

"Keep walking, don't run and don't turn back," Morefield said calmly.

We turned up a street, but two and a half blocks from the compound a revolutionary guard who was with the militants fired a shot into the air. We stopped walking. The group surrounded us, shouting "C I A! C I A!" They did not seem able to speak English. Blocking our path they moved in and began to push us around. Finally, with gestures and shoves, they made it clear that we had to go back with them to the compound. "Spy! Spy! C I A!" they shouted over and over again.

As we entered the compound through a gate leading into the courtyard, we came face to face with the revolutionary guard lieutenant who had waved us on when we left.

"What do you want these people for?" he asked the militants. "They're nothings. They work in the consulate."

Ignoring him, they pushed us into the courtyard where two militants were talking to a man dressed in religious garb. The mullah did not look at us. When they realized, despite his "disguise," that Lopez was a marine, they wanted to take him away separately. "We're all going together," said Morefield. "Don't take him away." They ignored Morefield as well and grabbed Lopez. I'm not sure where Lopez was taken.

The remaining five of us were led into one of the four

cottages inside the compound. The militants expected to find other hostages. When they found the cottages empty, they took us out and partly pushed and shoved us in the direction of the ambassador's residence. I saw a television crew filming the takeover. That infuriated me. I was angry, so angry. "These little punks, these kids," I muttered. When the Iranian government finally gets its act together I hope they throw the book at them, I thought. I wondered if they had applied for visas. I didn't recognize any of them. I began to feel uneasy.

When we got inside the ambassador's house, I saw twelve or thirteen people taken from the chancery, tied to chairs, some blindfolded, in the main rooms. Gary Lee and I were taken to a small bedroom where my pipe, lighter and checkbook were taken from me and put on the table. Then the militants tied our hands behind our backs with nylon cord. This was painful and made it hard to sit down. I sat on one bed; Gary sat on the bed facing me. They tied blindfolds, made with torn sheets, tightly around our eyes.

I said, "I'm hungry." A militant answered, "The Shah wouldn't let us have food."

"Are you alright, Gary?" I asked.

"My hands are falling off, but other than that . . . How are you doing? What the hell is happening?"

"I don't know. I didn't think it would go this far," I said, puzzled.

I called one of the militants over. "These ropes are cutting off our circulation," I said in Farsi. He untied my hands, and I felt the blood rush back into them; then he untied Gary's. Maybe now they're through playing cowboys and Indians, I thought. Then they tied us up again.

We sat there, wondering and waiting. For what? The

cavalry? A male voice asked, "Would you like some date?" I said, "Yes." He put the date in my mouth and said, "Spit the pit out."

It must have been about two or three o'clock when finally another voice asked us if we wanted something to eat and we said, "Yes." By now we had been captive for almost two hours. The militants were talking in rapid Farsi, too rapid for me to understand, but there was no mistaking their mood. It was one of excitement, elation. They sounded like kids who had just taken over a school and finally had the teachers where they wanted them.

They took the blindfolds off and led us downstairs to the kitchen. On the way we saw people in the embassy ballroom lying down or sitting, tied to chairs. In the kitchen, several women in chadors pulled steaks from the freezer, threw them in a pan for a few minutes and served them. The outside was burned and the inside was frozen.

We sat there, gnawing on our steaks because they wouldn't give us knives.

"Do you want beer?" asked a militant about my age. The beginnings of a new beard gave his face a rough look.

"Yes, I would. Thanks," I said. He never came back.

Afterward, we were taken back upstairs and tied up again. Gary and I started talking, but a militant interrupted us, speaking rapidly in broken English, "The Shah has ruined our country! The Shah is an American puppet! We want the Shah back. We've seized you because of the Shah!"

Another said, "You're all spies, working for the CIA."

I felt disgusted. The whole day seemed so ridiculous anyway. A bunch of kids running around armed with croquet mallets? Tying us up, then serving us frozen steaks? It just didn't make any sense. I would have been, and I suspect everyone else would have been, far more adamant with them about our diplomatic rights except for two things: normally, diplomatic personnel are protected by their host governments and it is a wise procedure to let the host government handle such a problem. And it was immediately obvious that diplomatic rights meant nothing to these people—they would have laughed in our faces if we had brought up such a concept.

So when the militants spouted their phrases, I only argued a little. I stupidly got into a conversation with a couple of the militants. One said, "You are trying to kill us. You build roads here bad, not like in U.S. You want all Iranians to die."

"You have so many traffic accidents because you are all crazy drivers," I answered.

Why wasn't anyone getting us out of this ridiculous mess? I spent the afternoon going over our predicament in my mind. I could just imagine the letter I would write if my hands weren't tied:

Dear Mom, Dad and Alex,

Sorry I haven't written sooner but I am a prisoner. I have been captured by a band of kids who seem to be running the Iranian government. I have explained to them that "diplomatic immunity" is a concept that all civilized nations honor. Their only comment was to tie all of us to the ambassador's chairs. We, of course, would be violating the diplomatic code and denying our thoughtful host country the opportunity to handle this "incident" themselves if we did anything, so we are going along with this farce. I'm sure the Iranian government and the Ayatollah, that religious fanatic, will be appalled at our treatment . . . as soon as they find out. By the way, just for your information, the news in this room is that Khomeini will be running for the office of President of the United States. . . .

On the second day, an Iranian film crew walked into the room. One of the militants standing near me held a shotgun to my head and said, "Don't worry, this is just for the cameras." But it didn't make me feel any better knowing that the shotgun was pressed into my temple. The crew started filming. Another one of our captors asked me, for their benefit, "How do you feel about all of this? What do you think about it?"

"I'm angry," I said, staring directly into the camera. "This should not be happening."

Our performance did not please the militants. I don't know if they hoped we would say, "This is just great being tied up in our own embassy in your wonderful country. Long live Khomeini," but judging from their maturity level, I think they expected something along those lines.

My Farsi wasn't good enough to make me loquacious, but evidently it was enough to have them gather around me. Pictures of Khomeini, wrapped in cellophane, still hung from their jackets. Over and over they told me that the United States would be an Islamic republic in five years, and that Khomeini would lead the U.S. into revolution. "The American people are waiting for Khomeini," one of them said. It was frustrating not being able to talk. They were not interested in an intellectual dialogue on why the idea that our next President was going to be the

Ayatollah was a loser concept. These were not dialogues; they were diatribes. I began to feel that things could get ugly.

There was a TV set in the bedroom we were in, and our guards turned it on for the evening news. The station showed films of the takeover and pictures of a Kurdish village. An American documentary on rocketry came on, dubbed in Farsi, and four or five militants watched it. Gary and I watched it, too.

When they led us down to dinner, they replaced the nylon cords with torn bedsheets, which were more comfortable. We sat down to a dinner of heated canned spaghetti from the embassy kitchen. I was glad they had given up on steak. We were returned to our room; this time our hands were tied in front of us, which was immediately more comfortable.

The same group gathered in our room again. They seemed to like it in there; one of them went over and lay on a bed, smoking a cigar, and another pointed at him and said, "Look at this guy. He thinks he's a king." Elated and unorganized, they ran back and forth all evening in small groups, holding heated discussions. I couldn't really understand everything they were saying, but the conversation definitely centered around us. They took turns shaking their heads in agreement or disagreeing violently, emphasizing their points by gesturing toward us, interrupting one another constantly. We knew they would have to release us as soon as this game they were playing was over. But now I began to think that release was not in the cards for us that night. Probably first thing in the morning.

We slept on a rug with a blanket thrown over us, our

hands still tied. Despite still feeling excited, after some restlessness, I was able to fall asleep.

The next morning, Gary told me he was sure a plane was on the way from the United States and we would be out in a day or two. I thought we'd be out sometime that day. "We've got to roll with the punches and take this in stride," he said. He was saying it as much for himself as for me, but I agreed with him and the exchange made us both feel cheerful.

We were taken to the kitchen for a breakfast of barbari bread—a long, flat, tasty Iranian bread that is baked fresh daily—and tea. On the way down, I saw Joan Walsh sitting on a couch in the ambassador's entry. Ann Swift rested nearby. They were guarded by a few of the women militants who wore full-length black chadors. Most of the hostages sat still tied to their chairs in the main rooms on the ground floor.

When we went back upstairs, we passed a room where I saw Bert Moore, the administrative counselor. "Are we going to be paid overtime?" I whispered smilingly.

He winked. "Yep, there'll be overtime." In my room I started reading Dr. Ali Shariatis's book on Islamic socialism. I pretended to myself that I was getting paid to read books.

I sat near a window that faced the compound and the snow-covered mountains in the back. It was a beautiful, clear morning. Around noon, the militants moved me, but not Gary, to a room across the hall. It was large and had two single beds, mahogany hard-backed chairs and an antique dresser—so far unscathed—in the corner. Seven people sat tied to the chairs facing the wall. Don Cooke was one, and Sergeant Hughes (one of the blacks who was to be

among the first released), Malcolm Kalb and Colonel Schaefer were some of the others. It was a strange scene: Americans tied up in their own embassy. It seemed like a good time for the posse to arrive and rescue us.

The two students who brought me over told me to sit down, as they pointed to a wooden chair with a straight, hard back. "Not very comfortable," I thought aloud, as they tied my hands to the arms of the chair.

"Don'ta speak, don'ta speak," or "No speak, no speak," one would hiss whenever one of us tried to say anything. My chair was near the door. I sat facing that wall all morning, counting the stains on it, feeling my anger mount. I wasn't frightened, just livid and bored. To be tied up like a criminal because you're an American didn't sit right with me.

At lunch I asked for the salt, and they refused to let Don give it to me because I had talked out loud. I began to feel my throat tighten; frustration, hatred and even fury filled me. This simply was not a rational situation.

After lunch we were tied up again, hands in front. I started to read the one available book, Merle Miller's *Plain Speaking*, about Harry Truman, but it was very difficult to turn the pages. I tried, but I couldn't imagine Truman in a situation like this. A little later one of the militants, without any explanation, grabbed the book out of my hands. Angrily, he pushed my chair forward as I leaned back and slapped down my feet which were propped against the wall. Then they walked over to Joe Hall and went through the same routine. We looked at each other and shrugged, What next? Don Cooke began to sing "The Battle Hymn of the Republic" and Colonel Schaefer hummed softly along with him. The words of the song filled the room; I felt as if I was hearing them that day for the first time ever. Charged with new energy, I sat up straighter in my chair. The mood in the room changed, our spirits were strong. Inexplicably, the guard who had taken my book away returned with copies of a few magazines, *Good Housekeeping* and *House and Garden,* which he distributed.

Time passed and the excitement I had felt at the beginning was fizzling down, almost like air going out of a balloon. I was calmer and I was slowly getting tired.

We had to ask permission to go to the bathroom. They took us across the hall, but if we took too long, they'd knock and look in. Night came. Another night? I thought. Doesn't anyone know we're here? They turned out the lights in the room but kept the ones in the hallway on. Someone was posted outside the door while another militant patrolled the balcony. The shades were kept closed. Several militants slept on the two beds in our room.

I slept fitfully, scenes of rescue playing in my mind through the night.

The third day we ate at the desk in our room instead of the kitchen. We were given forks and spoons, as though we were going to get into a sort of routine, and that made me uneasy. I kept thinking, My God, what's happening? This is supposed to be over by now. I no longer knew what to think.

By the next day, I could feel my confidence waning. I knew I was growing less defiant. I began to feel a knotted, tense sensation in my stomach before I went to sleep. I didn't want to get under my blanket because I knew this sensation would start. I tried to think of other things, but it hung there with me, all through my fitful dreams. It went away during the daylight when I was mostly bored. But my feelings were vacillating and I started imagining the worst—what if we were all going to be shot?

About one o'clock during the fifth night, they turned on the lights and said, "Come!" They put my blanket over my head and led me and several others to a car.

The car stopped after a minute, so I knew we were still in the compound. We were taken into a building and I knew it was the consulate. They pulled off our blindfolds and put us in the nonimmigrant visa waiting area along with twenty-five or thirty other hostages. I sat on the floor in a corner, my hands and, this time, my feet bound. We still had blankets. I tried to sleep, but thoughts and possibilities bothered me. Were we all herded in there because we were going to be released in the morning? Had the U.S. arranged to get us out?

Then the fear came. Were we going to be tried? Or moved? Were they going to torture us? Would I ever see America again? Finally, I dozed off.

In the morning, I woke up with my side and hip aching from the hard floor. I could hear the militants talking right outside the door. Something about the Shah . . . the U.S. . . . the Imam. They were still calling for the return of the Shah. My mind reeled with the impossibility of the situation. They couldn't be serious. No one would let them get away with it. The diplomatic community in every country would rise up and censure . . . I looked at the militants and realized again that they were not playing by any recognizable rules; censure, even if it came from God himself, would be just a joke to them.

Their own rules were not a joke, however. We were told we had to sit or lie down at all times. Two militants armed with sticks paced up and down, hitting the railings with the stick and making a loud, clanging sound. Another one sat at one end of the room holding a submachine gun. They alternated positions throughout the day.

This was one of the first times I had seen them armed, although we knew there were guns. It was not a reassuring sight, given their fascination with, and almost total ignorance of, weapons. When they walked with the gun, they kept it under their coats with only the barrel sticking out. With any luck, they'd wind up blowing themselves up.

One night they hung up a picture of the Shah with a noose around his neck. I didn't laugh. I began to imagine that that was what they had planned for us too.

"What's the poster for?" I asked the militant. He just smiled.

In the morning the poster was gone. My fear wasn't. I requested a pen and paper to write my last will and testament to my family. I didn't expect to see them again, and I remembered the last letter I wrote to them, complaining of a lack of mail. It seemed important to let them know how much they meant to me, that whatever I had accumulated in my twenty-eight years (which wasn't much, materially) was theirs. It was a dismal letter. I don't remember exactly what I said, but it went something like this: "I don't expect to ever be seeing you again; the little I have is yours. There is a will I wrote, before I left the States, in my safe-deposit box. I love you more than I can say. Thank you for being my parents."

The letter bespoke despair. Fortunately, the militants never mailed it. Don Cooke also wrote a letter. We asked to see a priest, but they wouldn't bring one. Although a

Russian Orthodox, I almost always took communion at either a Catholic or Episcopal church, so a priest from either would have suited me fine. I guess you could call me a twice-a-year Christian (Christmas and Easter). I know I didn't qualify as the most religious person ever taken hostage but I did have a deep belief and faith in God.

Some hostages seemed strong. Mike Metrinko, the political officer, was tough. He had already been held by militants when he was the United States consul in Tabriz and, in fact, had received a commendation for heroically saving an American from a mob in that city. When a big, overweight militant—nicknamed "Cro-Magnon Man"—strutted over to him and said, "Mr. Metrinko is one of the important people of the embassy—involved in many areas," Metrinko just smiled and said, "Yep." He didn't protest that he was nothing and should be left alone. The militant then listed the others he thought were important: Colonel Schaefer, Colonel Scott and Bob Ode. Ode was actually a retired consular officer who had come on temporary duty to Iran for forty days to replace the consul Cy Richardson, who had gone to Paris to visit his wife. Ode's age impressed them, and they pegged him for one of the more important members of the embassy. Mike Metrinko just sat there, with a smirk on his face and listened while the fat guard read the list. He nodded his head in agreement; "Absolutely right. We're all very important."

The militants had it in for him. They didn't like his feisty spirit. I heard the overweight bully ask him, "You speak perfect Persian. Why don't you ever speak Persian when the guards address you?" "I'm an American," he answered, "and English is my language. I'm only going to speak English—if I speak to you at all."

The next day when they took me to the bathroom, Mike was mopping the floor. He smiled at me and said, "Queen, don't tell anybody about this." I smiled and nodded. Later, he was put in solitary confinement and periodically roughed up, but they never killed his spirit. He saved his Farsi to curse the terrorists.

Don Cooke, the "rock jock," debated with them in Farsi. Once he said, "Why do you always come to me? My Farsi isn't good. Go to someone else."

He was sitting down, of course, since we weren't able to stand up. One of the guys debating him had a Beretta in a holster strapped onto his belt. Don looked at him and said, "You're Palestinian, you look Palestinian."

The man glared at Don and said, "No, we're Iranian students."

Don said, "No, you're not." He pointed to the pistol and said, "Is that your student ID card?"

The guy said, "We're students. When the Shah comes back, you'll be released."

Don said, "He's never coming back. You can shoot us now because he's not coming back."

The guy left with his partner; as they walked out, he said in Farsi, "He's very, very upset."

The main meal, a lunch of rice and sauce, was served around one o'clock. For dinner we ate soup and bread. Wesley Williams, a black marine, let his soup drip from his spoon to show how watery it was. Charlie Jones, another black, complained about the Iranian food. I remember him muttering, "We can't eat this as a steady diet."

The Iranians played up to the blacks. When two people

wanted to go to the bathroom, the Iranians said, "Blacks go first; blacks are important to us."

Once they went over to Charlie Jones, who was lying next to me, and one guy said to him, "We really love the blacks."

Charlie said, "Why am I here then?"

The militant told him that would be straightened out quickly.

Charlie said, "But you're white."

"No, no, I'm not white," the militant insisted.

Charlie: "Sure you are; you're white."

The guy said, "We know how you feel and we understand you."

Charlie looked at him. "You're white; what are you saying, you're not white? Where I come from, you're white."

So they gave up on Charlie.

They stayed away from Dave Walker, another one of the black marines, too. He looked tough; he looked mean; he looked like trouble. I used to wonder how anyone could be such a rock in this situation—but he was. When the Iranians spoke to him, he'd snarl.

On the third night, they brought in mattresses. Charlie Jones saw them and muttered, "Oh, shit!" I knew what he meant: we were going to be here longer than we hoped. They told us we couldn't leave the mattresses except to go to the bathroom.

I was shifted around the room, why I don't know. Sometimes they would take one or two captives from the consulate away and bring in new people. I looked around and saw Kevin Hermening, one of the marine sergeants;

Bill Keough, the former superintendent of the Teheran American School, his large frame spilling over his mattress; Colonel Schaefer was gone, I didn't know where. It was unnerving; in that situation any change that couldn't be explained was unsettling.

Cro-Magnon Man, who now always wore marine pants, having led the group that broke into the Marine Corps quarters on Bijon Street, came in one day and arrogantly asked the marines in the room, "You know who I am, don't you?" Several nodded. He then cleaned out everybody's pockets. I had four or five American singles and some Iranian bills. He took my wallet and let me keep the money. He also took my key chain, looked it over contemptuously and tossed it back. Everything was put in envelopes and taken who knows where.

The worst guard was one nicknamed "The Weasel," who knew English well. He looked like a rodent and he was a nasty SOB. During my first meeting with him, someone asked what the mobs outside were shouting. He smirked and said, "They're saying, 'Shoot them all! Shoot the spies!'" We had no way of knowing; the crowd's fanatical screaming had no discernible beginning or ending, and the ranting went on like a broken record.

One morning, he poured tea into my Styrofoam cup and purposely let it spill on my mattress. He smirked. When I asked him for a book, he tossed me one on rock gardening. When I daydreamed, he stopped me. "You can sleep or you can read," he said, "but you can't do nothing." I looked at him, picked up a book and pretended to read.

Naming the guards was a way of passing the time—albeit a negative way. A guard only received a nickname if he was gross enough to deserve it, either physically, morally or mentally. Weasel, with dark mustache, slightly protruding ears, and a small build, which emphasized his ferretlike features, deserved his nickname. Later I was describing Weasel to Joe Hall, and he said, "Oh, you mean Rat Face."

The nicknames served another purpose besides identifying the guards. It was a psychological device that helped us to feel we had some control and were not totally helpless. We could isolate their personality quirks, recognize them and maybe even use them to our advantage. A few of the guards eventually learned their unflattering nicknames and were bothered by them. Sometimes it made them treat us worse. We were pointing out traits that others had probably teased them about all their lives. But nicknames notwithstanding, Weasel, Hamid the Liar, Old Stony, Cro-Magnon Man, Gap Tooth, Bulging Eyes and the others held us completely in their power.

They gave us a selection of fifteen or twenty books. I chose a collection of Irwin Shaw's stories, Len Deighton's *Twinkle, Twinkle, Little Spy,* Doris Lessing's *Briefing for a Descent Into Hell,* and Leon Uris's *Trinity.* The books helped, but it was hard to concentrate, especially with the guards walking up and down all the time clanging their sticks.

Through the glass windows inside the building where we did visa interviews, we could see Iranians sifting and reading documents. They worked constantly. There was nothing in the consulate except correspondence, so it must have been boring reading, but they were having problems because, after the takeover, Iranians who had been interviewed for visas were coming back requesting their passports. We had had a system: when we accepted Iranians who had applied for visas, we took their passports, stamped them, and gave them back the next day. Now, one woman pounded on the window day after day saying, "I want my passport. I want my visa. I want my passport."

Metrinko said to Cro-Magnon Man, "Look at that woman. She wants her visa to go to the United States and there are thousands like her. It's crazy."

So the militants were irritated at having to find the passports and asked where they were. They took Don Cooke out to show them. Then they got me. We walked around the consulate. They asked about our computers. I showed them ours and said, "We store names of Iranians who we rejected for visas in this computer," but I'm sure they suspected it was some sort of secret CIA operation.

I showed them where the secretaries worked, and when we went downstairs, one of them asked me how much money I earned.

"About eleven hundred a month," I said.

He didn't believe me. "Don Cooke said you were earning thirteen hundred a month," he insisted.

I told him there had been a slight pay increase and I wasn't sure what my exact salary was.

"I don't believe you," he said.

I told him I had different state taxes from Don's, that Don's were lower, and the militant said, "All right." They took me back to the main room.

We hostages couldn't compare notes, of course, so I didn't know how the others were handling things, but I know my morale began to drop. We hadn't bathed for days, just washed our hands. I developed foul odors and was disgusted with myself. I imagined my skin was crawling with vermin; my clothes reeked of perspiration, and I gagged just thinking about how filthy I was. I remember praying, "My God, what happens if I get dysentery or diarrhea?" I worried about not being able to change my underpants. It seems strange that I thought about these things when I also thought I could be shot, but still I worried about not taking showers, changing clothes, and wearing the same underwear. To make up for it, I think, we went to the bathroom a lot, one at a time. I became obsessed with keeping the area around my mattress as clean as possible. Several times a day I searched to see if bugs or dirt of any kind had accumulated; just spotting crumbs from the breakfast bread was enough to send me into a fit of anxiety. My mind jumped from one gloomy precipice to the next until I saw myself—and all of us ragged, dirty figures—unfit to return to society.

I began to do more sleeping, a weird, heavy-feeling sleep that soon became a wish to sleep all the time. I felt if I could shut everything out, it couldn't be happening, a state psychologists call denial.

I wondered if I was hallucinating. One night I thought I heard militants pounding from the inside on the garage-type door that led to the street where the visa applicants came in. Dick Morefield had locked the door from the outside after we abandoned the building on the day of the takeover, and I was afraid if the militants got it open, they would try to put us in vans, sneak us out of here, and hold us in some secret location away from the Iranian government, which I figured would now have the compound surrounded with troops.

Kevin Hermening must have thought that they were trying to open it to release us. "You can get us out another way," he said to them. "There's another exit outside the building."

I said to myself, "God, Kevin, shut up. Who knows where they would hide us? No one will be able to find us." I prayed that they wouldn't take us out of the embassy. At least, this was familiar, and we could be rescued by the government at any time. But of course, I was wrong—the government was not trying to help us.

I think that my demoralization must have been showing and that the militants picked me as one of the weak ones, in sad shape. Bulging Eyes, a guard who spoke English and one of the leaders of the militants, took me to a small room and showed me a sheet of paper. He said, "This is a statement telling the American government to send back the Shah. No one else has signed it yet. We'd like you to sign it first." I was still firm enough to tell him I couldn't do that.

The militant said, "I thought your country was a free country. So why can't you sign it?"

"I don't *want* to," I said.

"Your country is supposed to be free and yet you can't sign this statement," he said.

Again I said, "No, I'm not going to sign the statement."

I was speaking too loud; my voice traveled into the room next door where the others sat. The guard told me to keep quiet. We talked for five minutes. My voice rose again, and he told me to keep quiet again. Then he gave up and brought me into the main room with the others. Joe Subic quietly clapped his hands, nodding in approval. I went back to my mattress.

The next day, the militants took me out again, this time to a distant room. They showed me the same petition with thirty signatures. One guy said, "Now, will you sign it? Your friends have." I said I would, but I told him I knew the United States government wouldn't send the Shah back to Iran. I was confident and smiled. "He'll go to another country," I said. "What will you do then?"

"We'll take care of that when it happens," he answered.

"Well, give me the paper," I said. "It doesn't make any difference anyway, so I'll sign it." I scribbled my name.

"What's this?" He stared at my signature.

"That's my name," I answered.

He said, "Nobody can read this."

I printed my name, still illegibly, and went back with the others.*

The next day, two Western-looking men came in. I thought maybe it had something to do with the petition. The two were ambassadors, one French, the other Swiss. The French ambassador asked me how I was doing, and I told him all right. He talked to a few more people before he left. I was ecstatic. It was going to be over now. This visit was probably just a formality to prove to the world we had been unharmed by the militants; next we would be released. My spirits soared.

Two women dressed in chadors came next. They said they were medical students and wanted to know if anyone had any problems. Charlie Jones said he had high blood pressure. They checked him and found he was right. They examined some other people and soon brought in a doctor to look at Charlie and put him on medication.

After that, the militants told us we were going for showers and issued everyone a toothbrush—mine was child-size—and some Crest toothpaste. The first shower felt

---

*The illegibility of my signature is why when I was first released, my name came out Richard Owen.

71

great, but I had to put the same stinking clothes back on, except for a little boy's pair of undershorts a militant gave me. I struggled into them. They felt humiliated and embarrassed. Why had they given me a pair of child's pants? I was a man, I told myself, not a child; but I felt helpless as a child as I struggled into them, after first washing them. They put a blanket over me and walked back to the consulate.

All this, I thought, was getting us in shape to be released. They didn't want people to know how we've really been treated, so they were cleaning us up. We got something else new—four cigarettes per day. I had never smoked cigarettes before, but I decided to start. Once I put the cigarette ashes in my Styrofoam cup and started a fire. The militants ran over and stepped on the cup to put it out.

We were even taken outside, to a little courtyard to walk back and forth and, though we were blindfolded, I could sense the air and the surroundings and realized how much I missed the outdoors. Back in the building, I missed the fresh air more than before and searched for a window until I found a small barred one way down at the other end of the room where the Iranians were still sifting through consulate documents. It seemed fantastic to me to see the clouds and watch the light coming through. I looked out the window as much as I could.

Over a period of two days, the militants began to move people out of the consulate. "Hurry up, hurry," they urged in Farsi. "No speak, no speak." I wondered why I was one of the last three left. Had the others been released? Was I staying in Iran? Were they keeping me for another reason? I felt nervous, but I held onto the hope that this was it, I'd be going home very soon.

Then they told Johnny McKeel, a marine sergeant, and

Corty Barnes, a communicator, and me to get up. They put blankets over our heads and took us by car to a yellow cottage. They put us into a flimsy, closed-in porch where it was quite cold.

A guard with a four-day stubble of beard entered.

"Are you releasing us?" I asked.

"No. Not until the Shah is sent back."

"But he will never be sent back," said McKeel.

"Yes, he will, unless your country has maybe forgotten all about you already. Your wonderful America doesn't care what happens to you. You're not important.

"If the Shah isn't sent back, then we will keep you here, and maybe after a year we will get tired of this and shoot a few of you to show we intend to get the Shah back," he said with a faint smile.

Corty Barnes told them coldly they had raided American territory and that is a declaration of war, they had created war between the United States and Iran, and we had nothing more to say to them.

They left us in the small back room tied to chairs, and I remember hearing very clearly a conversation in English in one of the far bedrooms. At first, I only heard meaningless words. Then I heard Katherine Gross say in her midwestern twang, "Come on, Ladell, let's get out of here."

Ladell Maples was one of the black marines. Katherine seemed free. Her voice was cheerful. I remember hearing the door open and then shut and I remember thinking, My God, she's been released. They're probably going to take us into the bedroom, interrogate us, give us a little talk about why the Shah is evil and why they have to change things and then release us too.

An hour later, we were told to get up and put the

blankets over our heads. It was dark, and as we were led into a car I thought we were going to be driven to the airport. We just had a short drive. I wasn't sure where we were, but I knew we were in the compound because the car didn't turn out of the driveway into the Teheran streets. We went into the ambassador's residence where we sat on wooden chairs for twenty minutes while the militants moved things around the room. They then took the blankets off. We were in the ballroom on the ground floor of the ambassador's residence.

On the walls were the black cats, witches and pumpkin decorations left over from the Halloween dance. A streamer of orange crepe paper swung crazily from the chandelier.

Seven of us stood there: myself, Corty Barnes, Johnny McKeel, Bill Keough, Phil Ward (a communicator), Kevin Hermening and another marine, Greg Persinger. A large Persian rug lay on the floor, and the drapes were closed. There were no mattresses. We each took a little place on the rug, and I fell asleep remembering dancing with a beautiful girl in this room only a month ago. If I really concentrated I could almost forget that there were militants sitting in the hall.

At twelve-thirty they'd bring us lunch, which by now consisted of Western food. It was our main meal. It was prepared by the embassy cook, a Pakistani named Joseph, who had voluntarily remained behind. We ate spaghetti and meatballs in a little plastic bowl, or a couple of hamburgers and peas and carrots, or beef stew. Occasionally, they'd have extra food and gave us seconds, and we always had tea. When we finished, they'd collect the plates. At eight-thirty they brought a bowl of soup and a slice of bread. Sometimes I had to use toilet paper for a napkin.

It got cold at night. The militants brought electric floor heaters, and I had two old Navy blankets, with U.S. stamped on them, which kept me warm enough. I had one that I used during the day as a cushion and the other one I put over me. I placed my feet near the heater that I shared with John McKeel, who lay next to me. In the morning I folded the blanket and put on my shoes to get to the bathroom. We became possessive about our areas. I didn't want any crumbs falling on mine and I kept it clean.

They gave us numbers—mine was forty-eight. At first I imagined maybe they were going to have a lottery and release people by drawing numbers. But it turned out their idea was to control and regulate us. They complained, too, that it was hard to remember our names. I remembered we had complained the same way when we started to learn *their* names. We had said that they were all named Mohammed, Ali, Akbar, or Hamid. Now they told us we all had the same type of name—Bill or Bob or Joe or Mike—and they couldn't remember ours either.

One night, several of them began questioning Kevin Hermening about an Iranian woman they said he knew.

"Why do you know her? How did you meet her?" asked the guard.

"I met her once," said Kevin. "She said hello, she said goodbye. That was it."

Later that night they moved him and I didn't see him again while I was in the ambassador's residence.

Every day I would ask a guard, "Are we close? Is it almost over?" They would say, "Maybe." Some would say, "They're talking." Others said nothing.

One morning, Weasel walked in and gave us some pistachio nuts. "In a day or two it'll be all over," he said.

My mood flew up; it was like being in heaven. I let my elation roll over me because Weasel was so awful there couldn't be any other reason he would be friendly except the truth. My God, I remember thinking, Weasel, *Weasel* giving me pistachio nuts and giving them to some other people too. It's really going to be over, I said to myself.

I counted the hours. He had said a day or two—forty-eight hours away at most. That night I wanted to sleep through the next forty-eight hours, and the next morning I thought, just one more day.

But the next day arrived and nothing happened. I waited. I told myself they're working on something, it will be in the afternoon, in an hour or two.

The afternoon passed and I was crestfallen. I felt as though I couldn't last another night. While I was waiting, I tried not to think; I knew if I did, I would fall apart. So I began to daydream.

Chapter 3

When I woke up the next morning, the drapes were drawn as usual. For a second I thought I was back in my bed at the Ardelan apartment before the takeover. I was disoriented, but my hands brought me back to reality—they were tied. Across the room, sitting, watching, were two militants with guns held loosely in their laps. The one nearest me was smoking, inhaling in short, shallow breaths, exhaling fast while he tapped his foot impatiently. These were the dancers calling the tune in the ballroom now.

I struggled to my feet and moved over to a desk and chair, which were just a couple of paces away and by the window. It seemed very important to me to see the light and the day outside. Sitting in the chair and stretching my feet out, I nudged the curtain just enough to let a stream of light flood in. The militant stood up and ambled down the ballroom floor toward me. Bending down by the curtain, he reached into his pocket, extracted a paper clip and secured the curtains together.

"Forget about out there," he said, turning around, "until the Shah is returned to Iran."

"The Shah's not coming back here," I said wearily. "Why would he?"

"If he doesn't come back, you'll stay," the militant said with finality.

Even though we had heard this litany before, somehow this morning it made me more nervous, more tense than before. Partly because the ambassadors, who had seemed a connection with reality, had seen us in all our desperation and simply, unbelievably, turned around and left. They had done nothing, and not only our exchanges with the militants, but the whole situation seemed to be going around in circles.

There seemed no rhyme or reason to what was happening. It was nearly impossible to talk to the others, but I tried, with a tiny hissed whisper here and there, to find out what they felt about our chances of being held indefinitely.

"This is a bitch," said Corty Barnes, "but as long as I have something to read, a few books, I'll be all right."

But John McKeel, the marine from Balch Springs, Texas, felt differently. "There is no way they are going to keep me forever!"

And so it went—each of us having his own reaction. There really was no choice for me except to hold on to hope and the values I believed in. I felt depressed but still thought we would be released soon. Overall, as a group, we seemed to be doing alright. I still thought the government would put pressure on the militants to release us—*if* our government was putting the pressure on Iran. After all, the militants had no real power, no real authority. The cats playing with the mice until the dog shows up. Our dog better show up soon.

They had cleared out all the furniture in the ballroom except for a few chairs, some small tables and a piano. They left some bookshelves and books at one end. We each claimed a space. I sat next to the glass doors; a small coffee table and wooden chair stood nearby. I wanted to lie down on the floor and read, but that was uncomfortable, so I managed to get the militants to bring another blanket to use as a cushion. I also managed to steal a pencil. Inside the cover of a book, I wanted to keep track of the days. "This can't go on more than two weeks" someone had said earlier. And, I thought, it had been two weeks now. Then it was two weeks and two days.

I tried to listen to the Iranians' conversations because they talked about us. One would argue in favor of releasing us, another against. My ears perked up and I would say, "Come on, release us." These conversations convinced me of one thing: the militants, not the government, were calling the shots.

The only way we could see the sky was when we went to the bathroom. It was off the foyer hall, and to get there, you passed a floor-length window. In one corner next to the bathroom were several boxes of decorations. They were for the Marine Corps ball that would have been held in the ballroom the last week of November. Streamers and bags of confetti filled one box, but it was the contents of the other box that caught my eye. It contained hundreds of tiny American flags. The flag of my country, I smiled to myself, still here no matter who happened to be occupying the ballroom at the moment.

Sometimes the militants escorted us to the bathroom; other times they just kept a close watch. I went more than I had to, just to look outside and try to see something, even though we couldn't really see anything. We could hear things, though.

We heard the mobs shouting in Farsi, "Death to the Carter," "Death to the Shah," "Death to America," and we heard constant chanting.

Sometimes, when I awakened in the mornings, I'd pinch myself and think this was a dream, it wasn't happening. You read about things like this in the papers and you see it on TV, happening to other people.

But it was happening to me. I was hearing speakers ranting and raving and I was hearing shots. The demonstrations were constant. We tried to read in spite of the racket, but it was irritating and distracting. I got so I could identify the speakers, and one guy reminded me of a car, stuck in the snow, spinning its wheels, speaking so extraordinarily fast that the words seemed to be slurred into one indistinguishable sound. The mobs would react—usually screaming—after he paused. They would yell, "Allah Akbar," meaning God is great.

We didn't try to communicate much with each other. The militants wouldn't let us move around at all and looked suspicious if we got up—they didn't like us ever to do that except when we moved to our table. Very rarely we whispered, but because the room was large, we could only do it if we were close to someone. The bulk of the time we just read.

The books were mostly teenage love stories from the

American High School library in Teheran. I am a voracious reader who'll read the back of a box of cereal if nothing else is available but this stuff almost cured me. Hour after hour of: Lance loves Lauri who loves Larry who is crazy about a cheerleader. Lauri tries out for the squad. Will she make it? Will Larry like her? And what about Lance? My mind, bombarded on one side by the militants and on the other by Lance and Lauri, needed a rest.

I tried to remember who was in my tenth grade geometry class, who was in my eleventh grade English class, who I graduated with. What was my college schedule in my first semester of my sophomore year? I wondered who my teachers were and which buildings the classes were held in. I thought about my tenth grade geometry teacher, Mr. Olivera, who was the cross-country coach and taught geometric concepts using cross-country distances for examples. He seemed to like all of us a lot and didn't mind taking time to answer questions like some of the teachers did. Good old Edgemont School and my tenth grade class—Steve Love, Glen Goodfriend, Barbara Philbrick. One girl was so pretty, I had a crush on her for years. I wondered what it would have been like to date her.

When I wasn't daydreaming or reading, I tried to remember the books I had read earlier upstairs in the ambassador's residence—the Len Deighton spy novel and McAllister's World War II books. I was not reading the Koran, so the militants brought me another book, a little paperback on Westerners as seen through the Koran. The author was a lightweight, writing, "The way the Westerners lavish care on their dogs shows they have no moral fiber."

Then the militants came by with Red Cross notes,

designed for POWs. I filled in the eight lines with a note to
my parents.* I said, "I love you. Don't worry. I'm okay and
eating fine." I figured my mother would want to know that
I was eating. This was about the time they brought us a
lunch of turkey with dressing and vegetables—it was
Thanksgiving. The Iranians wouldn't have thought of
Thanksgiving dinner or know how to cook it, so I knew the
embassy cook, Joseph, must have prepared it. There we sat,
using the ambassador's good china, facing the wall. I put
my plate on a little table; they untied our hands when we
ate. But the turkey brought home my new reality in a way
that nothing else could have.

I thought of my family's Thanksgiving dinner. Mom,
Dad, Alex, around the big dining room table. Mom
laughing at my father's annual joke: "This is the biggest
bird I ever had to carve," he'd say, as the knife slipped
through the breast as if it were butter. I felt so bad, as if all
that was forever lost to me. Now cracks began to appear in
my hopes.

They widened. Very early one morning, while it was still
dark, the militants put three or four of us in a van. When
the van stopped, we filed out the back and went down some
stairs. We were in the warehouse.

Embassy staffers had called the basement of this building
the Mushroom Inn because it was so hot, damp and humid
in the summer, and it was also completely underground
and windowless. They put me into a room with Phil Ward,
a communications technician. I stood there for a moment
and looked at our new "home." We were being buried alive
in a dungeon.

---

*The note was never mailed.

I couldn't hear a sound. The walls were thick; a cocoon of silence. The room had a rug that was obviously just moved in since it crept up the sides of the wall. Two mattresses lay on the floor. There was a little couch and a chair, too. They had put some books on the floor in my room. A week later, they brought in a little table and placed the books on the table. I saw about twenty-five books across the hall in the large room. Only fluorescent light, no air, but books—that was something.

Ward and I couldn't talk, and one of the guards sat next to the open door, but we saw other people filing down the hall during the day—among them Bill Keough, Bill Belk, Charlie Jones, Jerry Plotkin, almost all the marines including Jim Lopez and John McKeel. I had made a list in my mind of who was held hostage and who I had not yet seen, and I watched who went by and went over my mental list. I was quite sure that Kathy, Joe, Mark, Cora and Bob Anders had escaped and would curse myself for not having left with them. Were they still in Iran, I wondered? Maybe they got lucky and were home. Doors to the rooms in the Mushroom were never closed, and so I could see everyone there as they passed to and from the bathroom.

As the day wore on, we lay on our mattresses and I could feel apathy, like an enemy I no longer wanted to fight, rising in me. Yet part of me did want to struggle, to hold on. I compromised by trying not to think at all. I read, and again I used my daydreams to blot out any realistic thoughts.

I'd sit and think about who was in my high school American history classes, but not what I was going to do tomorrow. Who sat next to me in my English eleven class in college? What courses did I take in my first year of graduate school? I thought a lot about my best friend Pete Brown and Anne, his wife. Pete was my roommate at Hamilton College, and he and Anne had married after graduation and moved to Alaska.

Pete, Anne and I would go to the local pub in the evening and drink beer and agree that Hamilton was the best school and these were the best years of our lives. Pete had even called me when I first arrived in Teheran to tell me the fish were jumping and to get to Alaska as soon as I could.

I began to fantasize about the beautiful girls I used to see at college; how American they were in their Levi's and clean sneakers; about what great legs American girls have, long and slim. No other country had women with legs like that. American girls—white teeth, great smiles; they always seemed to be laughing, a laugh that said, Isn't it great to be alive? God, I thought, what I'd give to hear one of them laugh right now.

These daydreams helped to stave off the degradation of having to ask to go to the bathroom, or hearing a guard bark, "No speak!"

Reading, reading, reading kept me from the realization that I was still wearing that tiny pair of shorts I didn't like. The bathroom next to my room had showers—one of the few advantages of the Mushroom—and we were permitted to use them, but I was sick of never truly undressing or changing.

It was the same feeding schedule too. At 9:00 they flipped on the room light and brought breakfast—tea, barbari bread, and packets of butter. This Iranian bread was my favorite kind. They cut the bread in half, since it was two feet long and six inches wide. I waited until the butter got soft before I spread it. The jam was usually American—taken from the commissary—or sometimes a concoction made from rose petals that was very sweet. Other times we were given feta cheese. At first when we finished, they would take away our plates and wash them. Later we were each given our own plastic plate, cup, fork and spoon, and we would wash them in the bathroom sink. I wasn't sure where they washed the plates we had at first, and I didn't want to know how well they sanitized them.

Once in a while the militants let two of us in the bathroom together. A guard was supposed to watch us; sometimes they relaxed and we were able to whisper a few words, relay the latest rumor or ask how the other person was doing or feeling.

Later, after we were moved from the Mushroom, the militants used the Mushroom Inn as a firing range, shooting off their G-3s into sand bags. Their appetite for playing with weapons seemed to be insatiable. They spent hours just clicking their guns, a habit that decreased eventually, although we continued to hear shots going off in the night.

Four or five days later, after we got to the Mushroom, they moved a mattress and another person into my room in the middle of the night. We barely fit. I didn't know who had arrived, but in the morning I discovered it was Joe Hall, a warrant officer in the Defense Attaché Office (DAO). Phil, Joe and I were together for one day, but the next morning when I awakened, Phil was gone—the militants moved him next door. It made me uneasy when someone disappeared, and even though I saw him in another room when I passed by it on the way to the bathroom, I felt a great sense of unease—arbitrary moves like that added to my growing sense of helplessness. I felt worse several days later when I found out that not only Phil but also most of the original hostages had been moved during the night. The new group were military officers. About eight of us had not been moved, including Joe and me. Some of the department heads had come in, too. I saw Dick Morefield and Bert Moore, the administrative consular.

Joe Hall was my age, of medium build with dark hair and a newly grown beard that complemented his mustache. He was anxious to shave off the beard but couldn't because the militants still wouldn't let us have razors. Soon Joe became tied to my morale boost and I to his. The point was not to get too unnerved by whatever our captors had in store for us.

I think that the militants must have turned most of their hostility and venom against the American military officers. Why had they left us with them? Were they singling us out for something out of the ordinary?

We took our shoes and socks off each night before we crawled under our blankets. One morning, during my second week in the Mushroom, I awakened to find my shoes gone. In their place were thin plastic sandals from the Melli Shoe Company, an Iranian manufacturer. They had embossed pictures of elephants on the bottom. I didn't want to put them on my feet, and anyway, they were several sizes too small for me. They looked like shoes for someone in a mental ward or for someone who would not be going anywhere for a very long time. I felt frightened and helpless because I didn't know what this meant. I wanted my old shoes back; I didn't want to wear prisoner's shoes, shoes to be humiliated in. Or shot in? My mind reeled. In my mind, I saw a picture of myself in Vietnam pajama-style shirt and pants and the plastic slippers, lined up in front of a firing squad.

The militants finally took us out for some air, two at a time. They put blankets over our heads, and we walked down the length of the building past the others. They didn't guide us well; we kept bumping into walls. Upstairs, we got into a car and were driven to one of the tiny courtyards of the ambassador's residence.

After two weeks there, it seemed like a miracle to be out of the tomb, to see the puffy clouds drifting by, to hear the birds singing, the fork-tailed parrots squawking. Most of the trees stood bare, but the pines were green and the sun warmed our hair. After fifteen minutes, the blankets went back on and we were driven back to the tomb, away from the daylight again.

I strained to overhear the Iranians' conversations or the radio. My Farsi, although not very good, was good enough to pick up clues, and I whispered what I heard to Joe. One day I overheard two militants talking. I could make out enough words to surmise that some of the hostages were going to be shot. So this was it. No rescue, no chance to say goodbye, no last contact with the people I loved. I made up my mind not to tell Joe. I didn't know if it were true, and he couldn't do anything about it if it was.

That night I couldn't get to sleep. I kept waiting for it to happen . . . for them to burst into the room and take us out. I made myself stop thinking about dying and concentrated instead on all of the good things in my life— my friends, my parents, my home, my college days, baseball. And nothing happened. Maybe it was my Farsi; maybe it was their lies.

Shortly after the new people moved in, at the beginning of December, I heard something on the radio about a possible war brewing between the United States and Iran. They seemed to be talking about military ships moving in, and something about bombings. I thought the United States must be getting ready to bomb Teheran and send in the military—I thought we were going to war. I was excited; we would be rescued.

The militants seemed to think so, too; they began a great flurry of activity. They had votes nearly every other day, for about a week, on *jang,* which means war, and *azadee,* which means freedom. They would argue before they voted—I heard one young guy, about nineteen, having a heated discussion with an older one, right outside my door. The older one didn't think that they should free the Americans even if that meant war. The young one actually cried and said, "You are going to have thousands and thousands of people killed for fifty people."

When they argued, or voted, war won each time. Then they argued about how many of us to release, whether to release all or some. Around this time the talk was of "losing" us and I thought I heard them talking about getting plane tickets to fly us out. My room was next to the main communication phone, and one day I was sure some guys were talking about getting airline tickets—they had forty-seven but wanted fifty. Again I heard it that evening—they finally got forty-nine and then fifty. They mentioned Alitalia and Lufthansa.

Our excitement rose again. Could we really be going home the next morning? I really don't know whether Khomeini stepped in or whether the government was close to resolving the issue, but it seemed the government was pressuring the militants to resolve it. One evening, I heard a phone ring. The militant who answered it said, "It's Yazdi," referring to the former foreign minister under Prime Minister Bazargan. Another militant looked to the ceiling with disdain. The first one said, "I'll take the call."

Most of them were angry at their government, claiming that the CIA had infiltrated it. One night when it seemed we were close to release, one aggressive militant, a snotty little guy with a round face, big ears and a mustache said, "We've got one friend left." He meant Khomeini.

Another day during this period, one of the militants came downstairs agitated, shouting, "They're moving their troops on the compound." Another said, "Are they American troops?" The first one said he didn't know. Twenty minutes later one of them went up to check. He came back with the news that the troops were speaking Farsi, so they were Iranian.

I never learned where the troops came from. Maybe some revolutionary guards or regular army units had moved near the compound and then left, but by now my mood was fluctuating so wildly I couldn't sleep. I'd lie on my mattress until four o'clock in the morning trying to overhear a fragment of conversation. The militants knew that I was trying to listen in on them and they would ask each other loudly, "Which people do you think we should release first?" And they joked, too, about how poor my Farsi was.

But I didn't care. Even the tiniest hope kept my spirits soaring—or dropping—and I wasn't the only one that was overhearing and hoping. I said a silent prayer. At last. Home now not only meant my family's house but America. My big wonderful country. I didn't care what city they dropped me in, just as long as I could see Americans again.

But nothing happened. Tomorrow came, and I went into the bathroom and said, "We're going home" to the other hostage. A militant stood outside the door.

"No, you're not," the militant said slowly.

I could feel a sense of complete despair rolling through my body and spirit. Reality was not home and friends and country; it was a stifling room in a hole in the ground. I felt completely, utterly destroyed. For the first time, I thought of suicide.

Somehow I washed. Then I came back, threw the towel against the wall and fell on my mattress. My world of rules and regulations, honor, fair play, no longer existed. I felt a profound sense of loss and a grotesque fear of how I'd deal with that loss. I heard the Iranian outside say, "He's broken." Then he asked, "What do we tell him?"

"Just tell him he's not going home," his companion replied.

After that, I stopped counting the days. I didn't have a watch, but time lost its meaning—I measured the days by the meals and by the lights going on and off. I never saw the sun. We went outside only about once a week.

Then something odd happened two weeks before Christmas. I was taking a shower when I noticed my left arm and hand seemed slightly numb—as if they were still asleep. I clenched and unclenched my fist and stretched out my arm. The numbness did not go away. It was probably from sleeping too long on that side, I thought. It seemed strange, so I mentioned it to Joe.

"You ever have a numbness in your hand?" I whispered.

"You mean like pins and needles?" he said. "Like when the circulation is cut off?"

"No," I said. "More like what you'd feel if you plunged

your hand in snow and kept it there for a very long time."

He looked at me for a minute and then said off-handedly, "Why don't you get someone to look at it?"

"I'll wait on it. It will probably go away in a day or two." It didn't. Two days later the numbness seemed more pronounced, particularly in the left fingertips.

Each night I secretly took my bindings off when I got under the covers. In the morning I'd tie them again. Some of the guards didn't know how to tie a basic Boy Scout knot. Some tied my wrists very tightly together; others left them loose. But still the numbness didn't get better, so on the fifth day of this feeling, I asked to see the Iranian pharmacy student who sometimes came by.

A bearded man in his late twenties, he seemed especially gregarious and friendly. I described the sensation to him. He said that maybe it was the draft from a vent in the ceiling. Move your mattress, he told me, and you'll be all right. I moved my mattress, but it didn't help. I was still bound with torn bed sheets. I saw him a couple of times. He thought the bed sheets caused it, so they took them off and put up a sign in Farsi explaining that I shouldn't be bound.

Then they brought in the quack doctor. He was about forty-five and had been trained in America. I wondered if his hands were clean.

"It's nothing, it's nothing," he laughed with a shrug. "I'll give you pills and it will go away. I had the same thing once myself."

During the examination the doctor pointed to my eyes and spoke in a very agitated manner to the pharmacy student in the room. But when he spoke to me he had the same ludicrous grin on his face: "You've twisted your spine;

91

it's nothing, nothing. It'll go away." But he, too, said I shouldn't have my wrists tied.

"And how are you?" he asked Joe on the way out.

"I'm sick, too," said Joe. "Homesick. The cure is an airline ticket out of here."

I tried not to get upset with the diagnosis. Maybe I had twisted my spine. In any case, everything was so grim that this was just one more thing. I tried to ignore the sensation, but it got worse. The thought occurred to me that if I were getting really sick, none of these militant creeps would give a damn.

A week before Christmas, Akbar, a quiet, shy guard I had come to recognize because he was one of the nicer ones, even though he rarely came into the Mushroom, came by and asked if I'd like something from my apartment.

I made a list: blue jeans, changes of underwear, my "War Between the States" game and "Lord of the Rings" game, pipes, tobacco. I handed it to Akbar. I told him where everything was, or anyway where it was supposed to be. Most of the apartments near the embassy had been ransacked and for weeks I received nothing. But a month after Christmas Akbar brought me two pairs of jeans, a couple of shirts, a blue sweater, and underpants. They seemed truly like a gift from heaven. Joe didn't get anything he asked for because his apartment had been ransacked.

I knew Christmas Day was soon. I heard Mike Moeller singing "Jingle Bells" in the bathroom albeit sarcastically, and the mood in the Mushroom seemed strangely brighter. The militants brought us a selection of Christmas cards and a pen, and allowed us to write home for the first time. I wrote a card to my parents. When I finished, the militants took the pen away and read the note.

December 24, 1979

Dear Mom, Dad and Alex:

I don't know how to begin. I miss you all terribly much. This past week I was hoping, praying, pleading to God so hard that I would be able to return to you in time for Christmas, but I guess to no avail.

I hope you didn't get my last letter composed when everything was gloom and death here. That pall has lifted; now I feel overwhelmed by bitterness, frustration and longing for freedom. When is it going to end? The days just drag by overwhelmed by boredom and without meaning. But be of good cheer, this can't last forever and I will sometime, hopefully soon, regain my freedom and join you. It will be the happiest moment of my entire life. Until that day we must keep enduring with patience and hope. The very best of the New Year and God bless you all.

Love, Love, Love and Kisses,
Richard

It wasn't until Christmas Eve afternoon that I heard we'd be having Christmas services with ministers from the United States. "Tonight," said a militant, "you will have Christmas." I asked him who had given permission for this event and he said, "Khomeini." There was a dispute about it, of course. They wondered if they should put all fifty of us in one room for the Christmas service, and naturally most militants were adamantly against our being together.

The Iranian who was organizing the service appeared anxious to make it seem normal. The rumor was this was going to be a big propaganda thrust, and I knew it was, but it was a Christmas service nonetheless and a badly needed one for me.

"To be correct," he asked me, "what should we have? What time should it be?"

"Christmas Eve services are often held at midnight," I told him. "Who should be there? It's a time when families are together."

He agreed he'd suggest that the services should be at midnight.

Later they came by with a little pile of underpants from the commissary and I got to pick one pair that fit me. I put on my best pants and a shirt and brushed my hair with my hands. But supper came and no one came for me. The evening dragged by.

Joe was taken to an early service and came back with a bowl of pistachio nuts and candy. Outside our door I watched several militants eating Brach's hard candies, no doubt sent from America in Christmas packages for us. Twelve o'clock passed—I figured they had forgotten me or wouldn't allow me to participate. Depressed, despairing almost, I went to bed.

Finally at 1:30 they came for me. With Paul Needham, an air force captain; Sam Gillette, a navy communications petty officer; and Mike Moeller, the marine NCOIC (Noncommissioned officer in charge), I went to the largest room in the Mushroom Inn.

An artificial Christmas tree stood in the far corner

complete with American decorations. The ministers probably brought it with them, I thought. Anti-American propaganda slogans covered the walls. Twenty or thirty Iranians stood around, plus a TV camera and photographers.

We met Reverend Howard, a Protestant minister. Each of us took a chair. He said he was invited to hold a Christmas service for us. He realized that this could not be a joyous Christmas but he hoped he could bring some comfort and help to us. He distributed Communion, and I was the first to get my wafer and wine. When everyone had his, we went to a small table near the Christmas tree and sat down. Bowls of candies and some fruit stood on the table. Iranians hovered around.

We talked about football and baseball at first, then he said, "Please be aware that the American people know you are here and they support you completely."

I guess we didn't really comprehend the scale of this report's implications until Howard said, "It has become an emotional issue that is uniting our country. Don't be afraid; don't lose hope. All of America is praying for you."

I let this sink in. America not only knew but *cared*—still. Could this be possible? We were not forgotten? Not replaced on the front page of the newspapers and the six o'clock news with some new, more glamorous event? Not just relegated to a postage cancellation like "Help Fight T.B."? He said, ". . . an emotional issue that is uniting our country." I repeated his words until I believed them. This was the first time I knew, since we were captured, that our country cared—or even knew. It was so glorious to hear. It gave me a surge of support almost impossible to express, but it was life-giving—the best Christmas present, except for release itself, that I could possibly have had.

The minister asked if we wanted to sing Christmas carols, but none of us felt like performing for Iranian TV and we said no. We held hands and prayed the Lord's Prayer out loud instead. For the first time I felt I knew what the words "deliver us from evil" meant. The whole service lasted about twenty minutes. It wasn't glamorous but it helped me tremendously. At home I had gone to church sometimes on Sunday, but this was the most moving and meaningful twenty minutes I had experienced in a long time. I had a powerful feeling that God was with us all, even here in the Mushroom Inn.

When it was over the militants gave us each a little bowl and told us that we could bring candies back to our rooms. I took a couple of Marathon bars and other candies, because although I had never liked candy, these seemed such a delicacy now. Mike Moeller—we called him "the Gunny," short for the gunnery sergeant—told me to take fruit. "We haven't any sunshine," he said, "and you need it." I took apples and gum and filled up my little bowl with pistachio nuts. Then I walked back to my room, ate some pistachio nuts and went to bed.

The next morning they gave us what I called "Khomeini's Christmas card." It was a message from Khomeini in which he talked about Iran's militants capturing a nest of spies. Khomeini extolled the glorious achievement of these student followers of the Imam. He wrote, "Ring bells for spies," mocking President Carter's appeal to ring Christmas bells for us. I couldn't imagine Hallmark selling many of these. I was feeling especially low that morning because Christmas was always such a joyous occasion and here I was now buried in the tomb, thousands of miles from home. I asked for one of the song books that Reverend Howard had brought to the Christmas service. They were stamped on the back "The Brooklyn Savings Bank" and had been used as a promotional giveaway for the bank's customers. I smiled when the militant brought me one; my father had been born in Brooklyn. I thumbed through the book and picked a song we used to sing in elementary school, "We Three Kings of Orient Are."

I remembered spending days memorizing the song. As I remembered, I realized something else—my despair was lifting. I was trying to divorce myself from reality. I still would occasionally get a sinking feeling in the pit of my stomach, and I still had a nagging feeling that we could be shot at any minute. But my fear diminished. I tried to stop overhearing the conversations and no longer paid attention to the radio. And I was less depressed. I was retreating more and more from reality by turning to a semifantasy world of my own. It was much safer there.

One of the first times I realized this was when I noticed that I was beginning to see the militants as individuals. Now I actually felt that they were people. I picked out the few friendly ones like Akbar. I knew the unbending types, mostly indifferent. And there were a few decent human beings. In the Mushroom they had four-hour shifts. One named Mohammed from Mashad, a city in northern Iran, was friendly and somewhat easygoing. But he left in early February, disillusioned with the results of the takeover. He let us whisper sometimes. There was another militant from Mashad who once brought some candy his grandmother had given him to bring to us. Ahmad was a militant militant, he spoke English and was one of the leaders who blew hot and cold. One minute he'd be nice and the next cruel. It all depended on how his life was going at the moment. The hardcore slobs like Hamid the Liar, Weasel and Cro-Magnon Man never changed—they just acted like the cretins we knew them to be. Then there were a whole slew of annoying militants—self-important but not distinguishable. They were the ones who had passed out Khomeini's Christmas card and said things like, "Even though all the evidence is destroyed, we know you're all spies."

The one poster in my room was a fire-breathing serpent, the United States, with a white top hat and a bunch of Iranians running, holding a green banner and the rest with rifles attacking the serpent. Another poster by the bathroom was of a hand made of Iranian faces, choking Carter's neck, forcing out the Shah.

I started trying to communicate with Joe more. I used whispers and gestures and even looks. Sometimes I talked briefly to the guards, intending the conversation for Joe. Most of our communication was by whisper, though, when the guards stepped outside.

Sometimes the guard would catch on and yell the familiar "No speak, no speak" at us, but more often they didn't hear our whispering. We took that opportunity to exchange information about our families, where we lived, school, growing up, things like that. It brought the past and outside life back into our lives and made the Mushroom Inn seem a tiny bit more bearable.

The second letter I wrote to my parents, I tried to keep light, but my melancholy sometimes crept in.

January 23

Dear Mom, Dad and Alex:

No change here really. I am continuing to exist in this timeless void of a world. It is getting so I no longer know what day of the week it is. Oh well, life continues.

Lord only knows when I will be with you again, but I am still praying every night that it will be very soon. One of these days I know my prayers will be answered, it is a just a matter of time. Are you still planning to move?

Please describe everything when you find the new house; its size, number of rooms, amount of property, shorefront, etc. I have really no idea of what it will look like and am so eager for information. I hope everyone is in good health. How does Alex find Chicago now? It sounds like an exciting city, one I certainly intend to visit when I return. And of course it is the hometown for my baseball team, the Chicago White Sox. Luckily baseball season is still several months away and I certainly hope to be out before the first ball is thrown. I still intend to tour the United States when free; it is really a disgrace I have only lived in the Midwest and East Coast and never visited the rest, excepting Alaska of course. In the future I still intend to buy land up there, perhaps with the money that is right now accumulating in my bank in Virginia. I am certainly not spending any money here. Unfortunately I was still in the process of investigating Persian rugs when captured and had not yet set about buying any yet. So I will be coming home rather emptyhanded I am afraid. At this point I would settle for coming home only with the clothes on my back.

There is really so little to say about life here. I will soon be forced to start describing the food I had for lunch. We are still getting our ration of gum every other day.

Please say Hi to relatives and friends and thank anyone who might call for sympathy, etc. Send me pictures of yourself and the new house, when you pick it out. Believe me, I miss you as much today as I ever did.

Love, love, love and kisses,
Richard

Chapter 4

At the Christmas service I had had trouble holding the Communion cup. A few days after Christmas, I had just finished my breakfast bread and was holding a glass of tea in my left hand waiting for it to cool when suddenly Joe yelled, "Richard, the tea!" I looked down at the floor where the plastic glass lay; tea was all over the place.

"What the hell happened?" he asked, throwing me a towel to wipe up the mess.

"I don't know," I answered—and I didn't.

"No speak. No speak," said a guard from his post outside the door.

"Get the doctor back," whispered Joe. "I'm getting worried about you."

I had a sinking feeling about the whole thing. It was getting impossible to pretend that something wasn't wrong with me. Why, I wondered, was my left side, especially the palms and fingers of my hand, affected and not my right side too? I decided it had something to do with not enough exercise and resigned myself to losing the use of that arm permanently. Then I began to feel an irritating itching sensation along the left side of my torso. To relieve it, I scratched my chest until it bled. I looked up to see Joe staring at me, a very concerned look on his face. I shrugged—maybe I was dying, part by part.

The quack doctor came by to check me. He still didn't take any of it seriously, and he laughed the sensations off. And yet, they were spreading. I couldn't imagine what was wrong; still I thought at least it's the left side and not the right—so far. The doctor came again in early January. That time he gave me a two-week supply of vitamins B-6 and B-12, telling me again that I had obviously twisted my spine slightly. He still maintained that it would correct itself. Since we spent all our days and nights lying on the floor, only standing up to go to the bathroom or sitting up to read, this seemed like a reasonable explanation. It couldn't do our bodies any good to stay in an unnatural position like that; obviously our life-style was doing something bad to mine. But all I could do was use the technique that had served me so well recently—try to ignore the whole thing.

And for some reason my symptoms, even as they got worse, didn't seem to affect my attitude. One day Joe told me the vitamins must be doing me some sort of good because I seemed almost ebullient. I felt pleased, but I think there was another explanation: I was coping by not facing reality.

After Christmas, the militants started giving us razors

for as long as it took us to shave. They hadn't let us have razors before because they feared we would commit suicide or use them as weapons. I decided to keep my beard, but my hair was getting very long. I thought I was starting to look like one of Cro-Magnon Man's relatives—a frightening thought. I had always worn my hair short, so when an Iranian asked if anyone wanted a haircut, I volunteered to be the guinea pig.

Off we went to an adjacent room, and he started cutting. I sat quietly, feeling happy at all the mane that was dropping off and thinking how much better I would look. When he finished, he handed me a mirror; I was so shocked I could hardly believe it. It looked like he had put a bowl over my head and cut around it. I had gone from the Cro-Magnon look to Village Idiot in a few minutes. My barber shrugged and probably crossed hair stylist off his list of careers. When I returned to my room, Joe just stared, too shocked to laugh. The others were diplomatic about my new look, but I noticed no one else volunteered for one just like it. So there I was stuck with my embarrassing coiffure, and worse still, an Iranian photographer took pictures that appeared in *Time* and *Newsweek*—one of me and Joe arm wrestling, another of me reading Shakespeare in bed— bowl-shaped hair and all.

One day later that week, Hamid the Liar came in with a photocopy of a letter. "Read this," he said, passing it to Joe and then to me. The letter's author was obviously deranged; the letter said, among other things, that in 1941 American oil interests had been ready to seize Peru but the "benevolent Hitler" prevented them. It also said "everybody in Arlington Cemetery is doomed to go to hell," and berated

American policy in general. Hamid the Liar thought this was the greatest thing since sliced cheese. He made several photocopies and passed them around.

I began to worry that some crackpot would write a letter to the militants and say we were all spies; Hamid would believe it and convince the others it was true—he really was a stupid and immature guy. Wouldn't it be ironic, I thought, if we were shot because some nut decided to write a letter and say we should be.

On the evening of January 9, I heard a noise from the hall. I saw two guards leave. Golacinski whispered to me on his way to the bathroom, "Mail call."

Mail call? I wanted to start shouting or laughing, I was so happy. A letter coming from someone back home; their hands had actually touched the paper that I was going to have in a few minutes. I envisioned this carton of mail, full of loving words, promises of support, acknowledgment of where I was and what was happening. Maybe one from Pete and Anne. That would be so great if it was a postcard from Alaska. I thought about where I would place it—right above my bed so I could see it first thing in the morning. I just knew there would be lots of letters from my parents. What a relief it would be for me to know that they were okay. My mind had gone overboard imagining the strain and worry they were going through and what effect it was having on them. I would know some of my mother's letters had gotten through—there would be that unmistakable hint of her perfume on the letter; it would almost be as though she were really close . . . Enough, I shouldn't keep this up. I was setting myself up for a very big crash if there weren't any letters for me. The thought was so sobering that my elation just whimpered away.

Joe went first and he came back with a letter in twenty minutes. Half an hour later, they took me to the room where we held the Christmas service. Three hostages sat around a table, one seat apart, reading. They gave me a letter from my father, written not long after I was taken hostage. An "X" was marked on the envelope, which meant it had been censored. Nothing was crossed out. It contained no news, only three typed sentences: "Hang in there, Richard. Hang in tough. We love you son." I devoured each word, reading the letter over and over, holding the paper and looking at it.

I realized they probably would have censored "Hang in tough" if they had known what it meant. As it was my father's letter, it must have been full of U.S. news concerning our release. I reasoned it had to be good news or the militants would not have censored it. Bad news we were allowed to read; anything that would depress us further was okay. On the other hand, knowing my father, the letter could have contained some very pithy comments outlining his opinion of the militants in general and the Ayatollah in particular. No matter—it was a letter from home. It said they loved me. I knew that already but oh, how important it was to read it—almost as good as hearing it.

The two guards, Ahmad and Hamid, offered us salted nuts and candy while we read. After twenty minutes they led us back to our rooms. A new, blessed rule was in effect. We could now write three two-hundred-word letters a week, not sealing the envelopes. I wrote my first letter immediately—to my mother, father and Alex.

January 1980

Dear Mom, Dad & Alex:

I am so glad that I have received mail and no doubt will be soon flooded with more. (We can write up to three letters a week of 200 words each.) In some ways this imprisonment may be a great awakening, almost a beneficial experience for me because it has made me think so much more about life and what it means. There is so much which before this I always took for granted but which really is so important. I think people take life too easily and unobservantly until it is threatened or drastically altered. By being given this time to ponder life— and I don't mean to philosophize deeply about oneself, mankind and the universe, but just those little things I always assumed would always exist like certain friendships, and how much being with your family really means—I think I have improved greatly. Such pensive thoughts from me. What's happening? All I want now is to be free and with you to put all these great thoughts to practical application—and I will too.

Love, love, love and kisses,

Richard

I planned on receiving a reply in forty days—twenty for the letter to get to Maine, where my parents now lived, and twenty for the return trip to Teheran.*

---

* After forty days I started watching for the response to my first letter. It never came. The militants were giving us paper and envelopes whenever we asked for them, but they weren't mailing many letters out. I continued writing anyway, diligently printing every word for the censors, and once in an eternity I'd get a letter from my parents acknowledging one of mine.

Two days later, we had another mail call with candy and pistachio nuts. They handed me two letters, one from my parents and a postcard from Pete and Anne. I couldn't believe it, one of my fantasies had actually come true! The card was a picture of a bald eagle flying high over the treetops. I almost cried—the censors hadn't realized that was the strongest expression of freedom I could have received. I tacked the postcard over my mattress and looked at it often; I began to daydream about Alaska and flying out of here like an American eagle, high above the militants' heads. Whenever things got very bad I'd "go" to Alaska and picture myself camping with Pete beside a shimmering lake or hiking on the tundra.

Along with my letters and postcard was a bill from the American Philatelic Association for four dollars. (I collected a number of postcards, which I eventually taped on the wall above my mattress.) Now the letter writing and mail call helped me keep track of the time. I wrote letters on Monday, Wednesday and Saturday—two to my family and one to a friend (since I had no addresses with me, I wrote to the friends who wrote to me—if they included their return address.) I used a small calendar we got after Christmas, although Joe thought we shouldn't expect mail on a certain day, because we'd be sure to get our hopes smashed. I couldn't help it. I timed them anyway; it helped so much by now, a monotonous contrast to the earlier chaos. The militants flipped on the lights at 8:30 A.M., and I'd get out of bed then. Sometimes I had to wait to go to the bathroom because the guards still mostly allowed only one of us in at a time, but that didn't matter because breakfast usually arrived late, around 9. We had the usual barbari bread and jam, and sometimes foil-wrapped butter, handed to us on our own plates. One day a snotty guard, who dressed like a

Palestinian for our benefit, tossed the bread on the floor, dirtied now with mud tracks.

"You can keep throwing it there until the pile reaches the ceiling," I told him, "but if you want us to eat the bread and not die on you then hand it to us. We're not caged animals."

"You care so much to be clean but you don't care that you keep the Shah," he said.

After a while, he picked up the bread and put it on the sofa arm, where I precariously balanced my plate. I think he was worried that we wouldn't eat the bread and then they'd have to deal with that. We'd wash the dishes in the bathroom, with a dishwashing detergent. We had to scrounge for rags.

I had been smoking several times a day, always after our large meal. The militants had brought around some used pipes to choose from, and I picked one and cleaned it. Later they brought new pipes from the commissary and let me choose another. They also brought Half and Half—a half cigarette and half pipe tobacco. They told me it was the kind all Iranians liked and they figured we would too. It wasn't my favorite, but I wasn't going to give it back.

Every week or ten days the militants came by with a little shopping cart of new books, and in mid-January they brought checkers and chess sets and a Monopoly game. I am not really a big checker fan, but I do like Monopoly and I tried to get a game going. The militants would only allow three to play at a time, with one guard watching. We couldn't talk so we grunted and flashed the cards to make deals. Occasionally a word would escape before we could stop it. After a few days they took the Monopoly away. Their excuse was the dice—gambling is un-Islamic. I think they really feared that our grunts and groans had become a code for communicating.

Jimmy Lopez, who had just been moved in, gave up on a game and began to read a book one of the guards had let him have earlier. Without a warning, a different guard came over and knocked the book, a history text, out of his hands.

"U.S. history is all lies; read about Islam now," he said.

"You dumb son of a —" yelled Jimmy. "You better be glad I'm reading instead of wringing your neck."

"You are not allowed to yell at students," yelled Hamid the Liar.

"Yell at them?" yelled Jimmy. "I'd like to flush them head first down an American toilet."

They took Jimmy out for "counseling." Later he was brought back to the Mushroom undaunted.

Al Golacinski and Gary Lee were devoted to playing chess on a regular basis. Al used the games as an excuse for making certain points to the militants—they let him talk as long as they were playing. Their games were an evening ritual. We called them the Spassky–Fischer matches. Whenever Gary found himself losing, he'd try to get Al talking to the militants to break his concentration.

"Hey, Al, tell them what's going to happen," goaded Gary. The militants were all gathered around watching the American "barbarians" play and making comments in Farsi about which one was going to win.

"Eventually we'll be driven to desperation," said Al, looking at the militants. "You can't keep people locked up day and night in a place like this without an explosion. Look at it—we're in a dungeon. If you don't ease off—give us our mail and all of it—you're going to have trouble here.

We know people are writing to us and it's important we get it. What does it cost you?"

While Al was making his point, Gary was making his: "Check," said Gary, gloating.

The true checker champ was Sergeant Regis Ragan, who lived in the room opposite us. It was hard to beat him. I played a few times too, once with Hamid the Liar. He played with his rules, and I played with mine. According to his, he could jump his own men as well as his opponent's.

"In Iran we always play this way. These are my men and if I want to jump them it is up to me," he said, living up to his nickname.

"That's crazy," I said, "I never heard of jumping your own men."

"We are in Iran—you play this way now."

"I come from a long line of checker players, Hamid, and for me to jump my own men would border on heresy."

"Good, then it will be a test of Irani rules and American rules."

When he lost, he blamed my set of rules. Joe Hall and Paul Needham played a lot as a way of communicating. Often the guards would get bored watching them and turn away. So Paul and Joe could talk while they played. The Iranians finally caught on and took the set back.

About this time, I asked Akbar, the guard who had brought my things after Christmas, if he could get some more things from my apartment. Since the last windfall I had spent a lot of time compiling lists just in case I had another opportunity to make a request. Sometimes I made up fantasy lists: four gallons maple walnut ice cream; Alaska cracked crab; fresh corn on the cob, dripping with butter; a huge bacon, lettuce, and tomato sandwich; a clean mattress on a real bed; several cans of Dunhill tobacco. But this was not the list I gave to Akbar. I asked for my own pipes and tobacco and cigars and some games of my own. He looked at the list and said he didn't know if he could find everything.

"Would you like to go to your apartment and bring back what you need?" he asked.

I didn't know if he had gone crazy or what. Akbar was the most decent guard we had, but still I didn't trust any of them. Maybe they planned to film me in my apartment to prove to the United States that we were all living like kings. I just didn't know. I told him I wouldn't do that unless everyone could do it. He said that was impossible. It would be too dangerous to take everyone out on the street.

After that conversation I figured my chances of receiving the items on the list were pretty remote. Then, one day on my way back from the bathroom, I saw one of my pipes, tobacco and games on the table. I asked the guard if I could have them. He said I would have to wait until morning. When the new guard came on, I told him Akbar had brought these things for me. He shrugged and said fine. I grabbed the pile; it was like Christmas all over again.

There were two games—one based on Tolkien's Ring trilogy, the other my giant Civil War game, "War Between the States." This was the game I had started in my apartment. For a moment I felt if I had to, I could live the rest of my life lost in the two worlds they represented. My favorite was the Civil War game. It had a big map, a lot of counters, dice, and a 32-page rule book. It takes months to play. It was late so I just glanced at the rules to refresh my memory and examined the pieces. While the guard was gone, I showed the game to Joe, but he wasn't interested after he saw the rule book.

"It will take as long to play it as it took to fight it," he laughed.

The next morning I moved the couch and mattress to make room to spread out the map. The Iranians were intrigued by the game, but I was uneasy when they watched.

"What is this for?" one asked. "What are these mark-ers—named Grant, Lee, Sherman?"

I told them, as concisely as I could, about the Civil War. They said, "Oh, of course, Americans playing war." One asked if he could play, but when I showed him the rules, he shook his head and walked away. I was always nervous because of the dice, but the militants let me use them, saying it wasn't gambling as long as I rolled them myself. That worked out fine since no one wanted to play with me. So there I sat in an Iranian prison replaying the American Civil War.

Along with the games, Akbar had brought me my own tobacco, a brand I had bought when I was in graduate school in Ann Arbor, Michigan. I was careful not to waste it. After each smoke, I'd pull out the little bit of unburned tobacco at the bottom of the pipe and save it for the next smoke. At first, I had to ask for matches one at a time. Later they gave me one book at a time. Akbar also brought a pack of Antony and Cleopatra cigars, which I gave to Joe, a big cigar smoker.

I decided to ask Akbar for all my pipes. I owned twenty-four and a couple of pipe stands. I started writing notes to him, mentioning the pipes and a few other games. I even asked him for the pipe I had left in the ambassador's

residence the day of the takeover and drew pictures of it so
he could recognize it. Joe was very amused by all this, since
the situation we were in was hardly one for worrying about
pipes, but I thought it was worth a try.

January passed. I didn't consciously decide to accept my
situation, but without realizing it I was beginning to
acclimate myself to hostage life. Then February came.

On February 5, I received a curious piece of mail. It was
a card from my friends Pete and Sandy in Washington,
with whom I had spent many happy hours playing the
board games I enjoy so much. But it was addressed to my
parents! I didn't worry about how the card had gotten to
Teheran; I just sat down and wrote Pete and Sandy
immediately.

February 5, 1980

Dear Pete and Sandy,

I just received your card, the one mailed in
November and intended for my parents, with a
picture of me playing at Origins. Any mail from the
States means so much to me these days that I can't
thank you enough for writing, or question why your
card to my parents ended up in Teheran.

Life here is tolerable if one truly tries to make the
best of this bad situation and continues to maintain a
sense of humor and a hopeful, cheerful spirit. I think
it is necessary to accept the conditions and try, if
possible, for small improvements but without in any
way sacrificing one's pride, dignity, self-esteem and
loyalty to America and its government.

You will be pleased to hear that I was permitted
to have the giant game, "War Between the States,"

which I have been playing steadily for more than a week now. I have been unsuccessful in inducing anyone else to attempt to learn the rules, but even solitaire it provides me excellent entertainment. So beware, Pete, that by the time I return to Washington I will be an unqualified expert.

Most of the time, however, I spend reading, reading, reading. A few days ago the guards also brought us Monopoly and Risk, but no more than two and occasionally three are allowed per game. Speaking is completely forbidden, so when playing we communicate with periodic grunts, cries or groans, or by frantically waving cards or our hands. Such is a glimpse of life at the U.S. Embassy in Teheran these days.

All the best and hope, God willing,

to see you soon again,

Richard

On February 7, I went to the bathroom just after midnight and noticed something strange: the metal door which separated the larger room, where twelve hostages were kept, from my room and two other smaller rooms was closed. I lathered my face with soap, and suddenly I heard a loud knocking. I rinsed my face and turned around. A man wearing combat fatigues and carrying a semiautomatic rifle stood at the door. A white mask covered the lower part of his face.

"Move!" he shouted.

I wiped my hands.

"Get going! Move!" he yelled. He shoved me out the door and jabbed me in the back with his rifle toward the direction of the large room used for the Christmas service and mail calls.

"Get in . . . quick, move, move."

My heart sank when I looked at the scene inside. People were lined up, palms against the wall, feet spread. Behind them stood ten white-masked Iranians, their rifles pointed at my friends.

"Everyone lie down," ordered one who seemed to be the leader.

"You'll have to shoot me standing up," said Navy Commander Don Sharer as some of us started to lie down.

"Hands against the wall," the leader yelled, letting us stand. I didn't recognize their voices—these were not our regular guards. These were our executioners. I could feel the terror rising up in my throat, a sudden, violent thudding in my stomach, my heart pounding out of control. Seconds turned into minutes. We all seemed to be breathing in unison. I heard someone swallow, loud. It was me.

One of the men pushed me hard against the wall and kicked my feet apart. "Don't turn around, face the wall. Keep your arms up."

Then I heard a sudden, metallic click as the masked men locked the bolts on their rifles. They were ready, poised to kill us now. I could hear their fingers on the triggers. We were dead men. It was over.

"Ready, aim," someone ordered in Farsi. Deathly silence. I clenched my teeth and began to say the Lord's Prayer, waiting for the moment when the bullet would enter my back. None of the Americans cried, no one begged, no one asked for mercy. Just the terrible silence. It pounded in my ears, filled the room, held us in its pulsing grip. My back, chest, neck and face were covered with sweat. Nothing happened.

I heard movement but didn't dare turn around. From the corner of my eye I could see one hostage at a time being led from the room. Were they going to shoot us, one by one, outside? I heard the click of a bolt. Suddenly, something began to happen to my left arm. It felt odd, as if it didn't belong to the rest of my body. My arm began to fall; slowly it inched down the wall. Terrified, I tried in desperation to keep it up there. I couldn't. Again I heard a bolt click.

"He has a medical problem," said one of the unmasked militants to the men with the rifles. "Alright," someone said. The militant slapped my arm down hard. When it was my turn, the guard led me into a small room nearby and told me to strip. My mind had stopped, it seemed. I no longer had any interest in what was happening to me. I started to remove my shorts, but they stopped me. I watched, not caring, as they searched the pockets of my pants, then tossed them back to me. When I had my clothes on, they took me back to my room. It was a wreck.

My Civil War game was scattered everywhere. My pipes were knocked over and tobacco strewn all over the floor. A torn, stained mattress replaced the one I had been sleeping on. My fork was missing. I sat down on the mattress and bowed my head. I had come so close to death that it was hard to comprehend that I was alive now. Maybe I wasn't. I wondered if I was going to be able to recognize myself if this nightmare ever ended. Would I like the part that survived?

Now it was very quiet in the Mushroom. We had all gone through an intense experience, a vivid hell that I did not want ever to return to again. I'm sure all of us were feeling the same thing: shattering uncertainty, thankfulness that we were still alive, and pride that we had not "broken" in the face of death.

I made my bed slowly, with the one sheet and old military blanket they had given me, and then feeling very tired, I fell asleep.

The next morning I awoke at eight as usual, but it was a very subdued me, a very quiet person. I asked Mohammed, one of the more considerate guards, what had happened.

"I don't know," he shrugged. "It just happened. We had nothing to do with it. The others . . ."

His answer reminded me of the Nazi guards who pretended not to know what went on at the concentration camps; from then on we referred to that night as the "Gestapo raid." Later that day Akbar came into our room. "I am sorry for what happened. This is not Islam. We do not believe in this. Don't think Islam is like this," he said, apologizing.

I made a strong effort that day to lose myself in routine, and it wasn't too long before I felt superficially back to normal. My postcard of Alaska from Pete and Anne was still over my mattress, and I retreated in my mind to that peaceful scene as much as possible. When the Iranians told us they were fasting for the revolution and Khomeini (some claimed they were starving themselves and letting their children go three days without food), I couldn't have cared less what they said or did. They were fanatics, and I don't think even they knew when they would strike out at us again. Absolutely anything could set them off. Our lives were really in the hands of the asylum's inmates. My only purpose was not to let my mind and spirit be destroyed—no matter what happened.

In the next room, Sergeant Ragan was yelling for the guard. He had been stationed in Teheran since 1974 and was a Vietnam veteran.

"I demand you treat us under the rules of the Geneva Convention," he said, angrily.

The guard laughed. "We don't accept the Geneva Convention rules—we weren't there."

"You have to treat us as Prisoners of War and there are specific things you can and can't do. You cannot beat us, you can't ask us to betray our country, you can't torture us . . ."

"You are not POWs," said the guard, "you are hostages. We can release you, torture you, or kill you and no one can stop us."

At that moment, Mike Moeller knocked on the door to be taken to the bathroom. When the guard finally came to get him he began whistling "America the Beautiful" as loud as he could.

"You're all a bunch of barbarians," shouted Ragan.

"Don't insult the students," said the guard, very primly. "Insulting of students is not allowed."

"This place is a nuthouse," snarled Ragan, disgusted.

On Valentine's Day they brought us some cake and flowers and told us a group of Americans who opposed Carter had sent them. I nearly laughed in their faces. Inconsistent as usual, they gave us an empty jam jar to put the flowers in. Joe and I scooped the icing off the cake with our fingers and ate it, then ate the cake and kept the flowers until they completely faded. Valentine's Day—a day of love and cards and candy and romance. A very American day. I thought how wonderful it would be to get a card, all red hearts and cupids, from a sweetheart. In a way, I envied Joe, having a wife who would be waiting for him if we ever got out. On the other hand I was glad that I wasn't putting one more person through all this anxiety and worry. It was bad enough my parents and friends had to deal with it.

The guards noticed our attitude didn't change; we were not thankful or appreciative for their peace offerings. We felt nothing but contempt for them; children playing at war, over their heads with a situation bigger than they were.

In February I began to feel weak. I started dreading the car ride to the courtyard for outdoor exercise because it seemed to be making me nauseated. I had accepted the fact that my left arm seemed on the way to permanent paralysis, but this was something new and seemed totally unrelated. My head was covered by my blanket, which didn't help, and when I got outside I'd have to sit down and let the nausea ease. After a while I felt so sick and worried about vomiting, I didn't want to go at all. I remember the first time I refused. It was a rainy day, and I saw the others coming in soaked. I told the militant I wasn't going. He told me I was crazy.

"You must go or you will get weaker. The legs need to move—that's why we take you. You get good treatment here."

I told him he could shoot me, but I wasn't going anywhere. I guess he knew I meant it because he left me alone. I thought maybe the problem was lack of exercise between these visits outside. Like me, Joe Hall felt faint in the shower, and several times had to turn the hot water off and bow his head. When several people began to weave as they walked, a militant asked Joe what was wrong. "This

119

lousy place is killing us," he snapped, "and when we die so do you."

I'll never forget the look that guard gave him; I guess Joe had hit on a sore point. The militants, to get any bargaining power out of our captivity, had to keep us alive. We had no way of knowing what was going on, but we thought our parents, wives and relatives were probably putting pressure on our government to do something. Little did we know that the American people, by sending tons and tons of mail, gifts, telegrams, packages, were impressing the militants with our importance. The idea that fifty-three average nonwealthy Americans could be so important must have been an incomprehensible concept for them to accept.

"You're all getting ill," he said, upset. "We're going to be blamed for your illness."

After that they untied the others' hands and allowed us to walk around our rooms. I began to pace myself—walking back and forth for half an hour to an hour. Joe used to say "God damn, you're getting me dizzy with all that walking back and forth."

Our condition must have filtered to the higher-ups because soon the guards brought us a bicycle exerciser too, with a small odometer. Seven or eight of us used it, taking turns. My time was after dinner. At first I did two miles, then worked up to four. I could tighten the tension to make it more difficult to pedal, and surprisingly my arm didn't get better, but my strength returned after awhile. I'd either daydream or quietly sing melancholy songs while I ped-aled—"When Johnny Comes Marching Home," or something from *My Fair Lady*, or my favorite—"Bally Mena," a Harry Belafonte song about someone who drowns at sea.

Charlie Jones read while he pedaled. Mike Moeller whistled "The Marine Corps Hymn" or "America the Beautiful." Some would pedal like mad to rack up mileage before they faded out. The exerciser was right next to my room, and I'd hear the whir of the wheels going round and round all evening. It sounded like an exercise wheel in a hamster cage. I hoped we wouldn't wear it out.

My left hand was still the bugaboo at this point. My control over it had improved since December and January, but I still had difficulty picking up something heavy. By now it was clear I was going to have to live with it, and even though I sometimes wondered if my left arm might remain permanently paralyzed, I had a kind of nonchalant attitude toward it. There were so many other things to worry about.

For one thing, people had begun to disappear from the Mushroom. Colonel Schaefer, the senior attaché, was the first to go. I had seen him always on my way outside to the courtyard, or occasionally at the bathroom. Suddenly I wasn't seeing him anymore. Colonel Holland was the next to disappear.

"Where do you think they are?" I whispered to Joe. "Do you think they've been shot?" We could hear the shots ringing every night. Was that why?

"Something's up," said Joe. "Schaefer and Holland are tough though. They'll be okay."

Still I thought, tough only went so far. When they pulled that trigger you were dead. I worried about them. They had been a good, calm influence in the Mushroom and kept spirits up in little ways.

"Where are they?" I asked Weasel the next day.

121

"They are enemies of Iran and will be tried by our people," he said, with great glee. "Maybe you'll be next. We also have your boss, Bruce Laingen."

Schaefer and Laingen were both important members of the embassy staff. If they were tried they would receive a harsh judgment from the Revolutionary Court. Then the militants, encouraged by the people's cry for blood, would probably try us too. This was the logical step. I privately hoped there would be international coverage of any mock trials.

"You're the criminal," Joe said to Weasel.

"Put us on trial, but make sure the world is invited so they can see what kind of assholes are running this country," I said.

From across the hall, Mike Moeller called, "Hey, Hamid, I've got to go to the bathroom. I've got to take a dump." En route to this function, Mike would usually inform all within earshot that he was "going to have a Khomeini."

"No speak!" yelled Hamid.

Maybe to distract us, as they often did when we questioned them, maybe on a whim—you could never be sure with the militants—Hamid the Liar came in one day and asked if any of us wanted to organize a library. A library! It seemed the most extraordinary idea. But I didn't care and leaped at the chance. Hamid took me to the room where the Christmas ceremony and the Gestapo raid had taken place. Books, sometimes piled seven or eight feet high, were heaped several rows deep along two walls.

The books had been in the American High School in Teheran, a large school that had closed when the Shah was overthrown. Bill Keough, superintendent of the Islamabad

American School, had come to Teheran, where he had previously been superintendent of the huge Teheran American School, in early November to get the student records and to move this valuable library to the Mushroom Inn for storage when the takeover occurred. He was taken hostage, and the books had just been sitting there. In fact, I had been trying to get my hands on them ever since I saw them in there during the Christmas ceremony. Several times the militants had let us glance through a few of the ones within easy reach. It was my luck to grab a high school yearbook, but everything from classical works to cheap romances filled the stacks.

Hamid told me I could work in the library all day and choose two volunteers to work in each of the shifts— morning, afternoon and evening. Bill Keough said it made him too depressed to look at the books, but everyone else wanted to be chosen, even though in the beginning the job seemed overwhelming. There were so many books and no shelves. I asked Hamid for some, but he said no. I had very little space, as well; one whole corner of the room was filled with student records.

The first day we began separating the books by subject, then subdividing them further. The fiction we organized by author's last name, the history by chronology and topic: American, European and British history. Sports books were broken up by particular sports. We even included a category for books we didn't think people would be interested in. Several times my helpers pulled out a book on the Dewey Decimal System and handed it to me. I didn't mind the teasing; we were organizing a true library.

Soon our stacks got very big. They began to intermingle and there was no space to walk between them. And there were still hundreds of books we hadn't even looked at, including multiple copies of textbooks. We devised a new plan: we would make long rows on the floor, piling fifteen books to a stack. I wrote up signs for each pile.

I felt good having something to do, a project I could take hold of and develop. I was putting in the last book on the stack when Ahmad told me to stop and to go back to my room to make myself "to be presented." At this point, with my bowl haircut, old clothes and plastic sandals, I was hard pressed to look presentable; I went back to my room and settled for looking alert.

In a few minutes, an Ayatollah, Ayatollah Montazari—Khomeini's designated heir—strode in with a horde of militants crowding his heels like a flock of sheep and a translator in tow. He spoke in calm, even tones. "How are you?" translated the small, wiry man standing next to him, almost lost in the entourage. "How are you being treated? How is the food?"

Joe and I said "fine" to all three questions. The Ayatollah smiled beatifically while the militants behind him glowered at us.

"I hope the Shah returns soon so you can go home," he said, enunciating every word in Farsi. I didn't need the translator for that one. This was the first time the Shah had been mentioned for awhile.

"What was that all about?" Joe asked when they left. I didn't know, but I thought something must be bubbling in the government if suddenly everyone was interested in our cuisine and opinion of the Mushroom Inn. Next, the Ayatollah Khoeini, who I believe was the militants' mentor, walked through our corridor with the usual yapping group. It did seem like we had become the sight in

Teheran not to miss. Khoeini did not have any cameras filming his visit and seemed more interested in our strange living conditions than talking to any of us. He didn't stop or say anything.

I took advantage of these visits to ask for more library space, and finally Hamid relented and allowed us to expand further into the room.

We got him to agree as well to let us shift the boxes of student records moved from the American High School in Teheran before it shut down. We started culling the records as a break from the library work. I'd pretend I was a career counselor and try to decide which colleges the students should go to. We'd also look through the yearbook and rate the girls on a scale from one to ten—we hadn't seen a woman in a long time. We moved some of the boxes with a small lift mechanism, since they were quite heavy and difficult to handle. Hamid ordered us not to talk, and so we'd move the boxes and curse him under our breath.

The atmosphere in the library was relaxed, with only one militant assigned to watch us. The rule was that we could only talk about books, but some of the guards didn't speak English, and so we talked about anything we wanted to when those guards were around. A few guards were easygoing and let us talk and joke anyway. Charlie Jones, Mike Moeller, Colonel Roeder and Colonel Scott especially enjoyed working in the library, but some volunteers just did it because they were interested in particular kinds of books. Bert Moore set up his own science fiction section with books by Isaac Asimov.

In March, the militants brought us the Boston *Globe* sports section. We knew now that Americans were sending all kinds of things—bags and bags and bags of letters, cards, notes, food, puzzles—to occupy us, and knowing this really gave us a wonderful feeling. Sometimes the militants would hand the gifts over, but in many cases they tore them apart—giving us only four or five pages of a crossword puzzle book. I tried the puzzles when I didn't want to read. They challenged and frustrated me for hours, but I was determined to finish them.

Americans sent a boxful of Donald Duck, Daffy Duck and Elmer Fudd jigsaw puzzles, too, small ones that could come through the mail. We all did them, passing them around when we finished. Periodically, the militants gave out the gum packages we were sent, and Joe and I traded messages on the wrappers. He would write a few words, crumple the paper, and flick it to me. I would read it, then write my response. Sometimes we were given comics. There was a series running in "Doonesbury" that dealt with the militants. Usually they cut it from the page, but a couple of times they let it go through—when it didn't show the militants in a bad light.

In early March one of the Iranians brought a white rabbit, which he called "Mustafa Hargush" or "Donkey Ears." Hargush hopped around the halls free to roam wherever he liked. You could always tell where he had been by the trail of rabbit pellets he left behind. He particularly liked hopping on my game board. Once in the early hours of the morning I heard Joe yell, "Who's there? What the hell is happening?" I looked over to see Hargush sitting very comfortably on Joe's stomach until Joe jumped up and Hargush went flying.

The strain of being cooped up underground seemed to be getting to the militants, too, even though they only had four-hour shifts. I snickered to myself when I heard one of them say to the other, "Thank God, I'm leaving this place; I can't take it. Maybe I'll finally be able to get some studying done." Apparently, he was still trying to take a couple of classes. Other militants were actually upset with us for interrupting their education.

I doubt they went so far as to wonder about the Mushroom's effect on us, but they did in early March bring in a mimeographed form letter asking about our treatment. They wanted us to list our three big complaints and which grievances we would want most to be alleviated. I wondered where this list was going to wind up. I felt as if we were going to be here for a very long time if they were still trying to fix things on a permanent basis. But I filled it out, saying I could survive as it was, but my biggest complaints were lack of mail and not being able to talk or to go outside in the sunshine. I said I wanted more pipes and tobacco.

Then an Iranian government official came in to ask about our conditions. We told him about the lack of mail. This was becoming a real bone of contention since we were only receiving a small part of the mail being sent to us. Akbar, who was one of the best of the militant leaders, told us they had forty or fifty bags of mail that they couldn't give to us. It was too much to read, he said, and every piece had to be read before it could be handed over. Hamid the Liar wouldn't admit there was a backlog. According to him we were getting all the mail that was coming in. I told him about the forty or fifty bags and he demanded to know who had told us that. I shrugged my shoulders. Hamid then offered his own theory: the CIA was intercepting our mail and trying to torture us and our families. That was his line from then on. I later told him that my mother had written and that people from other countries were sending me mail and still these letters never arrived.

"CIA means black in Farsi," he said. "When you call someone *cia* it means an insult. Your CIA is black and evil."

After the questionnaire, we waited for the changes we had suggested to come through. Actually, we didn't wait very seriously—and, true to form, nothing improved. "Maybe they're just taking a poll for a magazine," whispered Joe. "What a typical hostage wants." "I know, I know," Joe said to Hamid. "No speak. No speak." Maybe, I thought, they're trying to find out what we like so they can take it away.

I didn't know what to make of this sort of activity. I suspected something was going on about getting us out, but I couldn't verify anything, and by that time I was purposely trying not to overhear conversations about release. Obviously it made no sense to go back to getting my hopes up and then having them dashed. I was making my world one of books and being back in school again; I wasn't thinking about the future.

We were all working, stacking books, when Hamid the Liar came running in. "We have found the toilet paper," he said, triumphantly.

"Good, Hamid," said Bill Keough, "cleanliness is next to godliness."

"No speak," said Hamid. "There are messages on the paper. You are planning to leave your rooms to escape. But," he said, patting his G-3, "I wish you try. I will fire my gun if you put your face out of your room."

I never saw these messages, but I'm sure that some of us communicated that way.

I buried myself in the library and my reading. We weren't supposed to take books to our rooms without checking with the militants, but again it depended on the guard. If I saw an interesting book, I'd put it aside and later take it to my room. So would the other workers. I was trying to structure my reading so that it progressed almost like a college course that became stricter as time went on. I forced myself to spend an hour daily on French vocabulary. I read Bruce Catton's Civil War trilogy and followed the battles on the map to my game. I read Browning and Wordsworth slowly, memorizing the poems. Earlier, I got hold of a volume of Shakespeare's plays. First, I reread the plays I had studied in high school and college, then I read the rest of the plays. I felt as if I had personally discovered Shakespeare. *Julius Caesar* was my favorite. I remember arguing in the library in whispers with Colonel Scott. He thought *The Merchant of Venice* was the best.

The library by now had become a passion with me. Making it a good one gave me a great sense of purpose. I would start after breakfast and work until ten at night, only stopping for meals. The militants had a cart they carried food on. When I saw the chuck wagon coming, I'd go back to my room and eat lunch or dinner and have a smoke. Sometimes I smoked in the library while I was working. My work clothes were jeans and a T-shirt, which I had to wash every day because it got so dirty from the dusty books. At the end of the day, I'd take a shower. I told the militants I needed more showers now that I was working. I hung up my underwear and T-shirt to dry in my room, tacking them up on the fiberboard above my mattress. When, in mid-March, I had almost gotten the books completely organized, Hamid the Liar came up with a

"Management" scheme. First, he would check through the library and make sure there were no CIA books, then he would let two people in for half an hour at a time to pick out a maximum of twenty books. All returned books would have to be put in a special place where Hamid could check for secret messages. He wrote a four-sentence "Library Procedure Sheet," which he typed (with numerous typos and grammatical errors), mimeographed and handed out.

ATTENTION: LIBRARY PROCEDURES
1. You may never to take more than 20-twenty-20 of books from the month.
2. You may never to write in the twenty books your messages.
3. To stack you found them return your books-20.
4. A student good in English will check for messages you should not write, if he find this library will be destroyed.

Hamid presented this memo with a great flourish and did not understand why we found it hilarious. Now we were ready to open; our first customer came in the next day. When the guards started letting people come in, they gave them about a half hour to pick the books they wanted. Then they had to stack the books so Hamid the Liar could check through them. He did this very diligently, hoping he would find something top-secret in the books. Occasionally he'd locate a pencil mark made by a long-ago reader. He'd hold the book up to the light and exclaim, "Hmmm. I think maybe this is something."

After you returned your allotted twenty books, you could take out twenty more. Hamid got very upset if you tried to take out nineteen or accidentally piled twenty-one in your arms. "Twenty books, twenty only," he'd yell.

I never expected Hamid to find any CIA books or variations on the theme of "Everything You've Always Wanted to Know About Being a Spy." But I did happen on one by Philip Agee, who had worked for the CIA. I gave it to Hamid before he could make the "discovery" for himself and ruin a good day of reading by grilling us about the author. He took it, remained unusually calm, and we never saw it again.

Some of the militants asked if I could find books for them. Most of them were engineering students and would ask for books on trigonometry or higher math and engineering. One wanted books on the sciences, another on art. When I found the books, I'd give them to the militants—if they were friendly.

One evening, though, Hamid told me I couldn't work in the library. I thought this was odd—nothing had happened and the system seemed to be working out. I stayed in my room and read. Suddenly someone closed the same metal door that I had noticed closed the night of the Gestapo raid. My mind saw all of us against that wall—my arm slowly and irrevocably slipping down—heard the click of the bolt on the gun, ready to fire. I told myself, you were not shot then and you won't be shot now, but it wasn't the most comforting of thoughts. I wasn't sure if I could believe my own advice. I knew the Gestapo raid had been held for one purpose—to subdue and terrorize us. It was not a shakedown, it was a pure terror tactic. I breathed in slowly and tried to remain calm, but I felt my heart lurch with the old, horrible familiar terror.

Minutes later, men wearing white masks and fatigues

and carrying G-3s barged in. "Come," they said, quietly. This time there was no pushing, shouting or shoving. I didn't feel so frightened, even though they lined us up against the wall in the library. They didn't lock the bolts on their rifles; I guessed they didn't have any ammunition in them. Again I had trouble keeping my left hand up. They let me put it down.

After frisking us, they told us to return to our rooms. My room had been ransacked but the mess was not as bad as before. The mattress was untouched, and they had been careful not to disturb my game. What they did take were all the books people had picked up from the library—even the book of rules from my Civil War game was gone. All I had left was my pocket New Testament and a calendar.

The next two or three days there was nothing to do but look at ceiling and walls. I couldn't play my game without the rule book. I asked what the purpose of the raid had been, but the militants wouldn't answer. I read the New Testament again, even though I had just finished reading it the previous month. Finally they let me go back to work because the white-masked men had dumped all the books they had taken from our rooms into the room where the guards slept. The guards were irritated with the raiders for making such a mess, and they wanted their room cleaned up. I retrieved my French textbook, the two volumes of Shakespeare, and the rule book and charts for my game. The other books went back to the library, and I was happy, thinking of going back to work. But it wasn't going to happen like that.

About 10:00 P.M. that evening the metal door was shut again. I got the same unsettled feeling; here we go again, I thought. But I knew I would never be as terrified as I was the night of the first Gestapo raid—the night we all died. I felt so much stronger now. Soon Ahmad came in and told us to pack our things. We were leaving in a few hours, he said. I pulled my postcards off the wall and spread out my blanket. In it I put all my possessions—my small collection of letters, my games, my ashtray, thumbtacks, plastic cup, plate, knife, fork and spoon, and tied up the four corners.

"Do you know where you are going?" asked Ahmad.

"We'd be the last to know," said Joe, picking up his cigars.

"Do you think you're going home now?" Ahmad's tone was mocking.

"No," I said wearily. "We don't think we're going home. Would you like to tell us where we're headed this time?"

He held up his fists close to his face and pretended to be peering through bars; his eyes darted furtively from left to right. As a mime, Ahmad had a long way to go, but we got the message: We were going to jail. We tried to keep our spirits up by joking. After several hours, the metal door was opened again, and we saw other hostages file past with their belongings in bundles. Ahmad motioned that it was time for us to go, too. He put blankets over our heads and led us to a small car. We were put in the back seat and driven a short distance. I knew we were still inside the compound, but I couldn't tell where. Ahmad led us up a flight of stairs and into a room. It was dark. He flicked on a light, then he took off our blankets and said, "These are your new quarters. You're allowed to talk now."

"You mean we can talk all the time?" I asked him.

"Yes," he said, and added, "when you need something, just knock on the door." He left. Joe and I looked at each other. "Allow me to formally introduce myself," I said, "a slight oversight these many months—my name is Richard Queen."

"And I'm Joe Hall," he answered. "Howdy-do."

We stood there grinning, shaking hands.

Chapter 5

Mattresses lay on the floor. Chairs and a table stood against the wall. I still couldn't guess where we were, but Joe said we were in the chancery. We could hear the traffic outside and the window was bricked over. One side of the chancery was along Taleghani Street. The bricking had been done before the takeover as a security precaution. The bars Ahmad had referred to were those outside several of the chancery windows, and so we weren't being taken to jail after all, to our immense relief.

It was unbelievable to hear the cars pass by and the horns honking, to know that we were a part of the world again. For a while we just stood and listened, almost stunned. The realization that we could talk, after so many months of silence, came more slowly. We hadn't forgotten how, but it had become automatic to stop ourselves, to communicate in other ways. I had become adept at nodding agreement or

the eloquent shrug; Joe had mastered the dunk shot—
throwing a gum wrapper (on which he had written a
message) directly into one of my sandals; we were both
expert whisperers as well. Now we spoke in short sentences,
then we soon used longer ones, talking nonstop, saying the
things that had been building up for so long—inconse-
quential, emotional, almost feverish talk—but wonderful
beyond words.

"Maple walnut ice cream—it's my favorite," I said. "I'm
going to eat tons of it when we get out of here."

"I'm married to the prettiest—her name is Cherlynn and
she's in Silver Spring, Maryland, right now. Actually
there's no spring in Silver Spring but what the hell . . ."

"And the White Sox," I interrupted him. "The White
Sox and maple walnut ice cream. Another thing is Alaska.
Joe, you've got to go there with me. As soon as I get out
I'm going to buy some land there . . ."

"I know she's worried so much about what's happening
here, and we don't have any family near us. Everyone's in
Little Falls, Minnesota, now, but I grew up in Bend,
Oregon."

We stopped suddenly and laughed for ten minutes.

"Okay," said Joe. "I think it goes this way. You say
something and I listen; then I say something and you
listen. They call it . . ."

"Con-ver-sa-tion," we both said together. I told him to
go first. I couldn't get my thoughts organized so quickly.

"Okay. I was born in Bend, as I said. I love cigars and
I'm really a cleanliness nut. I was really glad to be rooming
with you because you keep your area almost as clean as I
keep mine. What else? Boy, have I been out of practice.
This talking business isn't that easy. Cherlynn and I had

lots of plans, but then I was offered Teheran. I sure wish I had turned them down, now. Cherlynn was really afraid for me to come here, but I thought—" He paused and shrugged. "I guess it doesn't matter what I thought. Here I am."

"Well, I'm not married. I have a mother and father and a brother, Alex, who's one year younger. That's my immediate family. I was born in Washington, DC, and grew up in New York State. My parents have sold our home and moved to Maine. I guess I feel awful about that. Here I am thinking about them in a house and neighborhood they aren't living in anymore."

"Yeah, that can be rough," admitted Joe. "I guess I've lived in so many houses in so many states I wouldn't know which one to think about first. This is one," he said glancing at our room, "I'd like to forget."

"But you have to admit it beats the Mushroom Inn."

We unpacked, still talking. Wherever I had moved, I took everything I could. I'd add nails and tacks to my little box of possessions. If I didn't get a hammer, I'd use some hard object to hang up my pictures. Sometimes the militants would give me nails if I asked, but I didn't want to take any chances. Who knew what was going to come up in the future? This time I knocked on the door and asked for tape to put my pictures on the wall. The militants brought it without any argument—who knows why?—and they brought some tea as well. Joe and I then talked again for hours before we went to sleep.

The next morning I heard the traffic again as I woke up and saw a little crack of sunlight through the bricks. It was so small that when we flicked on the lights in the room, we couldn't see the sun at all, but it was precious. We could hear birds singing and two young girls walking along, laughing and talking to each other. I knew then that I really was waking to the sounds of an everyday morning, the first time I had heard those kinds of sounds in almost four months. I lay there soaking it all in, feeling pure pleasure.

When I wanted to go to the bathroom, I knocked and the militants took me across the hall. They had whitewashed the bathroom windows, but the tops were pushed down. I could look out and see that it was a clear, crisp, beautiful day. Snow-capped mountains stood in the distance. I stayed in the bathroom long after I had finished my morning routine, just to look at the mountains and to soak up the sun. All day I kept coming back. I discovered that if I stood on the toilet seat, I could look out the other window into the compound itself.

Soon Joe found a broom and started sweeping, accompanied by traffic noises and piercing parakeet caws and the sound of planes. Again we talked all day long and through the evening until we went to bed. That night I went again into the bathroom, looked up and saw the stars. It was a lovely sight.

There was a big office desk in the room. I opened it and found a pair of marine pants. They fit me perfectly—thirty-four waist, thirty-four inseam. They belonged to John McKeel; his name was stenciled inside. I had no idea why he left them, but I added them to my collection. We found other things, as well—extra papers, rubber bands. They were insignificant items, but we took them all, feeling like celebrating.

We ate our meals at the desk. The militants announced meal time and came to collect our plates. Minutes later they were back with our food, and we sat down to eat. It was hard not to think that something would happen to take all this away, but for the moment we didn't want to worry anymore. We were too busy savoring everything.

The next morning my eyes were watering and I had almost a choking feeling. Joe had it too. During the takeover a lot of tear gas had been thrown into the room and had settled into the carpet. We didn't notice it when we first walked in, but we had stirred it up when we cleaned the rug. Because there was no ventilation, the fumes hung in the room.

The militants noticed it, too, and moved us down the hallway to another room facing the street—a much better room with a clean rug and whitewashed windows, which nevertheless let in a lot of light. We were so elated we were almost floating on air. Joe got them to bring him a vacuum cleaner—it actually worked—and cleaned as hard as he could. It was very difficult, if not impossible, to find a working vacuum cleaner. The Iranians all claimed to be engineers or engineering students, but it seemed to us they broke everything they touched. For example, when the plug didn't fit the socket, they'd cut off the wire instead of trying a new plug. So you'd be left with two wires in the wall socket. We had to put them gingerly into the wall, hoping we wouldn't have a spark, explosion or God knows what else. They did the same thing with a space heater we once asked for. Anything unbroken—in particular, anything mechanical that was unbroken—was a real rarity. Inspired by the idea of living like humans again, we put up our pictures and postcards on the wall.

And then Hamid the Liar punctured our balloon. He walked into the room and told us we were moving.

139

"Get your things. Quick," he said, very pleased with himself. "It's too bad you got to go because you just fixed it up good."

"What are you guys trying to prove?" said Joe, ripping his postcards from the wall. "You act like a bunch of jerks."

Hamid left, and later Akbar just happened to drop by. Joe said, "Listen, Akbar, see what you can do. Hamid is just playing Napoleon."

Akbar shrugged, "I will see."

Now we could see outside without even having to go to the bathroom. It was wonderful to look out and see the sun. Akbar left us there all afternoon and through dinner, but after dinner he didn't come back, and while I was smoking my pipe and Joe his cigar, Hamid the Liar walked in again.

"Pack up," he said, "you're moving, and you," he pointed at Joe, "are going back to the Mushroom."

Joe and I looked at each other. I thought they couldn't get to me again but I was wrong. The hurt welled up inside of me, and I felt as if I were losing a brother. We had been through so much together—all those long, dreary weeks in the Mushroom, where even though we couldn't talk, we had come to know and rely on each other. Now, after our long conversations, we had found out that although many of our interests were different, we were alike in the ways that counted, in the ways that had made the Mushroom bearable. Both of us were steady types, not particularly excitable. Both of us believed in trying to be as self-reliant as we could and just taking each day as it came. And after four months we had gotten so used to rooming together that it seemed almost like our own little support system protecting us against the terrifying and unexpected twists

140

of our captivity. We never discussed it, but we both dreaded being separated. We both knew we had survived the Mushroom because of our "partnership."

Joe picked up his things. "It was great being with you," he said.

"It was great being with you," I answered. Then I watched him move out. I felt awful.

In five minutes Hamid was back.

"You're moving in with some of the chiefs, and we'll give you a deck of cards," he told me.

"I'd rather stay with Joe," I said.

"You won't get your cards that way," he answered.

"Too bad," I said. "I'd rather be with Joe."

I had packed, reluctantly, and now Hamid put a blanket over my head, led me downstairs and made me wait on a bench. I heard two people walk out. I could just see their feet, but I knew one was Charlie Jones. He was the only black in the chancery. The other, I found out later, was Greg Persinger.

I was next. The militants led me into a room and took off the blanket. Then they moved someone else in. They took off his blanket. It was Joe. We just stood there again, incredulous and overjoyed, and then I found my voice.

"Fancy meeting you here," I said. He laughed, sounding as pleased as I did.

When we glanced around, our hearts sank. We were in the basement of the chancery. The rug was filthy, and in one corner a pipe had burst earlier, soaking the walls and leaving a lot of dirt. Underneath the yellowed spray paint on the walls, we could make out anti–Khomeini statements and cartoons. We guessed that Jim Lopez and Steve Kirtley had been the previous occupants. Jim was a pretty good artist, and we could recognize his drawings. In one he had drawn Khomeini with a head in the shape of a mushroom cloud. In another a religious figure was jumping up and down, spewing smoke before a mob of people. We could make out the words: *"Viva la rioja, blanca y azul,"* which in Spanish means, "Long live the red, white and blue." On the opposite wall, Kirtley had drawn an American eagle. The militants had filled in their own slogans: "Death to America. Death to the Carter."

The room did have one advantage—the militants hadn't whitewashed the windows, and we could open the one that wasn't broken. Because it faced a brick retaining wall below ground level, we couldn't see anything at street level, which was why the window wasn't whitewashed. But if we looked up through it, we could still see the sun, the sky and the trees. We went to bed that night with mixed feelings. We had been moved to a hole, but we were together, and we were out of the Mushroom.

The next morning I woke up to a whole windowful of sunlight coming down from above the retaining wall. I put my mattress right next to the window so sunlight could strike me and lay there, watching it play across my clothes and watching the room light up.

Again we had a big office desk, two small night tables, a couple of stuffed office chairs, a swivel chair and a hard-backed one. At least we had furniture. I suggested to Joe that maybe the militants would give us some paint and brushes so we could try to fix the walls up. Joe wasn't enthusiastic. He had liked the other room so much that this latest move had temporarily taken the housekeeping fervor out of him. I asked Hamid anyway, and surprisingly he said yes and promptly brought us one brush and a can of white enamel paint. The paint was designed for use on metal surfaces, but it worked. I think his idea was that we would just cover up the drawings, but we decided to paint the whole room.

We got an old Persian newspaper to protect the rug and went right to work. It took a day and a half to cover all the walls, and we had to ask for extra paint, but when we finished, the whole room looked much lighter and more cheerful. Even Joe's depression lifted a great deal at the sight. During the day Joe found a broom and started sweeping up the room. He knew I was not up to using a broom with both hands, so he insisted on doing it. Besides, Joe really loved to clean, and I don't think he really trusted anyone to do the job as thoroughly as he would.

That night Hamid the Liar came in with a can of spray paint. I thought, my God, he's going to spray slogans on our newly painted walls. Instead, he childishly sprayed the air in front of Joe and me with a quick, short blast. That was Hamid, a twelve-year-old mind in a twenty-four-year-old body. It was useless to wonder why he did those infuriating things, so Joe and I didn't even discuss it. We just exchanged glances. But it was typical Hamid behavior, an example of how he endeared himself to us all.

I put up my photographs and postcards. My parents had sent a picture of the new house in Maine, which helped me a lot. Now I could imagine them in their actual setting and not at the old house as I had been doing. It still was hard to give up the old memory because I really had nothing to replace it except this picture. So much had changed for me, and for a moment I felt truly homeless. I finished putting the last card up while Joe watched. He said he wasn't going to put his up anymore; it would probably trigger another

143

move. But my housekeeping instinct was still going strong, and I asked the militants for some paintings or posters to decorate the walls, hoping they wouldn't just bring us propaganda posters.

Next—I was becoming insatiable—I remembered a travel poster I had seen before the takeover in one of the basement offices of the chancery. It was a big, lovely picture of Mount McKinley, with "Alaska" printed on the bottom. I had asked one of the Iranian secretaries if I could have it. Jokingly she had said yes—for a visa—and so it had stayed right where it was. Now I asked one of the militants to look for it. He nodded but he didn't come back, so I asked other militants who came by if they could find the picture for me. Finally, after three or four tries, I described the poster to yet another guard.

"It's a picture of a very beautiful mountain," I said, tracing a mountain in the air with my finger. "Mount McKinley. At the bottom of the poster it says 'ALASKA' in big letters."

"Alaska," he repeated. "It's very cold in Alaska. You go there?"

"As soon as I get out of this place," I said, giving up on the poster.

"Then you won't be there soon," he said and left.

About two hours later he came back with it. He said he had been looking for it all that time. I asked for a hammer and nail and I put it up next to my mattress, reflecting on the astonishing paradoxes of the Iranians' behavior—one minute spraying us with paint, the next taking two hours to search out a poster for our room, and I decided that the inconsistencies reflected more than naïveté and lack of education. Most of the militants were simply very childish.

One day Hamid came in with Ayatollah Khamanei, a

leader of the Islamic Republican Party, and a whole retinue of militants. The Ayatollah asked a few perfunctory questions, and I practiced some of my Farsi on him. Afterward, Hamid came into our room very upset.

"You," he said, pointing at me, "have insulted an Ayatollah." I could see Joe raising his eyebrows in mock surprise. "You must speak perfect Farsi to talk to an Ayatollah—it is not a time to practice. I will teach you. When he comes back you must say, 'I'm having a good time here. I enjoy it here. The students are treating me very, very well. I have no complaints.'"

"Fine, Hamid, I will be glad to learn Farsi, but I'd like to make up my own answers to whatever questions the next Ayatollah you bring in here asks me."

That was our last Ayatollah.

For the first week or so, the adjustment to being out of the Mushroom preoccupied me, and getting a good sense of our political situation was hard. The militants were talking very little around us and in the bathroom we learned very little, even though once I was forgotten in there. I washed up and was ready to knock for the guard when the door opened and in came Kevin Hermening, the youngest hostage. He asked how I was and told me that he had just seen his mother, who had come to Teheran maybe a day or two before. I didn't understand how this was possible. The only visitors we had been allowed to have so far were ministers and the ambassadors and, of course, the wandering Ayatollahs. Maybe, I thought, Mrs. Timm had come on her own to see Kevin. I hoped my mother wouldn't come. As much as I was yearning to see her and my father, I didn't want my country or the other hostages compromised in any way because of me.

Kevin and I talked about who I was rooming with and

how everything was going. He then left, while I stayed. A minute later Al Golacinski came in. The militants closed the door. Al asked how my arm was, and I said, "Better."

Evidently word had gotten around the Mushroom that I had a medical problem. After the Gestapo raid everybody figured it was something wrong with my arm—no one realized the whole left side of my body was affected. Al asked who I was rooming with. He told me who he was rooming with and which other people he had seen in the chancery basement. We gathered that a lot of the military officers who had been with us in the Mushroom were here too.

After he left, I waited another couple of minutes and knocked on the door. The Iranians were surprised. One guy hit the top of his forehead with his hand, realizing his mistake. I could hear them arguing about what went wrong. As far as I could understand it, they were doing the Iranian version of "Who's on First?"

"Forty-eight is still in there? Who with?"

"No, no, I took thirty-five. You were supposed to get forty-eight."

"There is no thirty-five. Thirty-five was one of the released."

"No thirty-five? You're crazy."

Meanwhile the door was wide open and I could see whoever was in the hall. That happened a lot. The militants went through their Mickey Mouse routine, then blew it with a wide open door.

We guessed that Navy Commander Don Sharer and Duane Gillette, a navy enlisted man we called "Sam," were our neighbors because Sharer had once been walked into our room by mistake by the militants. Not only did they forget our numbers, they forgot which rooms they had assigned us to. This is not so unusual as they kept changing our rooms depending on their whim. Not long afterward I heard three or four knocks—light knocks on the wall next to my bed. I responded with three or four light knocks. Thirty seconds later I heard two or three pounding sounds. I decided that didn't sound right; it could be an Iranian. I remembered what happened when Lopez was trying to call Golacinski in the chancery during the takeover; an Iranian had tried to impersonate Golacinski. I gave up on knocking.

Life developed a routine again, if a slightly modified one. I got up early and read. Lately I had been intent on finishing as much of Thomas Hardy as I could and was now reading *Tess of the D'Urbervilles*. Hardy wasn't exactly the cheeriest author to read, but his characters got a lot of experience dealing with misfortune, which made his books doubly interesting to me at this time. After the usual bread and jam breakfast, we were taken with towels over our heads to the bathroom. When we finished, we knocked on the door. I had this recurring thought that everyone would be released while I was in the bathroom waiting for a guard to get me out.

Joe and I were having normally paced conversations now, with no more of the frantic efforts to talk continuously sixteen or eighteen hours a day. We played checkers and chess here, too, but neither of us were real buffs, despite what I had told Hamid earlier. I set my Civil War game up again and started a game beginning at 1861. Joe still maintained that refighting the Civil War was not number one on his list of things to do, even in this place where there was not all that much to do. He said if I kept up my obsession with the Civil War he was going to start calling me General Sherman.

I got a little package from a friend containing a game called "The Creature That Ate Sheboygan." I imagined the Iranians were rather confused when they opened the package to censor it and saw the cover drawing of a monster attacking a city, but it didn't keep them from giving it to me. By now, I think they were accustomed to my game-playing. This game had a little map and some counters. One person would play the Creature, and the other would play the Sheboygan police and the National Guard. I taught Joe how it worked, and we played it in the evenings, just before our smoking hour, alternating sides.

Joe referred to the game often in his letters to Cherlynn, and before long I became known to her as The Man from Sheboygan. Earlier, when we were first allowed to talk, Joe and I decided that it might be a good idea to develop some kind of code in case one of us was released first. If Joe got out, he was supposed to contact my mother, and she would write and say she was going to Oregon, Joe's home state. If I got out, the message from Cherlynn would say she's going to Maine—where my parents live. As it turned out "The Man from Sheboygan" was all we needed.

Mail was still coming in, but without the ceremonious deliveries of the Mushroom. Now the militants simply came in with a couple of letters every week or so and handed them out. Joe and I knew we still weren't getting a lot of our mail, even though Hamid the Liar insisted we were. After a while we didn't even bother telling him the contrary. I saved my letters—mostly from my family, a few from strangers—and read them so many times that I practically memorized them.

I also received a packet containing six notes written by students in the seventh grade at St. John's School in Brooklyn. What a fantastic delight it was to read their notes. On the same day I received a letter from my mother that gave Joe and me our biggest laugh of the day. Mother, caught up in decorating the new house, wanted me to arbitrate a Wedgwood blue vs. royal blue dining room color conflict. Since I had absolutely no conception of what either color looked like I begged off.

"Maybe we ought to put the question to the guards," Joe said, laughing.

Sometimes the bathroom right across the hall was filled, so they took us to another bathroom. When they led me across the hall, I couldn't see a thing because here, unlike the Mushroom, we had to wear towels over our heads. Sometimes, accidentally or on purpose, the militants led us into one of the chairs or desks where the guards sat, letting us get bruised or banged up. But I could see where my feet were going, and by looking down, I learned where the carpet ended and the bare floor began. I learned to be careful and not catch my foot at these places, which could cause a really messy fall. The bathroom ritual—knocking, wearing towels on our heads—was meant to be degrading, but we refused to be degraded and made a joke of it instead.

Nothing seemed to change as the days went by, but, surprisingly, to me at least, Joe and I were both growing calmer. It was not something we talked about. It was just a feeling, I think, that since there was nothing we could do about our situation, we were not about to discuss it between ourselves or with the Iranians either. That had all been done and had gotten us nowhere. For me, again, the decision was probably an unconscious one that kept any

149

tiny, nagging thoughts that we might never be released from turning into panic. I think it kept me from falling apart, a combination of emotional survival and stubborn pride.

We did talk, though, usually after dinner. About ten o'clock, we had what we called our smoking hour. We would turn off the bright fluorescent overhead light and leave on a dim desk lamp. I took my pipe; Joe, his cigar. We sat back for a couple of hours, just smoking and telling each other stories about our past lives.

"I always knew I wanted to be in the army," he said, the end of his cigar glowing in the semidarkness. "So I joined up right after high school. Since then I've been just about everywhere. I guess my favorite tour was Greece. I was on the military attaché staff there too. The water over there is so blue—a different kind of blue from here. I think about that a lot now. When I'm not dreaming about Cherlynn I dream about that blue water in Greece."

"I wanted to be in the army, too," I said, "but my eyesight fouled me up every time I applied; I passed the exam for West Point but was turned down because of my vision. I joined ROTC and wanted to make the army my career, but again my poor eyesight caused me problems. Eventually they put me in the best of the quartermaster corps, POL, petroleum oil lubricant. Funny the hostages didn't turn me down because of my eyesight. There must be a lower standard for hostages than for the army."

"Well, I'm in the army and I'm a hostage. And I can tell you this—being a hostage is a lot tougher. Maybe they should start giving entrance exams," said Joe, smiling to himself at the thought.

Joe had been watching me smoke for a while when he

decided to take up a pipe again. I gave him my extra pipe. Akbar brought him a second lighter from the store. We smoked the Half and Half tobacco the militants provided us.

I tried to keep the window open at least part of the day. I didn't want the room to turn into a chimneyless smokehouse. I also liked getting a breeze. That was something we never got in the Mushroom. It was still a thrill to hear the sounds of the birds and the traffic and the airplanes—all the sounds that made me feel a part of the world again. The thrill lasted a long time, and although it beckoned us alluringly, it also helped me enjoy the never-never land I had set up for myself.

We took our showers back in the Mushroom, every week or so. Hamid the Liar told us to tell him when we had gone seven days without a shower, since that was supposed to be the maximum, and on our way to the Mushroom showers, we walked by the library. I noticed that the library had started to deteriorate. When the Iranians looked for books, they weren't always neat about it. If they found a book at the bottom of a pile, they'd just pull it out and the pile would tumble down. Sometimes the guards would let me have ten to fifteen minutes in the library, and, since I knew where all the books were, I could quickly find the ones I wanted, but I didn't, of course, have time to straighten things up. I really missed using the library.

One day in early April, shortly before Easter, Hamid the Liar asked me if I wanted to build a library in the chancery. Naturally I said yes, and Joe decided to help. Hamid took us, towels over our heads, to an office room upstairs at the end of the chancery. Beautiful wooden shelves with glass doors stood along the walls, and a big office desk sat in the

151

center. It was a much smaller room than the one in the Mushroom, and I knew we couldn't fit all the books in. Hamid said that was all the space we'd get. He also said the books had to be standing properly.

He was adamant. "Just put them on," he said and even started doing it himself. We wondered what was up when he spent the next few nights shelving all alone and brought in a couch and a nice glass table with a vase of flowers.

Then we found out. Hamid wasn't interested in building a library for our sake; he was interested in making a showcase to demonstrate how well we were being treated as hostages, in preparation for the imminent Easter visit of some ministers from the United States. Khomeini had invited them to come.

I wrote a hopeful letter to my parents just before the Easter festivities.

April 5, 1980

Dear Mom, Dad and Alex,

Tomorrow is Easter, and I am expecting some religious services, hopefully similar to the one I attended on Christmas. I anticipate that we will have ministers from America, and am greatly looking forward to seeing them; even if we are forbidden to talk about what is happening in the world today, it will nonetheless be a tremendous boon to speak to someone so recently arrived from home.

I certainly can't complain about conditions here, especially after the improvements we recently have been experiencing, but holidays such as Easter and Christmas which normally should be such festive and joyous occasions naturally make me feel especially lonely and homesick. My mood now though is infinitely better than it was at Christmas.

Please mail me a package containing various Macbarren pipe tobaccos, especially Scottish Blend and Royal Twist. Thanks.

Happy Easter, God Bless and love, love, love,

Richard

The services were similar to the ones at Christmas. We went upstairs in groups of four, and again I was in the last group. I had combed my hair and put on the marine pants—they were my dressiest—and my best shirt hours before Joe and I were called. Gary Lee and Bob Engelmann were with us. When we came in we saw a table in the far corner with the two ministers—Reverend Thompson and Father Rupiper—seated at one end. The four of us sat at the other.

Again, the service was simple and moving. We received Communion and spiritually it meant a lot to me. Still there was an unreal side to it—our degrading captivity displayed before two people from the States, who were free to come and go as they pleased. They met with us, comforted and blessed us, while Iranian television cameras and newspeople watched, pushing and shoving in the back of the room.

When the service was over, Reverend Thompson embraced us with tears in his eyes, and Father Rupiper said, "I wish I had the strength to stay here with you. This is a real test, a test of one's faith." I thought that was a kind thing to say.

The militants then showed us to a table at the back of the room full of all sorts of sweets, candies, cakes and fruit. They told us we were the last group, and so I piled a paper plate with the cake and fruit, and packed my pockets—shirt, front and back—with candies and chocolate bars. When I finished, the pockets were bulging and I couldn't sit down for fear of squashing everything. Because the militants were filming us and joking and laughing with us, I was afraid that films of me stuffing my pockets would be shown in the United States, but luckily they weren't. Joe and I debated whether to take a whole cake, since there were some uncut cakes left, but for the same reason we decided not to. Instead we cut out a huge piece. We walked away, in fact, with everything we could carry, knowing the Iranians would eat it if we didn't. Better us than them.

When I got back to my room I divided the chocolates into different types—Krackle, Reese Peanut Butter Cups, almond bars—and put them into a drawer, because we didn't want the Iranians to see them and take what they wanted for themselves. We had to eat the cake quickly, and kept on eating it even when it got hard. Each day Joe and I would debate which bar to have. We'd split it carefully and usually ate it in the evening with our tea. One militant we called the Moocher found us with a bar and asked if he could have a piece. We had to give him one.

I tried not to dwell on the fact that we had spent three major holidays in captivity—Thanksgiving, Christmas and now Easter; if I did my mind would jump ahead to a lifetime of these staged celebrations, and I couldn't deal with that. Both Joe and I discussed the problem, which helped. He felt, as I did, that to write home and constantly complain to people who loved us, who worried about us, would be grossly unfair. On the other hand, we could not lie and say things were great.

I thought about what I could say, reworked it in my

mind. I knew by then I had readjusted enough to cope. I knew what was happening to me, but my parents didn't, of course, and imagination can be one's worst enemy. Therefore I tried to include some humor in my letters, to ease their fears, and never mentioned my illness to them. I put a few thoughts—much more brave and positive than I was feeling—in a letter to my folks.

April 12, 1980

Dear Mom, Dad and Alex:

Now that the excitement of Easter has calmed down, life has resumed its everyday routine as the visions of America stirred by my conversations with the priests again recede to the recesses of my mind. Hostage life must be my life now, so the easier and more completely I accept that, the better things will be here: It only causes unnecessary anguish and hardship to fight this obvious fact. Accepting the moral presented in the parable of the willowy reed and the unbending oak in the storm is the best solution to surviving this situation. And, I must add, I have adopted this very well indeed, so much so that for the past four months or so life has not been very burdensome at all.

Love, love and more love,
Richard

I tried not to listen to the loudspeaker outside our window that broadcast propaganda into the courtyard, even though snatches of news were broadcast on it, too. From what I could understand, America was imposing new sanctions against Iran. Of course, the news was always slanted pro–Iran. "The American devil has been beaten trying to cripple the brave followers of Islam." Or variations on that theme. In Iranian news, Iran always triumphs, so it wasn't something you wanted to hear day after day after day. Instead I set out to organize the library. Now the ministers were gone and Hamid had stopped worrying about it. Even inside the chancery, snatches of release talk were floating around again, and I decided to submerge my thoughts in an organized program of reading and study instead of getting worked into a frenzy of endless and useless speculation.

Later that day I received a startling letter from my mother. It said, among other things:

Pete Brown asked me not to mention this, but I feel I must. When you were captured, we waited so long to hear that you were alive and well. But no word came. I called Pete and Anne and told them I was frantic with worry. He said they both were worried, too, and would find out what was going on.

He called back later to say that he and Anne talked; they agreed Pete should go to Teheran to find you. He was going to get press credentials! Everything was prepared for his trip, but the day before he was to leave, I received the first letter from you—finally we knew something.

I thought you should know how much Pete and Anne love you.

I reread that letter so many times—the immensity of what my friends were willing to do overwhelmed me with emotion. I had to let them know as soon as possible what their gesture had meant to me. Maybe, I thought, one of the Red Cross people could take the letter back with him. I asked Ahmad if this would be possible. He came back and said, "Yes, but you must write it now—and only two lines." How could I express in two lines all that was in my heart? I wept unashamedly as I wrote:

Dearest Anne and Pete:
My God, what friends you are.

Then I handed it to the guard.

It was around this time that a delegate from the Red Cross visited us, checking on our welfare. He was escorted by the quack doctor. I tried to describe the symptoms of my illness to the Red Cross representative, but the quack doctor cut me off and escorted him out of the room. I didn't push it because, as I told Don Hohman, "I assume the quack doctor has told the Red Cross I am ill."

Don replied, "No, I don't think he did. You should have pushed it."

I groaned. "You're right, dammit." But it was too late.

Life settled back quickly into the dreary routine. Only the challenge of getting the chancery library completely organized held my interest. There were several hundred fiction titles, plus a shelf for anthropology and ones for sociology, history, government, etc., like a regular library. The marines had gone back to the Mushroom library and brought all the sports books over, and so we had plenty of those as well. All in all, we had a reasonable collection. It included some new books sent from the United States, which I could identify because I'd find half-opened book parcels with books that hadn't been stamped "Teheran

American High School Library." Someone had sent twenty-
five copies of *Spooky Speaks,* a book about a talking poodle.
We also received a lot of what I call pulp fiction—romances
that all seemed to be called *Savage, Sacred Love* or *Sacred,
Savage Love.* They seemed to revolve around the theme of a
young woman of unquestionable purity falling in love with
a reprobate who spends the major part of the book trying
to make her purity not so unquestionable. I thought if we
all read those books as a steady diet while we were hostages,
our minds would be reduced to pudding without the
Iranians having to do a thing.

Hamid the Liar devised a new system for checking out
books: all of us got a four-digit number, so we wouldn't
know how many people were being held. We knew
anyway, although writing in books hadn't worked. The
library had several thousand books, and so it was hard to
know which one would be picked up again. I found one
note written by a marine. In it he said that Don Hohman,
the army medic, was on a hunger strike, and that three or
four of the marines were going to join him. The marine
who wrote the note got the date wrong, so they started
their hunger strike after Don had finished his. When I
picked up the book, it was three months after any of the
hunger strikes—not very timely information.

We did know by the grapevine that there were about
fifty of us, although we didn't know everyone's name. I
found out John Graves, an international communications
officer, was a hostage when he wrote the four-digit number
and his name on a slip of paper. Everyone was to leave a slip
of paper with their number written on it inside their
returned books. I collected the numbers and tried to
decipher whatever I could from them. As the librarian, it

was my job to go through returned books to make sure nobody had written messages in them. If an Iranian was present, I flipped through the books. Otherwise, I just put them back on the shelves. The work gave me a good feeling of being in touch with everyone, and I also felt I was doing something to help everybody—an alternative to just sitting around and feeling sorry for myself. If the library was organized, you could find a specific book and not just have to grab whatever was handy. This way you could control what you read and, thereby, what you felt for the rest of the day. But for once, Joe and I didn't agree.

"You know the library's just a publicity stunt for the militants," he said.

"Sure it is," I answered. "But it helps us, too."

He disagreed again. "People don't care what they read. It doesn't make any difference to them."

That really hurt. It was as though the very foundation I had built my world on had been badly shaken. I said I knew it made a difference. "At least to me," I said. "I don't want to read pulp fiction." But I was upset enough to want proof, so much later, when I roomed with Bob Ode and Don Hohman, I asked them if they cared which books they read. When they said yes, I felt better, even though I knew on one level how childish resolving the argument was. And I knew it was our situation that was making these things matter so much.

The weather was getting warmer. The window over Joe's bed wouldn't open, but mine did. There were no screens, and it was the rainy season, so we had to close the window when the sun went down to keep out the swarms of mosquitoes.

The militants brought us an electric mosquito killer that

159

had a pad, which, when plugged in, heated up and emitted fumes. It was effective, but we only got it once every eight or nine days for a night or two, so the rest of the time we'd have mosquito safaris at bedtime. We didn't want to swat them on our newly painted walls, and so we tried to get them flying before we squashed them. The ones we missed buzzed around our room and kept us awake.

Although our doors in the chancery were kept closed, very few of the Iranians knocked before they came in. Most just opened the door and said what they wanted, or just entered. Early on, they would make regular checks to see if we had escaped. They would come in, and Joe or I would say, "No, we haven't run away. We're still here." Where they thought we could run to, I don't know, because the windows had bars that had been put on before the takeover to keep out intruders. Unfortunately, the bars also kept us inside.

Later on the militants scraped the whitewash from the window in our door and put a flap down, so they could see in without our seeing out. But compared to the Mushroom, this was the epitome of privacy; in the Mushroom we had been watched twenty-four hours a day.

Because of my interest in the library and books, one of the guards complained that I was reading too much. It was a complaint I had heard before. He had something else in mind. He told me that some of my friends were learning really important things but I was learning nothing. Twice he came in and complained.

"You don't really learn the truth," he said, holding up a pamphlet with Khomeini's face on it; "here is your chance to find out what lies you've been told by your government."

I looked up from my book, Charles Dickens's *Nicholas*

Nickleby, and told him I'd catch up on his "truth" later, the "truth" of the Iranian revolution.

Around that time a tomcat began to visit us. He got near our windows and moaned and yowled. At first we thought somebody was beating a child. I tried throwing water on him, but I couldn't reach that high; then he climbed to a crawl space above our ceiling. Occasionally a ferocious cat fight would erupt right after we dozed off. We wondered if it was our forlorn cat being attacked.

We were in some ways lucky to have the same small group of about forty guards around us all the time. After a while, they got to know us by face and a few addressed us by name. I knew several of their names and recognized all of their faces. They no longer labeled Joe and me as spies. Although they still wrote slogans like "Spies' Nest" and "Death to the Carter" on the walls, I think they had gone through the records and realized that despite their ingrained suspicions, we were what we said we were, so they no longer accused us personally.

Once I asked if any visa plates were still in the consulate. Hamid the Liar told me the consulate was out of bounds. They had locked it up because there was nothing in it. This didn't square with their propaganda about all of us being spies who had been plotting to overthrow the Iranian revolutionary government. That rhetoric was for the public.

Around this time I grew hopeful that my left side was getting better. I attributed it to exercise and generally better conditions. After about three weeks in the chancery, the Iranians had even put a Ping-Pong table in the room next to ours. If we wanted, we could play Ping-Pong, but only between ourselves, not with any of the other hostages.

There was also going to be an exercise bicycle, they said, and some weights. Joe didn't play Ping-Pong, so he and I only played once. I had already been using the room as an exercise room. It was rather small. I'd walk around the perimeter, fifty laps one way and fifty the other. When the bicycle arrived, I'd ride a little bit, or try to do sit-ups. I could do a fair number, but I was getting lazy with them. I'd find excuses to postpone doing them in the morning. Then I'd postpone them for the whole day. Push-ups were the worst problem I had with my left hand and arm. I had trouble controlling that side; sometimes it collapsed.

But I could play Ping-Pong, if I served by placing the ball in the palm of my left hand, turning the hand over, letting the ball drop in front of me and hitting it. A few of the Iranians started asking me to play, and in spite of my physical problem, I won half my games. Some Iranians really knew how to play the game well, but most just liked to slam the ball. They didn't know how to do this properly, so instead of the ball bouncing back on the table on the return of the slam, it would go sailing up into space and bounce off the wall. They threw away their points. We'd count in Farsi, and some of them really didn't like losing to me or to any of the hostages. One I beat complained about my serve. I told him I couldn't use my hand. The majority were better sports.

Sometimes the militants would come in and look at our pictures and ask a few questions. Joe had put up pictures of his wife; they'd want to know who she was and if he had any children. He would answer yes or no, saying little more, but I'd have longer conversations with them. We'd talk about the village in Maine where my parents had recently moved and the Iranians' villages and families. I considered these conversations a good thing. They let the militants know that we were human beings like them, with families and homes. It was a tactic I remembered from the training course in handling terrorism given by the State Department just before I left for Teheran. The instructor's most important point in the hostage survival session was that a hostage should try to establish some contact with his captors. Any simple personal relationship made the captors see you not as a nameless, faceless enemy agent but as an individual.

I didn't shy away from that sort of contact, but I did shy away from political discussions. The militants were not well educated or at all sophisticated. Some came in and tried to make a propaganda point, expounding on the evils of the United States and the evils of the Shah. They would harangue us for a minute or two. We'd look at them, smile, and nod our heads, and then they'd go away because we didn't give a response. Other times we became irritated and said, "Go away" or "Nonsense," and they'd tell us, "No, you're wrong."

In one political discussion, I told a militant that Iran was going to be in trouble with the Soviets. I knew from a letter my father had sent, which the militants had obviously forgotten to censor, that the Soviets had invaded Afghanistan and said so. He denied it at first, and then he agreed. I told him there was a good chance the Russians would invade Iran.

"We'll destroy them if they do," he said.

"They'll roll right over you," I told him.

We talked about Iranian weapons being supplied by the United States. The militant maintained that American oil companies and bankers wouldn't allow Iranian oil to fall to the Soviets, regardless of what the Iranians did with us. Then he said that Iran would fight to the last man, woman and child to stop the Soviets. The discussion ended.

One day one of the guards who was convinced the United States would someday become a Moslem republic came and asked if I was going to sue the American government.

I said, "Why?"

"There are some people around here already working out lawsuits," he said. "Aren't you going to sue too?"

Joe and I both said no.

"Well, a lot of your friends are already planning suits," he maintained, "and some are planning a coup for when they get back to the United States. They're going to overthrow the government and set up a people's democracy."

We asked about these alleged "conversions" during the one interesting political discussion we had, sometime in mid-April. "Kansas," one of the "supervisors"—supervisors being those who could speak English fairly well—came in and asked if Joe and I would like to discuss politics. We said we would. Nothing happened so we asked when the discussion was going to take place. The supervisor said in a short time. We were not to worry. He seemed to be putting it off. Finally one afternoon he came in with two others: Little Hamid, an Iranian who had been educated in the United States, and a second Iranian whom I didn't recognize. They could all speak English quite well, particularly Kansas, who also had been educated in the States.

They stressed their position—the evils of the Shah, the United States' responsibility for supporting the Shah, how the Shah had destroyed Iran. The United States was responsible for this destruction, they said, because it supported the Shah. The purpose of the embassy seizure was to expose the corrupting influence America had had in Iran. They said they hoped that the seizure would have an effect on the United States itself.

Joe and I said, "You don't know what you're doing to your own country. You're destroying it. Iran's in chaos and it can't afford to be isolated."

Even though I had no idea what was going on outside, I was sure this was causing Iran to be isolated from the diplomatic community and from the rest of the world, West and East. I guessed that most of the other embassies had closed down in Teheran. (I was wrong. Some had, and a number of others had trimmed their staffs.) I said, "This revolution of yours will fail because your country depends on outside resources. You can't grow all the goods you need, and you depend on trade with other nations for industrial goods—people of the West and the United States. Your military is supplied with American weapons and planes, British and American tanks, so you have a strong connection with the West, particularly with the United States. You can't just suddenly cut it off."

I said I worked in the consulate and I knew how many Iranians were trying to get to United States schools. I reminded him that they couldn't educate all the Iranians who wanted to be educated because Iranian universities were too small. I said that if the United States broke off relations with Iran, those ambitious people who wanted to advance would have nowhere to go. It was this young, volatile population they would have to worry about. These people would soon become frustrated and realize the revolution wasn't going to produce the heaven it had promised. They wouldn't be able to get decent jobs or to advance in life. They couldn't even go to the United States or leave the country. Iran would be a boiler about to explode.

He said, "No, you don't realize how deeply the Iranian people support this revolution, particularly the young. They are the corps of our revolution." He went on to discuss the United States.

Joe or I said, "You don't realize that you won't get support from the United States."

The usual response was, "The American people are ready for revolution: they're waiting for Khomeini to come lead them."

I said, "You don't really believe that the American people are going to rise up and support a Khomeini."

The student educated in the United States said, "No, some of us realize that, for example, on the American campuses, we have no support. All American students want to do is go out and get a good job. They don't have revolutionary fervor. We don't expect anything from them. We know the United States, the American people, are not going to rise up and join us." It was one of the few times that I heard a realistic statement about America from one of the militants.

I think all three of them realized what conditions were like in the United States and how the American people felt about the hostage-taking. "Kansas" hinted that the American people were supporting us and that Iran couldn't expect anything from American college students or American people in general. He even said, "The blacks have let us down. They're not supporting us, either. Don't you realize you'll have to change your government?" he asked us.

Joe or I said, "No. We have an elective system. If our people want the government to change they will vote a change."

The militant then said, "Well, you're just too patriotic if you don't realize that your country is controlled by the bankers and oil interests, that they're the ones who control who votes and who gets elected."

We said, "You don't understand the American system. You have a better understanding than most of your friends, but they don't understand it at all. They know as much about the United States as I know about the far side of the moon."

Before we finished I asked if they really thought some of the hostages were plotting to overthrow the government when they returned to the United States.

One of them said, "No, of course, we realize they aren't. Some just say that to see if they can get out of here. It's all nonsense." Still I was sure that the person who told us believed it—an indication of how naïve so many of the "students" were. Most of them had never left Iran; many never wanted to leave. They'd say, "Iran is my home and I never want to cross its borders." Their world was extremely provincial. The people we had just spoken with were better educated and more realistic. Our discussion wasn't heated and it was actually one of the most level-headed talks I had ever engaged in with any of the militants. It ended ambiguously, with no real conclusion.

Chapter 6

In April it got warmer. We went out more regularly and once we briefly got a volleyball to play around with because there were photographers present. Usually we spent about a half hour walking around and shooting the breeze in the two walled-in courtyards, both rather small. One had been the ambassador's garden. When the takeover occurred, there was nothing much growing there except for chives, which I dug up, took back to my room and ate with our salads whenever we got them. Eventually they were trampled on by too many people to be edible.

As time passed, my hair started to get long again and my beard got scraggly. I had never liked long hair, but I wasn't about to let the Iranians cut it again. Instead, Joe and I decided to do a little barbering for each other. We had to ask six people for scissors, but eventually they doled some out and razors as well, so Joe could cut off his beard. That way we maintained at least a civilized appearance.

We didn't like to use the bathroom the Iranians used. It was usually a disastrous mess; indeed, just walking in the door we'd be bowled over by the stink. They made us use it when ours were full, but we got to where we'd rather wait. Luckily, I never ran into the toilet paper problem that a number of other hostages encountered. Sometimes they'd have to wait a whole day for paper. The thing was to always check for such things before you committed yourself.

There were always the day-to-day minor inconveniences—really small annoyances on top of everything else, like finding no soap in the bathroom and then having to wait two to three days to get it, or having to wash our dishes in the sink along with our clothes. Sometimes we'd be given fabric softener instead of dishwashing soap. I'm sure the militants got it from the commissary in the compound without realizing what they were taking because the bottles were the same size, shape and color, and the labels were similar. It was impossible to wash plates with fabric softener, so instead, we used a bar of Ivory soap. If I hadn't sneaked in a dish rag I found in the Mushroom while I was taking a shower, we would have had to scrub everything with our fingers.

One afternoon, Hamid the Liar came down and asked if we wanted to see a movie. Of course we said yes. The movie was supposed to be ready in ten minutes. An hour later, we were led upstairs with towels over our heads, walking in a train with Joe's hand on my shoulder and one of the militants leading me. Corty Barnes, Bill Keough and Don Cooke sat in the movie room. It's the custom to take off your shoes before you walk on rugs, so we took off our sandals and sat on the floor. No talking was allowed. We saw a cops-and-robbers TV serial called *Chips* and afterward

Hamid put the towels over our heads and took us back down to the room.

The next week we saw a propaganda movie on the Islamic revolution, again with the same people. And then Hamid the Liar announced that he had an American comedy for us. It was *Annie Hall*, a Woody Allen movie about a love affair that fades. I had seen it already in the States, but this time we were going to see it under very different circumstances. After the first half, Hamid the Liar said, "This is awful, it's corrupt, it's disgusting. We can't allow you to see this sex. We'll have to destroy the movie." We never saw the second half.

The week after, Hamid came in and snapped his fingers the way he always did and said, "Movies, movies, movies. Let's go." We sat through a propaganda film with Hamid narrating. When he came by the next week announcing another movie, I said no. I was tired of being promised regular movies and seeing propaganda instead.

The following week one of the guards came in with several pens filled with shredded decommissioned dollars in the stem. It was sent from someone in the United States.

"You can use this pen for your letters," he told us, "but don't take the money out and try to put it back together again."

Joe and I just looked at him and burst out laughing. The students' naïveté knew no bounds.

One time they brought us a tape recorder with some music cartridges—country and western, and classical. We got them in the evening, and the militants retrieved them in the morning. Having music was a great treat. We'd play the tapes over and over again unless neither of us liked them.

Then one day Hamid the Liar came in and said, "I have a tape from Joe's wife." He whispered to me, "Watch this; I bet he breaks down and cries."

Joe was very excited, of course, but he asked me to stay and listen, too. It was a short tape that his wife had made on the phone, and the Iranians had recorded it. Her voice was warm and hopeful. "I love you Joe. I know you'll be home soon. Everything is fine here. Don't worry about me. Just know that I love you and we'll be together soon." Joe did break down and cry; he was ecstatic when he heard Cherlynn's affirming, positive words. And so was I. As I wiped away my tears, I realized Cherlynn was smart enough to know that the last thing her husband would want to hear would be a tearful, worried message. What I heard on that tape was the undefeated spirit of an American woman saying, "We're going to win this yet. Hang on." Hamid must have recognized it, too, because even though he was moved, he was disappointed with our elation and left the room.

We listened to it several times, then I went to the Ping-Pong room while Joe made a tape of his own. He gave it to the Iranians to send back to the States.

From our room, Joe and I could see the militants patrolling the pathway above the retaining wall and also see some of the taller buildings and trees across the street.

The militant we nicknamed the Moocher was an easy, overweight guy who used to come by and shoot the breeze before he went on duty. Sometimes he'd throw rocks at our window to get our attention because he always wanted something—cigarettes, which we didn't have, or some of our Off spray for mosquitoes. The first time he used it, he sprayed on too much and almost killed us along with the bugs. After a while, we had to pretend we had run out because he was borrowing everything. After Easter, when he had glommed our Easter candy, we started hiding our chocolates from him, too. He quit asking for things when he got sick on one of the cheap cigars we gave him.

I remember another one, Nader, who was really quite nice and somewhat shy. He was very slight, clean-shaven and had doleful eyes. He had never been out of Iran and only recently had left his village, which was about 150 miles from Teheran.

"What is New York like? What is Washington like?" he'd ask. "Is it like what you see in movies?"

One morning he came in holding something in his hand. "Here," he said, handing us a small cloth filled with candy, "for both of you. It's candy from my grandmother. She lives in Mashhad, and I visit her last week. She wants you to have these so you won't be sad for your home."

Some of the militants would go away on weekends and visit their families, wherever they were. More and more it was becoming apparent that they couldn't wait for their weekends to get away from their prison duty.

Nader was quiet usually. He would never propagandize. But once he came in and asked if we wanted a picture of Khomeini for our walls. We hadn't had any propaganda posters in our rooms since we left the Mushroom, and he said it with complete innocence, as though he thought we would really want Khomeini staring over our beds. I said, "No, he's your leader, not mine."

But he said, "Khomeini is a leader of the world."

I repeated, "No, no, no." We left it at that.

There was another guy in his twenties, named Rashid, who was somewhat narcissistic. Once I was in the bathroom with him when he looked in the mirror and asked, "Do you think I'm going bald?" There was absolutely no way he was going bald, and even if he was, it was ten years down the road.

He used to like to flex his muscles. One time when I was in the library, he challenged me to an arm-wrestling match. I have quite a strong right arm from my years of playing softball, and I beat him on the first one. He immediately challenged me again. There were a couple of militants looking on and joking because he lost to me, especially since it was known that I had a medical problem. I don't think they knew it wasn't my right side that was being affected—just the left. The second time, we had a tie. The third time, he pulled a quick count and won by cheating.

This guy, obviously a great believer in ethical behavior, was going to be a lawyer. Several times he asked me about applying to schools in the U.S. He wanted to know what his chances were if he applied to Harvard Law School. I didn't know how to take this at first. Here he was, holding me hostage, and asking about his chances of going to school—in particular, Harvard Law School, and wanting my help looking up different schools.

We had *Barron's Guide to Colleges* in the library, and I figured what the hell and gave it to him. He looked through it, and now he asked, seriously, if I could help him get into an American law school. He even gave me his name and address and then had second thoughts. He was afraid the militants' security people might find it on me and become suspicious of him.

He thanked me and told me, I thought somewhat wistfully, that he knew a lot about the States from books

173

and movies. "It's funny. I have looked at your movies in the Mushroom—every Saturday night. I watched your TV shows, too. All the time I like *The Wild, Wild West*. This is the best one. Did you see the time Artemis saved West— they were on this train going fantastically fast."

He was quite disappointed when I told him I'd never seen the show.

Another time he saw me looking at a painting by a turn-of-the-century American artist, Robert Henri. The name of the picture was *Mary* and it was of a lively looking young blond girl with a mischievous face. I wondered about her. If she felt confined, a hostage to the cumbersome clothing and mores of the time. It would be great, I thought, to have her suddenly materialize and we could talk to one another or . . . I suddenly wanted very much to hold someone and feel them holding me. I came out of my reverie to hear Rashid say, "Yes, I agree, she's absolutely lovely, but think how old and wrinkled she'd be if she were alive now." We then got into a rather melancholic discussion of how beauty fades and how the painting had captured the freshness of youth.

It occurred to me that our youth, Rashid's and mine, was slipping away too as we wasted all of this precious time playing hostage and guard. Rashid was from a very wealthy family who believed in the revolution, and he was a true follower of Khomeini. I found it hard to reconcile this information with his love of Western ways—cars, TV, movies. Somehow I couldn't see him practicing law in Khomeini's Iran. Not the law of the twentieth century anyway. When Rashid was not talking about his "school and career" plans he liked to discuss the merits of European cars as compared to American ones. He seemed surprised that my father did not drive a Cadillac or something similar. "In order to get girls you must have a good car," he advised. He said his spare time was spent riding in his father's Mercedes. He knew I liked fishing and so we talked about that and sports in general, as well.

There was a graduate mining student who was about twenty-seven and still single. I asked him why he hadn't married; so many of them married early, and he was very handsome. He said he didn't believe the Khomeini line that you had to marry early and produce children for Iran. Neither was he going to let his family arrange his marriage, he said. When he found the right girl, he was going to marry her and that was that.

Old Stony was another militant. He was fairly young, about twenty-one, and small, like many Iranians. He was always trying to impress us with his toughness. When we wanted to go to the bathroom, he would grip our arms tightly while the other militants would only take our sleeves.

He always had this stone face. One time, he caught us calling him "Old Stony," and he got stonier than ever. His retaliation was to tell us the bathroom was full whenever we asked to be taken to it, or to say that he'd come back later and then never show. This happened two or three times.

There was a really slimy character we called the Driver because he would drive us to the showers. He was slick. He would lie without the least bit of shame, and his face never showed anything. Unlike Hamid the Liar, he was intelligent.

One time Kansas (he had been educated at the University of Chicago and then the University of Kansas) came in and asked if I would come upstairs and listen to a tape. He said it was pirated from California and he couldn't understand it all. Since he spoke English so well, I wondered why he wanted me to hear the tape.

I couldn't understand all the words either; the tape said something about a peanut farmer in the White House. Then there were references to the fifty-three taken in Teheran. It went something like, "American women and men, all taken prisoners in Teheran. We don't need the Arabs' oil." Then I realized it was a neo-isolationist song— we should withdraw from our overseas commitments around the world. Just say the hell with the Middle East. I found this message very appealing and had to laugh that the militant who let me hear it (one of the more sophisticated of them all) thought it would be a protest song against the American government and the "peanut farmer in the White House" when, in fact, it was just the opposite.

Kansas took me back down to my room, not speaking. He was very upset that I had heard the tape and realized the support it represented. I went back and told Joe about it and we both agreed. It made our day.

After a while, the average militant I ran into was at best a small nuisance. You'd ask for something and you'd never get it. If the militant didn't go out of his way to make things difficult, he certainly didn't make any effort to make things easier. Once in a while, you'd find someone you didn't have to ask again and again for something, but most of them just forgot about you. The trouble was you were so dependent upon them for everything.

One evening in mid-April, the door opened and a couple of militants came in bringing a mattress. We were getting another roommate, they told us. Soon Charlie Jones came in carrying a little plastic bag with all the belongings he had accumulated as a hostage. We talked a little bit, then Charlie announced that he was a night person. He slept all day and stayed up all night.

We said, "Oh, God, we're the opposite; we don't maintain a vampire schedule." Charlie thought a while and then he agreed to spend his nights in the Ping-Pong room, awake, and his days sleeping in our room.

The next morning we found him already asleep when we woke up. The militants had kicked him out of the Ping-Pong room at about three-thirty. Our plan hadn't worked. He agreed to follow our general routine, but now we would keep the lights on an hour later than usual at night, which meant one o'clock, and Charlie would adopt a normal schedule of sleeping at night and staying awake during the day.

Soon after Charlie arrived, we were given a deck of cards, even though the militants had often said they considered playing cards un-Islamic. The first few days, we played around the clock until I grew tired of it and wanted to get back to my morning reading sessions. Charlie's and Joe's response was that they couldn't play poker with only two people. I went back to my reading anyway, and they'd make snide comments about me being a Jesuit monk.

Charlie was a communicator in charge of maintaining embassy communications with Washington. Both he and Joe had been overseas during much of their careers, so they had a lot to talk about. In fact, they used to talk all day long about old friends and old places, and I couldn't really concentrate while they talked and played rummy, so I tried putting my fingers to my ears. That didn't work so I tried a torn piece of cloth. That didn't work too well either. I was reading, but I wasn't reading very carefully. I was studying French in the mornings along with my scheduled reading, but finally I gave in and played poker with Charlie and Joe in the late afternoons and evenings.

Charlie was usually the winner. Luckily, we decided to play for pennies only, or I would have been out a fair amount of money. As it was, I lost $7.50 to Charlie and Joe lost $8.50. I'm not a bad poker player and neither is Joe, but Charlie was definitely better than either of us.

He was also very stubborn. Except for his medicines, which he put on the night table next to his bed, he never unpacked his few possessions from the plastic bag that he brought with him the first day he moved into our room because he didn't believe he wasn't going to be moved again, even though a militants told him he wasn't.

Charlie never wanted us to wake him up for breakfast, but one morning, a militant came in with some eggs—the first time ever. Joe and I had often joked about the fancy meals we were getting, and we'd fantasize elaborate breakfasts and dinners. Charlie had heard these fantasies several times, so when we woke him up to tell him about the eggs, he didn't believe us. We had to show him a plateful of the eggs. He shot out of bed and told the guard he wanted breakfast too. From then on, we had permission to wake him up whenever eggs came along.

We had a feeling, now, that our situation was improving. Even the militants seemed more relaxed. One day, one of the militants who was generally relaxed came in our room with a friend of his. He had always been fairly pleasant. They said, "The American people and the Iranian people really like each other. It's just our governments that are causing the problems." I couldn't believe it. He'd said "our" governments. That was the first I'd heard anything like that from any of the militants before—agreeing that his government was as culpable as ours.

There was a feeling in the air that we had reached a new stage, and for the first time, we began to discuss our future. We would talk after dinner, and we even would make bets on when we would be getting out. Joe thought May. I bet on June. Charlie guessed July.

So it didn't surprise me when, on the evening of April 25, as I was reading and trying not to listen to the radio that was attached to a loudspeaker outside, a broadcast caught my attention. The newscaster was talking about American planes from Saudi Arabia. Signs of reaction to it began to fill the chancery—we could hear commotion everywhere, constant movement and banging on doors, and I even caught a glimpse of somebody being moved out when I went to the bathroom.

This was it! The planes were coming for us. We were either going to be released or the U.S. was going to blow Iran off the face of the map. In my mind, I saw planes flying low over the city, ready to take all of Teheran hostage . . . Wait a minute—my imagination was really racing down that runway. We wouldn't be coming in to destroy Teheran. An agreement had been worked out. Of course, that was it. The planes would land, a government official would escort us out, and, oh, my God it would all be over. We're going home. I had to tell Joe and Charlie: Planes from Saudi Arabia were coming in to take us home.

They got very excited, as excited as I was, and when a guard came in and said we were moving, I jumped to my feet. Charlie, of course, had never unpacked, but the guard told Joe and me to take only a few things because our other

179

things would be brought to us. We spread our blankets and filled them up like Santa Claus sacks, thinking we'd never see anything we didn't take with us.

It was almost like a divorce, having to split everything up. I offered some leftover chocolates to Charlie, but he didn't want them. Another guard came in and said Charlie was going to be moving first. I was so excited, I could hardly sit still. I was allowing my feelings to surface and all my hopes burst forth when Charlie left. Joe and I would be next, I thought.

It was after eleven, then midnight. Finally, exhausted, we unrolled our mattresses and fell asleep. At three A.M., Hamid the Liar came in and asked why we hadn't packed. He told me to get ready because I was moving out alone. Suddenly, I knew what they were doing—separating Joe and me. Heavy-hearted, we divided everything. "You get the crunchy chocolates and I get the almonds. Who gets the cards and the checker game?" We shook hands for the last time. Then I was taken upstairs and put in a room by myself. I knew there would be no release.

I was on the second floor. The windows were white-washed, but I could pull down their tops. The bottom halves had two heavy metal sheets and sand in between. These had been there before the takeover as protection against snipers. From the top, I could still see the mountains, which were still snow covered, and although it was a beautiful sight, I felt lonely. I missed Joe.

The room had been a large office. It contained an office desk, a chair, a couple of end tables and several mattresses. I asked for a vacuum cleaner, but as usual, they were all broken, so I used a broom. Soon Hamid the Liar—how I hated him—came around and I asked where Joe was. All he would say was that Joe had been moved somewhere, too.

I asked for an ashtray and pulled out my books to read, feeling saddened that these monotonous routines were becoming my only structure. But I knew I had to follow them—anything else would send me really down, or worse, into despair. And lurking deep in my mind or not, despair is not my style. I wasn't going to give in.

So I read. I didn't hear much traffic, and although in a way I missed the street sounds, it was more peaceful for reading. The prayer call came from a distance, too, bouncing off the mountains, like an echo. I'm over six feet two inches; just by moving back in the room, I could look out over the metal sheets on the window. In the background was a bright blue sky with scattered puffs of clouds. It was fairly warm but not yet hot.

The bathroom was across the hall, facing the street. I couldn't see anybody else around, and when I asked to work in the library, the militants said no. The next day, it was the same. I spent my time reading or daydreaming and pacing back and forth across the room. Downstairs, I'd used the Ping-Pong room to pace. Now, my room was big enough to pace where I was. So I paced and daydreamed. Now there was no one to say, "For God's sake stop the pacing." I missed Joe so much it made this time much more unbearable than those horrible weeks in the Mushroom. I remembered him telling me that when he was a little boy his father took him to Alaska for six months; he lived there and went to school and fished and hunted. I suddenly saw the two of us, free at last, hiking through the pines, fishing in the rivers, drinking beer. I could smell the cedar; I could see us around the campfire. I wanted so much to be free, I could feel it. The feeling hurt. The pain of reality broke through and scattered my Alaska images. I was a hostage in Teheran, Iran. A long way from Alaska.

After several days, I was allowed to go to the library. The first thing I noticed was the empty table. Since the procedure was to stack returned books with a number sticking out, I could see that no books had been returned since I was there last.

The whole building seemed ominously quiet. I knew I wasn't totally alone because I heard someone knocking on the door across from me, but the routine sounds of hostage life were gone. I tried not to speculate, but I couldn't imagine why I was alone here. My questions grew when I discovered, at a movie Hamid finally arranged, that the person living across from me was Bob Ode, a retired officer from the State Department in Washington who had only been working in the consulate on a temporary assignment when he had been taken hostage. He was much older. I was further puzzled one afternoon when the guard brought Jerry Miele, who seemed depressed, into my room. He sat and daydreamed and didn't talk. I had been rationing myself to one half a chocolate bar a day, but I brought out one anyway. At first, Jerry wouldn't eat it, but then we polished off a couple of bars. That evening, he was moved out again.

I remained alone for about eight to ten days, feeling bothered, as usual, that the militants moved Jerry out without explaining why. That was always the case with changes—they gave you an uneasy feeling about what was coming next.

Soon, Hamid moved Bob to a room next to mine, and the connecting door was opened up. In effect, we had a two-room suite.

Bob Ode, the oldest hostage, had spent twenty-eight years in the State Department. He ticked off the countries: "Liberia, Poland, Britain, Iceland, Italy, Canada, Switzerland, West Germany—and never have I experienced anything as outrageous as this." He felt very frustrated that after five months we were still hostages. He told me that in December he'd written a letter to the Washington *Post* appealing for "prompt action" and telling the world that we were being tied up day and night. I was amazed that the Iranians had let the letter through.

A mild looking man who wore glasses and who had a receding hairline, Bob was filled with an anger belied by his looks. "I refuse to accept this situation. The Iranians be damned," he'd say. Like all of us he had a lot of emotion that needed to be released.

As usual, I'd positioned my mattress so I got the full sun every morning, and after breakfast, I'd smoke and read and then Bob would come into my room for lunch. Time was all ours, of course, and so we'd talk and eat a leisurely meal. We'd alternate doing the dishes.

Soon Don Hohman was moved into the room on the other side of Bob's. The army medic, Don had always had a very short crew cut. Now his red hair was very long and he wore a long beard. He kept pretty much to himself, not even eating meals with us. Hamid the Liar had warned us that he was a crazy man, but the truth was, Don just couldn't tolerate Hamid. Bob Ode and I would keep our anger to ourselves, but not Don. He and Hamid would get into shoving matches. Hamid's punishment for Don was no mail. He also reduced ours. When we would get ours, we'd share it with Don. But altogether, Don went seventy-five days without getting a letter or even a postcard.

For health reasons, Hohman refused to eat the meat. He said it made him sick. "This stuff is really terrible for you," he told me. When the militants would come by to collect the plates of food I'd say in Farsi, "Don Hohman can't eat meat, so if you could just give him vegetables, that would be great." You'd think they would remember after being told three or four times, but every time they'd come back with a plateful of meat.

My left arm and side were holding about the same—no better, no worse—but noting Bob's heart condition, I realized the militants had put an army medic with the two of us for a reason. Probably this was the sick bay, or we were, at least, the ones to keep an eye on. Don could do it for them. I wondered if they really believed I had only "twisted my spine," but I felt more worried about the ones who had left the chancery because obviously there'd been no release, so where had they gone? And why?

About this time, one of the militants came in and said, "Joe Hall sends you his best. He's doing fine." He wouldn't say where Joe was, but he did say that Bob Engelmann and Gary Lee were living upstairs. I knew they were rooming together, but the way he said it, I didn't believe him.

In fact, we were almost certain we were the only hostages left in the building, even though the militants had never told us about the rescue attempt or about where they had taken everybody. Then we found out that Kate Koob and Ann Swift were across the hall.

So, ours really was a sort of holding place, I realized, for those the Iranians thought were the "weaker" sex—Ann and Kate—and maybe for those they figured were the hostages with medical problems, together with the medic to treat us if a problem arose.

Bob was the first to encounter Ann and Kate. The militants walked him into the bathroom while Ann was there. She was fully clothed and washing her face. She turned around and told the guard outside the door, "Hey, boys, this isn't supposed to happen!" They just took Bob right out again and when he returned to the room, he couldn't understand why, when it was the first time since the takeover they had seen each other, she would have such a reaction. She wasn't even undressed. "Granted that I'm old," he said, "but I'm not that ugly!" Some weeks later, the same thing happened to Don Hohman, but this time he and Ann talked a minute or two before the guard realized his mistake. He told her he was rooming with me and Don.

The women had their own female guards. I think the women militants were more diligent than the men guarding us. They would stand right outside the bathroom door and yell at their male colleagues for wandering off. Even so, the women had their slipups: They were responsible for our two visits with Ann.

We had been given a couple of games, including a brand-new Scrabble set sent from the United States, and we started playing Scrabble as a daily event. First, it was the afternoon Scrabble game, then it became the evening game. One night Hamid the Liar came in and said he'd like to play. After that, we switched back to the afternoons to avoid him.

We really enjoyed these games. Sometimes one of us would use a word the rest weren't sure existed, and it would be challenged. According to the Scrabble rules, if the challenge is upheld, the person who used the word loses his turn. If the word does exist, then the challenger loses a turn. I remember several words that surprised us. Bob Ode, in desperation, used "kine," thinking it referred to movies, and it turned out to be an old English word for cattle. I used "zit," and when Bob said he'd never heard of it, Don said, "You just haven't been around." Bob was afraid he'd lose a turn, so he didn't challenge me, but later, when we looked up "zit," it wasn't in the dictionary we had.

We asked Hamid the Liar if we could play Risk or Scrabble with the two women. He said, "Absolutely not." First, he denied that there were any women in the building, and then he said, "No, it's impossible, you can't associate with the women."

But we did get involved with Ann and Kate after all, by fighting over the bathroom. The trouble was that there were only two sinks; one was hopelessly ruined and the other had its drainpipe removed. Before we had arrived, the drainpipe had clogged, and the Iranians had torn it out instead of trying to unclog it. Now a bucket sat under the sink, and the water drained right into the bucket. This meant we had to empty out the bucket a lot.

We complained that the women would always fill up the bowl and then leave it for us to empty, but one morning in the bathroom, we found a note in a woman's handwriting. It said, "Who do you think cleans up the bathroom? Elves?" They thought we were total slobs and were especially irritated because they *were* cleaning out the bathroom. After we had all been released, I found out that the militants had been using the sink, too.

Our biggest complaint, though, was that we couldn't get into the bathroom. In the mornings, especially, we would sometimes have to wait half an hour or forty-five minutes to get in. I used to get up early just to be sure I would beat the women to it. It got to be a joke, even with the Iranians. They would tell us to go back to sleep if one of the women was in the bathroom. We used to say among ourselves, "My God, what are they doing in there?" We felt they were gussying themselves up, putting on makeup, going out to a big dance. We would sometimes smell perfume in the air. Later, we realized that one of the female militants was testing the perfume—and unaware she should put on only a little at a time.

Eventually the plumbing broke in our shower in the Mushroom Inn. The pipe didn't drain, so instead of calling a plumber or trying to fix it, the militants smashed it, and the water flowed out onto the bathroom floor.

I liked to do my wash every day, and I finally found a large plastic tub that I could use for washing myself and my clothes. I only had two or three pairs of underwear, so I rotated washing them and stood in the tub to do my sponge bath. Such little things made up our days now, as early spring dragged into May. Time moved very slowly. Although we didn't get any newspapers, we did sometimes get the baseball magazine *Sporting News*. One of the hostages had asked his wife to send it to him, and instead, that great magazine company sent six copies, airmail special delivery, every week to the compound.

I loved it when I got it. I've always been a baseball fan. Through *Sporting News*, I'd follow as best I could what was happening in the baseball world—keeping up with the statistics, seeing who were the goats and who were the stars, and how the Chicago White Sox were doing. Sometimes I'd pick up some information about what was happening outside the sports world as well, but mostly I read it for the sports.

At least as the weather changed we were getting more

fresh fruit. Don put his orange pits in the sand stuffed in our metal-sheeted windows, which were in a direct line with the sun. He was hoping to grow some orange trees, but nothing happened.

In June, yellow roses began to bloom outside, and one of the militants gave us some, even though Hamid the Liar told us the other guy wasn't supposed to cut them because they belonged to the Islamic revolution and not to America anymore. We ignored Hamid.

By now, our original guards had all left except for Hamid the Liar. Of course, he wasn't actually our guard, but he was in charge of us. When he stopped giving out our mail completely, I complained to the other militants, which made Hamid very angry. One afternoon, he drove me and Bob Ode to the courtyard to exercise. On the way, he told his lieutenant in Farsi, "Watch this; they've just had a big lunch. I'm going to get them sick." Before I got in the car, he had made sure the towel was wrapped very tightly around my head so that I was almost suffocating, then put the car in reverse, floored it, stopped it, put it forward and back again, and did sort of a jerky back and forth motion for about two to three minutes. Another time, I complained to Ali, who was now the cook's helper, and the next day, Hamid came by and said, "Don't complain to anybody anymore. It can only get you into trouble. If you complain, then you're going to be left with Ali, who can't read English, and you'll never get any mail."

This didn't stop me, so Hamid would come in regularly and make criticisms of the United States or Carter. Once he came in while Bob and I were playing Scrabble, and he said there had been riots in the United States and twelve people had been killed in Miami. "Maybe this is the start of a revolution," he concluded.

"We don't believe you; you're just lying," we said.

Then he got out the Teheran *Times.*

"You don't think we'd believe an Iranian paper, do you?" I said.

"Well, it's really happening," Hamid answered.

We went around and around like that, with him telling me that the United States was ripe for revolution and me telling him that Iran was falling apart. We certainly could tell there was beginning to be trouble of some kind. One night I noticed one of the militants carrying a G-3 as he stood guard inside. I had rarely seen any of them carry one of these German-made army rifles inside the building before, although a couple of times, they actually fired one inside the building, making a terrific noise. Later I was awakened by machine-gun bursts right outside the compound. Don and I didn't know what it was. We decided the militants were practicing war games, or perhaps some group was attacking the compound.

Hamid strutted into the room carrying a light machine gun on a bipod. He held it up to us, saying "Isn't this something!" He was like a kid with a toy. He actually told me that it was a special treat for me to see the weapon and that I shouldn't tell any of the other hostages he had shown it to me! I had, in fact, already operated one, but Hamid insisted on giving me a demonstration of how it worked. It was machismo at its worst. In fact, he wanted me to play around with it. I said, "Why don't you be careful? You guys are always playing with your weapons." I knew about a couple of other militants who had accidentally been hit by people playing games with rifles. One was shot in the hand, the other in the head. Hamid was upset that I knew so much about their mistakes.

By this time, the noisy demonstrations outside were happening less frequently and were less spontaneous. Now, instead of a large number of people shouting one theme over and over again, you'd have male and female cheerleaders. A women's section would shout a long slogan, then a men's group would return it. It all had to have been carefully rehearsed beforehand.

One day, the "Death to America, death to the Carter, death to the Shah" slogans were replaced by "Death to Iraq." I listened and I thought, This is nice; maybe they took the Iraqi embassy. But when I asked one of the militants why they were criticizing Iraq, he answered, "The father of Iraq is the Soviet Union and the mother is the United States."

I said, "Come on, we don't have full diplomatic relations with Iraq." The two of us argued back and forth, stalemated, but still I figured something new was up.

Earlier that day, Bob and I had heard a siren when we were about to leave the Mushroom after taking a shower. I could tell it was coming from the compound. Immediately Hamid the Liar started laughing and joking and banging on a piano that stood in the garage where our car was parked. It was obvious he didn't want us to hear the siren, but of course he only drew my attention to it. We couldn't see anything, but we heard the siren stop inside the compound. We were then taken back inside the Mushroom and, after a while, driven to the chancery. On the way, we were delayed by some militants. Someone in the car asked in Farsi what was happening. Another answered, "It's Iraq, again." Hamid the Liar quickly told everyone to shut up because he knew I could understand them.

One afternoon in mid-June, we noticed a lot of shouting coming from a soccer stadium two or three blocks north of us. The shouts died down. They were followed by a chanting that grew louder and louder. You could hear the frenzy building, and for a moment I was glad I was inside and not in the middle of it. Volleys of shots punctuated the chanting; then shouting in all directions, the wail of an ambulance siren.

One of the militants came by and closed our windows. We asked why. "Um, air pollution," he said, looking worried and anxious.

Don Hohman had seen Hamid the Liar standing outside the building with a G-3 in his hand. He looked very impressed with his weapon, as if he thought he could defend the compound all by himself. Later, Hamid explained the shots as revolutionary guards firing into the air. I reminded him of the ambulance sirens, but he insisted no one had been hurt.

A few days later, a helicopter flew overhead and the compound opened up like the Fourth of July. Don could see a couple of girls with a light machine gun on a tripod, standing below our window. They'd fire a burst of fifteen to twenty rounds and then giggle. They thought guns were exciting, something we had noticed before. In fact, the militants were always fascinated with weapons. In the early stages of the takeover, they had spent hours just clicking the safeties of their guns, a habit that later decreased only slightly, and we still heard shots going off at night. I noticed a bullet hole in my room, where a bullet had earlier hit the top of the metal window frame and then the

191

doorway. The window glass in the doorway had to be taped together, but no one explained where the bullet had come from.

Probably one of the reasons Hamid the Liar—and so many of the others—did things to try to humiliate us was that we knew so much. Even more frustrating to them was the fact that we never gave in to them and never backed down; instead, to keep my sanity, I made fun of the situation—to myself I called it playing Mickey Mouse games on the Good Ship Lollipop. Obviously the militants used the towels and the guided trips to the bathroom as ways of degrading us, but so much else was so ludicrous that I had to adopt an attitude of Anything Goes or playing Simon Says to keep from going crazy. And it worked.

I think a few of the militants realized how silly it was too. Maybe they were just tired of the whole ridiculous routine—leading people around to the bathroom . . . with towels on their heads! By now, most of them didn't really check to see if we could see out the sides except for Hamid the Liar and some of his henchmen. Sometimes, I'd go to the bathroom across the hall with the towel on my head and afterward, I'd knock and knock to be brought back. No one would come, so I'd just start laughing, put the towel over my head, open the bathroom door and walk across the hallway by myself.

One time when I was brought to exercise and shower, I walked into the ambassador's residence and the guard didn't make me put the towel on at all. After I finished my shower, I walked around the ambassador's residence. I was still searching for the pipe I had left there on the first day of the takeover. Only when I got ready to leave did the militant put the towel over my head.

The fascination with cars was the same as with guns in the embassy compound. Hamid got hold of a car and drove it into the ground. You could always tell when he was driving because he'd floor it and then hit the brakes when he came to a speed bump. The car with its backfires began to sound like a bass drum. One time he wanted us to clean it, but I refused. His response was that we used it too. I answered, "Sure, but we don't get to see it." He then brought up the time I spilled shampoo on his back seat, but I still wouldn't give in. He was going to have to clean his car himself.

When he wanted us to clean the swimming pool, his offer was that if we cleaned it, we could use it. I didn't believe him, and I refused to do that, too. The militants seemed to be trying to maintain at least the exterior of the compound. They'd go out and clean sometimes and periodically water the lawns, but there was trash all over the place, especially in front of the buildings. Most of the compound looked like a junk heap.

In May the weather began getting hot. I really hate the heat, and I asked for a fan. Finally, someone came in with a humidifier—the kind you poured water into. But first we needed a current converter because the fan ran on the Iranian system they had at the chancery. Finally, I got a converter. I plugged in the humidifier and out came a gray-black smoke, cascading like a waterfall. Someone had put oil in the humidifier, and it had heated up.

I joked that that was what you got when you have so many engineers running the place. The militant who wanted to go to Harvard Law School said, "Yes, you're right. There are too many engineers around here." He got us another converter, and this one, to my great relief, worked and the humidifier kept my room cooler. The only problem was getting the buckets of water from the bathroom. The water would slop all over everywhere, and that made Ann and Kate more upset than ever about the messy bathroom.

One night, after a really hot day, the weather broke: we had a thunderstorm. Don and Bob came into my room, and I turned off the lights. It was like seeing a spectacular light show as we watched the storm rolling over the hills of northern Teheran and thundering toward us. In a wonderful way, our confinement had made us take notice of things we wouldn't normally have paid attention to. Here, looking at the lightning, hearing the thunder, and seeing the wild clouds boiling up from far away where people were living, working and sleeping; and feeling cool, just as they must be feeling cool, we were like blind men seeing for the first time. That extra sensitivity is still with me. I look more closely at the world now that I've known what it is to be cut off from it.

Chapter 7

As summer came on, my humidifier wasn't enough to cool the room. I had noticed a big fan that was going unused in the library. It stood five feet tall and sounded like a propeller from an old B-24. A militant agreed to let me have it. It came in two parts—a stand with a big base that was quite heavy and a pole with the fan on top. With some help from the militant, I got it back to my room.

Even at low speed it put out a lot of wind. I couldn't put it on directly or everything would be blowing off the walls, so I had it swirling around. It was enough to cool our three-room suite and very useful for blocking out the sound of a demonstration outside; on high speed it sounded like you were in the middle of a hurricane.

So, my room all set for summer, I might have predicted what happened next: Hamid the Liar came in and said I had to move. I was to double up with Bob Ode, though we would still be connected to Don Hohman's room. Of course, there wasn't a need to pack up everything. I just transferred it all across to Bob's room, but again I had to pull down all my pictures. By now I couldn't remember how many times I had gone through the routine—take down the pictures, ask for more tape, put them up again, nail in the Alaska poster. I hauled in the fan and Don took the dehumidifier.

I put up my postcards—insurance against propaganda posters—and I would purposely space them out so they would cover most of the wall. In the library I found some Easter cards that had never been distributed, and although they were addressed to all the hostages in general, I put some of them up, too. I also put up photographs, among them a picture of my parents and their new home in Maine. One day Hamid came in and looked at the picture a long time. "It's too bad," he said, "but you will never see your parents again. You will never see that house."

I knew it was only Hamid the Liar, spouting off, but still it wasn't what I wanted to hear. I received a photo from good friends of their new baby girl and I put that up on the wall as well. A militant whom I had never seen before came and looked over my photos as Hamid the Liar and others had done. He saw the picture of the baby and asked, "Where's your wife?"

"I'm not married," I said.

He looked again at the baby and said, "You don't have a wife?"

"No," I told him.

He said, "The baby has blue eyes, right? And you have blue eyes, too?"

I could get the drift of what he was saying. "That's a friend's baby," I said. "Not mine."

He didn't speak English very well, and I'm not sure he ever got my point, but I got his: You Americans are so corrupt and un-Islamic.

Don and Bob and I, like college roommates, had occasional little spats, but mostly we got along very well. One thing we all agreed on was that the pregnant black cat which spent her days in our bathroom was smelly. She would use the sand between the metal sheets in the bedroom window for a litter box. She belonged to one of the female guards and we liked having her around, but we were all afraid of walking into the bathroom with a towel over our heads and tripping over her or, if she had them, her kittens. The kittens were, from the looks of her, long overdue but never arrived while I was there. I was looking forward to that event. A furry little pet would be something I could lavish affection on. I laughed when I thought back to my obsession with cleanliness the first days of the takeover. Now I had relaxed enough to think of raising a cat.

Around this time Hamid told us we would have to make our own meals. It turned out that Joseph, the Pakistani, had left, but Hamid didn't say that. He just gave us cans of fruit and some shrimp, but mostly cans of chili beans. He also came around with cans of cake frosting, which I tasted and found quite good. In fact, on the first day I ate so much on my fingers, I felt sick. The perfect well-balanced diet, we used to joke.

Fortunately, Ali, the Iranian who had assisted Joseph, came to our rescue. He agreed to cook our dinners and so they became our main meal. We got some American food, but mainly rice and bean sauce. Rice was always the staple, though breakfast remained an Iranian meal: bread and jam and butter.

One day a guard gave me a book of essays about the Iranian revolution called *Iran Erupts*. It included articles by Bani-Sadr, and Ghotbzadeh, and was written from the point of view of the more moderate revolutionary politicians. The person who gave it to me was more sophisticated and intelligent than the average militant.

I read a couple of the articles. One talked about how Iran had to play one superpower against the other and couldn't allow the United States or the Soviet Union to have a pretext for invading Iran. I commented that the hostage-taking was a perfect pretext for an invasion. The militant said he didn't agree with everything in the book, but I don't think he had read it very carefully, because none of the essays supported the revolutionary line. Instead they argued that the militants were playing a dangerous game for Iran. When I pointed this out to the militant, he discounted it.

One evening one of the guards came in and asked, "What does 'OK' mean? 'WC' means water closet. What does 'OK' mean?"

I said it was an American expression meaning everything is alright. He said, "I know that, but I don't know what it means."

He liked the word a lot, so I told him to check the dictionary in the library. He came back about twenty minutes later and said, "It means 'Old Kinderhook.'" I couldn't imagine what he was referring to. I thought maybe his English was confused, but when I checked the dictionary it proved him right. Old Kinderhook referred to an 1840 political campaign, when Martin Van Buren's people were trying to get him drafted for the presidency. He came from the town of Kinderhook in upstate New York and his party became Old Kinderhook. After that, he would sometimes say "Old Kinderhook" instead of "okay."

Hamid was getting more obnoxious, if that was possible. By now he was doing things like calling out "Mail, mail, mail," and throwing our letters across the room. He was probably hoping we would run and scream and pick them up, which Don, who still wasn't getting any mail, had every right to do. But Don wasn't going to give him that pleasure, and we weren't either. We just waited until he left and then retrieved our letters.

Later that particular week Hamid the Liar came in and told us we had received a letter and some gifts from Mohammad Ali. We couldn't believe that Ali had taken time not only to write to us, but to send gifts as well; I was also amazed the militants gave them to us.

One of the militants said, "Mohammad Ali must be a famous CIA agent, isn't he?"

I would have laughed but the guard was serious. "No," I answered, "he's a heavyweight boxer. A real champion."

"I don't believe you," he said. "A champion would not send you gifts."

There wasn't much point in arguing. They believed what they wanted to believe. Don and Bob and I put on the shirts Ali had sent us and found in the pocket of one a small metal American flag. I took the flag and wore it the whole time I was in the chancery. The letter was terrific; it told us to "hang in there." Ali had also sent us a pineapple, according to his letter. But we never received it. The militants said it "rattled." I believe they just ate it.

One night early in June Hamid handed out several letters to each of us, and—wonder of wonders—he gave one to Don. Don was completely flabbergasted. We couldn't

199

figure out this change of heart until Akbar arrived the next day and told us that from then on he'd be in charge, and, among other things, he'd be giving us more mail. To say we were pleased would be putting it mildly, because Akbar was the most considerate of the militants and certainly the only one who ever actually listened to us.

That night some militants came into our room.

"I see Hamid's been replaced," I said.

Their answer was, "He's very tired"—a frequently used expression that meant more than being tired.

I asked, "How can he be tired? All he ever did was drive that car."

They laughed and nodded their heads in agreement.

Hamid was one of those people nobody could stand, including most of the other militants. Earlier I had heard a conversation between two militants in which they sarcastically called him "Hamid the King." In this, his domain, his only friends were SOBs in their own right.

Toward the end of his reign, some of those friends had helped Hamid try to make us wear double blindfolds when we went to exercise and to take showers. Instead we refused to go out at all. Hamid's friends then backed down, and Hamid never came to take us anymore. It was a face-saving gesture. He didn't want to see us after his double-blindfold plan had come to naught.

We asked Akbar about the double blindfolds, and he couldn't believe Hamid had tried to do that. All we had to wear, he said, was the same old towel.

Akbar was very soft-spoken and shy. He had a smooth-shaven face that was still handsome despite a slight break in his nose that hadn't healed properly. His English was very good and, unlike that of the others, was free of sarcasm, threats or propagandizing diatribes. He was single but planning to get married as soon as he could to a "beautiful girl from my village—not modern, very pure," he said, emphatically.

He promised to get us things that Hamid the Liar had refused to get. Don Hohman wanted his medicine. He said if he had his medicine he could eat the meat. He had to eat something, and his vegetable plate just never materialized. Don was extremely thin. I prayed they would bring him the pills. I wanted pipe tobacco and back issues of *Sporting News*. We got the tobacco, the pills and the magazines, but Don still refused to eat meat. He was afraid Hamid would be back any day, realize he was eating meat and take away the medication. It would have been a typical Hamid the Liar ploy.*

The improvement was so dramatic that we feared that Akbar might overwork himself. He did everything—drove us to exercise and the showers, brought our food in, took care of our mail. I got fifteen letters in the first week he was there. He also told us we could write as many letters as we wanted and he would send them, only warning us that he had a limited time to read them. Bob and I decided to stick to our old system of writing three times a week, but Don would write more, because he hadn't been writing while Hamid was around, since he didn't want Hamid tearing the letters up. I wrote to my parents and told them the good news about Akbar. I felt pleased that for once I had something positive to write about.

---

*We found out later that Hamid had been completely replaced. Akbar told us to forget about him, that he was now just a janitor and handyman around the compound. I felt even that was too good for him.

June 21, 1980

Dear Mom, Dad and Alex:

This morning we (myself and my two roommates) received some excellent news that has already made our day so bright. We now have a new student supervising our needs, in particular our mail. He is one of the most considerate and conscientious of all the Iranians with us, and I feel absolutely confident that he will try to make our living here as painless and as tolerable as possible. As long as he stays with us I am sure the weeks and months will pass quickly and smoothly. He already promised we will begin to receive all our mail and that whatever letters we write will be posted. What an inestimable improvement. I hope to soon be deluged in mail so please have everyone continue to write.

I am continuing to nurse carefully the three tins of tobacco you sent me (posted 4 June and received eleven days later) because my own tobacco, which I had from before the embassy takeover, is almost finished. I guess the first package of pipe tobacco never reached my hands. The students have given me other tobacco from time to time, but I am not too enamored of it. Please continue to periodically mail me more tobacco because pipe smoking is an outstanding pacifier for me. Keep the yellow ribbon around the old oak tree and God bless,

Love, love and love again with kisses,
Richard

Along with more mail, Akbar started giving us *Time* and *Newsweek*. He would cut out all the articles dealing with

Iran, but would forget to cut out the table of contents. From that we first learned of the rescue attempt. The missing article was "Why the Rescue Mission in Iran Failed." My mind wrote the missing article as we tried to guess among ourselves what had happened. We decided that the planes had made it to Saudi Arabia and then what? Perhaps the press leaked the plans and they were called off. Maybe they got to Saudi Arabia and decided the risk was too high. Or they couldn't find all of us. We were all moved to have this concrete example that the United States had not forgotten us; at the same time we thought things must have really bogged down in the negotiations if a rescue attempt had been planned. We had no idea they'd gotten inside Iran, or that there had been such terrible casualties.

By now we were getting even more Iranian food, because Ali, who had been cooking Western food, went back to his village. After a while Akbar asked if any of us knew how to cook. Bob and Don said no, but I volunteered, because although I'm not great, I thought I could put out basic meals.

They decided I should alternate with Kate and Ann, and the next day I arrived at work in the compound kitchen. It was a mess. Spilled ketchup and drippings were everywhere, and all I could find to cook was a five-gallon container of canned ravioli. My plans to make something inspiring faded, but Don, at least, got a tolerable omelet.

Next day it was the women's turn. I like to think they somehow got more ingredients to make a much better meal, but after we took turns for several days like that, with the women putting out elaborate dinners, Akbar said the women wouldn't be needing my help anymore. I was too grateful to feel hurt because Kate Koob really knows how to cook and Ann Swift was her very good helper.

I was grateful, too, because shortly after the women started cooking, I lost my balance and was sometimes so nauseated I couldn't eat anything. The Iranians' explanation to Kate and Ann was that I didn't like their food and wanted Iranian food instead, but I knew what it really was—my disease was getting worse.

Late in June I got a tape from my parents, unprepared and extemporaneous. It was great to hear their voices.

"We love you Richard," said my mother. "I know you'll be home soon. You are going to love the new house in Maine. Please take care of yourself . . . we're praying for you."

"Everyone is thinking of you, Richard," said my father, huskily. "The whole country."

I thought he was exaggerating a little about the "whole country"—little did I know. Akbar asked if I wanted to make a tape to send back to them. As it turned out, I became too sick to make one.

The numbness that had previously been confined to my left side had begun affecting my right hand sometime in May. It started with the fingertips, then became a very slight numbness in my whole right hand. Luckily, I could still write and perform my normal tasks even though I'm right-handed. I could live without having too much dexterity on the left and so I still kept my nonchalant attitude.

I had talked to Don Hohman about it, though, since he was a medic. He had said he didn't know what it was but that it was possible to have a stroke on the other side of the body too—although very unlikely. The militant medical student, more conscientious than the quack doctor they'd had looking at me, had also been baffled.

My symptoms did fit in with a stroke on the right side of the brain—paralysis of the left half of the body—but I was noticing problems in hearing with my right ear. My balance was being affected, too, so I knew something was truly wrong. One day I thought it would be a good idea to get my mind off what was happening by playing with my Civil War game. I got up from my bed, took a few steps and got very dizzy. I reached out to grab something to hold on to, but nothing was there and I fell. I wasn't hurt—just surprised and stunned. What was going on? I asked Don about the ear. He told me he thought I had an infection in the canal. (Actually, he thought right off the bat that I had had a stroke, but being a good medic, Don didn't want to alarm me.) He told Akbar and the medical student that I needed some medicine—Sudafed or Actifed. They got it for me and I started taking Sudafed. I figured the infection would go away. It didn't.

After two or three days I tried the Actifed. Again there were no results. My balance was getting worse and worse and I was starting to feel nauseated just walking around, especially with the towel on my head. Going to the bathroom became a real problem. I dreaded it. I'd stagger to the bathroom and vomit. I had to lean against the walls to keep from falling.

I was too nauseated to read. I was pretty much just lying in bed all day and all night. I had to lie flat on my back, because even when I'd turn my head, I'd become so nauseated I'd vomit. I decided that maybe the air circulation from the fan was causing the problem so I turned it off, but that didn't make any difference either. I couldn't figure it out. I had stopped eating but I couldn't stop vomiting. Was it all tied in together—the numbness, the dizziness and now this continual vomiting?

I remember the Fourth of July came and there I was lying flat on my back unable to move, unable to eat. I was wondering how long I could last like this, and at the same time, everything seemed unreal. I had become very fatalistic.

One morning, shortly after the Fourth, I opened my eyes slowly so I wouldn't get nauseated and saw Don sitting at the foot of my bed, frowning.

"Richard, you've been vomiting for days. I've been trying to get you a real doctor but they won't listen. I'm going to try again—I don't think we have much time. If they still won't listen I'm going to cause some trouble. The important thing is to get you to a hospital and quick."

I was too out of it to respond; whatever anyone could do to stop this plunging elevator I was on was all right with me. Don must have convinced them because that evening a doctor came in with several militants, including Akbar and the medical student.

The medical student had come by every day or two but had never examined me; in my opinion he was not really competent to do so. Don and Bob were there as well, and Don had brought in the humidifier from his room. I turned my head to look at the doctor and got so nauseated I vomited.

That was quite an introduction. The doctor ignored the mess and just started examining me. He had been trained in the United States and spoke very good English.

He said, "Describe your symptoms," and then looked in my eyes. Evidently the eye reveals a lot, especially with a nervous system problem. He seemed to see something wrong. He then looked into my ear and asked me to do some basic physical tests—mainly walking up and down the room to test my balance. The whole exam lasted about twenty minutes. And then the doctor left with the militants.

Bob and Don stayed on with me, trying to make me comfortable and cheer me up. About an hour later Akbar came back. "You're going to the hospital tomorrow morning," he said.

I believed him, because he was truthful, and I got ready for bed hoping they could figure out what was wrong. Before I went to bed, Bob gave me a broom handle and told me I should hit the door with it if there were any problems and he'd come to help.

By then I had become afraid of falling asleep because I knew I'd turn over in the night and wake up vomiting. I just watched the sunset as best I could and daydreamed, until finally I dozed.

In the morning I couldn't eat breakfast. About nine or ten o'clock I got up, and several militants helped me by putting the towel over my head for me. I staggered down the corridor, and Don said, "I hope they put you in an ambulance at least."

Akbar and another militant draped my arms over their shoulders and I half-walked, half was carried outside to the van. I didn't care where I was going or what they were going to do with me; I knew I was dying. The van took off, and I knew we were headed north because Teheran is built on the foothills of the Elburz Mountains, and the north is much higher than the south—so much so that in the summer there is a real temperature difference between the two areas.

I was lying flat on the back seat, unable to even enjoy the street sounds on this first trip through the city after seven months of captivity. I had the towel off my head though. At the hospital a revolutionary guard checked us through. "We wait here for the elevator," said Akbar. "Don't fall; here it is, get in." He and the other guard helped me in the small elevator and we rose slowly to the third floor. My head was swimming. "Now you will be fine, in here," he said, leading me into a small room. It was very hot and close. The hospital odors—a combination of disinfectants and sweaty patients—assaulted my sense of smell. I felt like vomiting. "It's very hot here," I gasped.

"Air conditioning is broken," he said, helping me in the bed. "They'll fix it soon—probably tomorrow."

The nurse came in and gave me water. "Can't you get rid of that thing," she snapped at the militant seated in the corner with his G-3 casually resting on his lap. "This patient is not going anywhere." The guard shrugged and grabbed a towel which he wrapped around the gun. All I could see was part of the heavy black barrel sticking out. Somehow it looked more ominous that way.

Soon the director of the hospital and five or six doctors and some medical students—a total of eleven people—came in. Several of the students were female. The director welcomed me to Martyrs' Hospital, newly named after the Shah's fall.

They immediately reran some of the same tests that had been conducted by the doctor who visited me at the embassy: the balance test, a test to see if I could touch my nose with my finger, and others. Throughout, the doctors explained to the medical students what they were looking for. I couldn't understand what they were saying, and I didn't know what to think about my illness. It looked like a strange ailment. Although Don hadn't known what it was, I found out later that for several days before they took me to the hospital he had told Akbar I needed help. He had, in fact, thought I might be dying, and I felt deeply grateful to him. He's a conscientious medic. I remember him telling me he would have to treat Khomeini if he was ever asked to, because of the oath he had taken as a medical man.

After the doctors and the medical students had gone, I was left with Akbar and another militant. The other militant was armed with a submachine gun, and Akbar had a .45 in his belt. The only other time I had seen Akbar carry a gun was two weeks before when he had taken several of us to the showers.

Now Akbar stood watch in my room and the other militant stayed out on the terrace, switching positions every so often, on guard every minute. Since I couldn't sit up, much less run away, I asked them what they were worried about. They said they feared a kidnap threat by an anti-Khomeini group that wanted some bargaining power.

After the first night I was taken to a much larger room, one of the best in the hospital, with a balcony which overlooked the grounds. Numerous bouquets of flowers sat on the window ledge and the sheets on the bed were dirty. I commented on the flowers. They answered, "They're not for you. They're for Ayatollah Khalkhali." He was known as the hanging judge. That morning he had had an automobile accident and had used this room. That explained the sheets. I no longer enjoyed the flowers.

But at least the bathroom was close by, even though it was tiny and messy, with cockroaches crawling along the walls. I was too miserable to care because still no one would tell me anything about my illness or how long I'd be in the hospital. Occasionally a doctor checked in and a nurse would take my temperature, but most of the time I just lay there and daydreamed. Lassitude had taken over—talking or reading seemed much too complicated.

The nurses all had to wear white head coverings, like long babushkas—badges of Khomeini's new regime. They complained vehemently to Akbar.

"This is terrible. We can't work, we can't be free to move, to help the patients," said the nurse who had given me water on my first day. "Why do you torture us with these new requirements?"

I couldn't catch all of what they said, but I got the gist—the revolution was ruining women's lives. Every day they brought me lunch and dinner. It was simple food; rice, sauce and soup. I could only eat the soup. Soon I stopped eating altogether. The food just made me vomit. The nurses asked if there was something wrong with the way they prepared it. I told them no.

By now I was so miserable I had to keep my mind distracted by singing old army ditties—marching songs— that I'd learned in the military. I'd sing, "A hundred bottles of beer on the wall, a hundred bottles of beer, if one of those bottles should happen to fall, ninety-nine bottles of beer on the wall" until I reached "no bottles of beer on the wall." Then I'd start again—to keep my thoughts from nausea.

The second day the nurses started giving me antinausea shots in the morning, the afternoon and the evening, along with some pills that were also supposed to help. One of the medicines had a terrifying effect. It made me think I was going under for the third time. I was drowning and no one could help me. I tried to shout "Help," but the words wouldn't come. My vision blurred, then I saw double images. There were two Akbars and both of them had machine guns pointed at me. Then something worse happened: I lost control of my head. It would start to turn to the right, slowly, until it couldn't turn anymore. I grabbed my chin with my hand to straighten my head out. It felt as if it belonged on the body of a ventriloquist's dummy. I would say to myself, "You're going to look at that object right in front of you. Mind over matter." The minute I'd put my hand down, my head would slowly move away until it landed on my pillow, like something possessed. My God, what was happening to me?

Next I started grinding my teeth. I couldn't stop it. I'd tell myself, "Don't grind your teeth," but I couldn't help it. I'd put my tongue between my teeth, and all I'd do was grind my tongue. It was more than frightening. I thought my mind was beginning to stop working and I would soon no longer be able to control my body. "Akbar," I yelled, "look what's happening."

He watched my head roll to the side, heard my teeth grinding furiously and stood there, transfixed. Even with my blurry vision I could see the horror in his eyes. He ran off down the hall for the doctors. Two doctors came in. Every doctor but one that I'd encountered at the hospital spoke perfect English. They'd been trained in the United States and seemed very competent, unlike the nurses and technicians. The two conferred for a moment and decided that one of the antinausea pills was causing this reaction.

They would stop the dosage at once.

On the third day I was taken downstairs for a brain scan. Akbar and the other Iranian guard went with me. I vomited. When they put me in a machine that needed me to move my head a little bit, I vomited again. The whole procedure lasted ten minutes.

Now I was being fed intravenously. When one bag of red fluid was empty, they'd attach another. I'd use the intravenous stand as a crutch on the way to the bathroom.

I'll never forget the metallic taste of the fluid as I vomited it up. The doctors couldn't seem to stop my constant nausea; none of their medications was working.

It is a custom in Iranian hospitals for patients who are able to walk to visit others who can't. A man of about twenty-six came in carrying his intravenous stand, assisted by a technician. He didn't speak English, so Akbar acted as a translator. The man said he was a revolutionary guard who had been stabbed in a fight with a leftist group and he wanted to know who I was. All I could say was, "I'm Richard Queen, from the United States, currently being held against my will by—who knows?" I couldn't concentrate on our conversation, but that didn't seem to bother him.

"The leftists are crazy," he said, thrusting his stabbed arm in my face. "See what they do? They don't listen to Khomeini. They don't want to keep the revolution pure. They want to control everything—no Imam, no religion. They don't say this—but that's what they want.

"Pray the leftists don't get you," he warned.

At this point I felt there wasn't much of me to get.

After a while, I began to lose the thread of what he was saying and realized that Akbar was only translating every fifth or sixth word—at least that's what it sounded like. Eventually Akbar stopped translating altogether and the two of them ignored me. They had quite an animated conversation for about half an hour. Then the man left.

Akbar said that in a way it was good I was in the hospital. "The other students think it is wrong I get your mail and bring you things. They said you are all hostages and should not be treated like innocent people."

I had been hearing a man across the hall crying and I found out he had had his legs amputated. It made me very sad.

The next day I was examined by a psychiatrist. I don't know what his prognosis was, but I was certain my problem wasn't psychological.

That evening a man who looked like Fidel Castro came in. He wore a revolutionary army guard's fatigues, with a special patch and a hat. Two other revolutionary guards were with him. In good English he asked who I was, and how I was doing.

He then said, "Do you know who I am?" He was surprised that I didn't.

"My name is Abdul Sharif," he told me.

He was head of the western front of the revolutionary guard, and at the hospital he had been guarding Ayatollah Khalkhali. He said he had served with the Palestine Liberation Organization for several years fighting Israel, and now he asked me, "Why do the Christian nations support Israel?"

I kept on vomiting but tried to answer. "We can't look upon them just as Christian nations. We try to be secular."

"But they are Christians," he said. "Don't they understand the struggle of the Palestinians?" He was so intent on making his political point that he continued to quiz me in spite of my obvious sickness.

He offered to give me a Bible. I declined but later I wished I hadn't. He was very knowledgeable about the New Testament and quoted verses from it.

Either Akbar or his nice-looking companion, the graduate engineering student, was always with me, one sleeping on the bed, the other on a chaise longue on the little terrace outside. Once Akbar said, "I wonder if Hamid is in here. He certainly belongs in this hospital." I completely agreed with him.

But then on the morning of July 11, I woke up and Akbar announced that I was going home. Home—that's a funny word for it, I thought. Home used to mean so much to me. Now my home was a commandeered chancery in the middle of Teheran.

"With all this?" I said, nodding at the intravenous tubes above me and the needles in my arms.

"No, you are going home, to your home."

I couldn't comprehend it. If it were Hamid the Liar telling me this I wouldn't have even listened, but Akbar? He always was pretty straight with us.

"America," said Akbar, frustrated by my incomprehension. "Ayatollah Khomeini has decided to release you to your parents." He read the message explaining my release. It said I was being released for "medical reasons, to go to a better medical facility."

It seemed true, still I didn't accept it. Then he turned on the radio, and we heard it announced. I was still skeptical. After two hundred and fifty days in Iran what he was saying came too suddenly.

"As soon as a representative from Bani-Sadr's government arrives," Akbar was saying, "we're going to sign you over to him, and you're going to be on your way home to America."

My mind wouldn't think. Certainly it couldn't absorb the concept of going home. Home? It was almost an unreal idea, one I had pushed down so far in order to survive that I couldn't summon it up again. At least not so quickly.

Then one of the leaders of the militants came in and spoke to me for about five minutes—a last political harangue. He was sophisticated and somewhat older, and I had seen him before. One of his front teeth was missing.

He said, "My people and the American people get along very well, but the government . . . the CIA is trying to destroy our revolution. No one tried to harass or kill the Americans who were leaving Teheran at the time of the Shah's overthrow. They had nothing against the United States, but the United States is trying to destroy the revolution."

I just listened, trying to fight back the nausea. I was trying my best to put everything together. Things were happening so fast. Finally, he said, "When you go back, speak the truth." He apologized for the militants' behavior.* He apologized for the first two months of the takeover, although he didn't mention anything about the Gestapo raid, and I was too sick to bring it up.

"We tried to treat you well," he said. "The first two months were chaotic here—it was so disorganized."

After he left, a Swiss doctor from the Red Cross gave me

---

* Later I found out that he gave this same kind of speech, apologizing for the even worse conditions that prevailed after I left, to many of the other hostages just before they were released.

a quick check-over to make sure I could fly. Based on what he had been told, he said he thought I had a virus in the brain or maybe a virus in the spine. I took the news without reacting. Too much was happening for it to register. I felt shaky and weak but excited. At least, I thought, I won't die in Iran. A representative from the Bani-Sadr government came in to ask how I was. We packed my toothbrush, a couple of pairs of underpants, and a can of crushed pineapple, a present from Akbar. I remember telling him he should make Kate Koob the new librarian.

That was it. A protocol officer in the Foreign Ministry and a hospital orderly walked down the steps with me to a waiting car. The government representative got behind the wheel. I sat in the back. Someone—I assumed he was one of the militants—sat next to me. He didn't say a word. The mood in the car was tense.

We took off. The representative drove like a madman, weaving in and out of traffic, honking his horn and cursing in rapid Farsi. His hand clenched the wheel so tightly his knuckles were white. "We've got to hurry," he said, screeching around a corner, barely missing two women in chadors. People scurried across the street to get out of the way. "A Swissair plane is waiting at the airport. They've been holding it for an hour already. That costs about a thousand dollars a minute. They may not hold it much longer—you know how the Swiss are about money."

I leaned forward to get a last look at Teheran and the militant jerked me back. "Stay away from the window, you're not out of Teheran yet."

I saw the airport just ahead.

"We're going through the VIP lounge—there's no time for Customs," he said, quickly.

We pulled up to a gate that led directly to the runway. Three reporters—one Japanese, one Iranian, one Dane—and two cameramen stood blocking our path. No American reporters were left in Iran. "What's your name?" they asked.

"Queen, Richard Queen."

"How are you feeling?"

"Fine."

When they asked me what my medical problem was, I said, "I believe I have a virus in the brain."

"Enough," said the government representative and drove the car through, right onto the field. I could see the plane, waiting, straight ahead. We were almost there. He stopped the car and helped me out. "Quickly, quickly," he urged.

At that moment the plane taxied down the runway and took off. My heart sank; I couldn't believe it. Was this a joke? I couldn't go back to the compound—back to captivity again. They'd have to kill me first.

"This way, this way," he said, leading me to the right.

Then I saw it—the most beautiful plane in the world, ready to go—waiting for me.

"Remember to write to Bruce Laingen—he feels bad that he's not with the others," the protocol officer told me. I guessed he was the same official who had worked with Laingen, Vic Tomseth and Mike Howland at the Foreign Ministry. Then he said, "Goodbye." The militant standing alongside was as mute as ever.

A Swiss embassy employee ran toward me. The Swiss had agreed to represent American interests in Iran after the hostage takeover. "How are you?" he asked. I couldn't answer him. Nothing was sinking in except one thing: I was on a plane and I was going home. Home.

"We have a couple of seats for you," he said. They were in First Class . . . I sat next to the window. Mr. Kaufman, who was in charge of American interests at the Swiss embassy in Teheran, sat next to me.

Immediately, the ramp went up, and we taxied to the runway. In moments I was in the air. Two hours before I had lain in Martyrs' Hospital, never dreaming of freedom. Although I hadn't felt sick while I rode in the car or boarded the plane, I felt my nausea return as the plane headed into the sky, so I couldn't look out, much as I wanted to see the last of Teheran. I had vertigo, too, and I felt a fear I can't explain.

Two stewardesses greeted me, and I talked a little bit with them. One good-looking blonde wanted to know where I was planning to live when I got back. I told her I was going back to Washington, DC. She wrote her name and number on a piece of paper and leaned across the seat to hand it to me; her face so close to mine was a knock-out—deep-brown, almost black eyes fringed with thick lashes. My mind raced.

Soon they brought a Swiss breakfast. I picked at some fruit and then some cereal. I hadn't been able to eat for eight to ten days in Iran, but now presented with this cornucopia of food, I felt my appetite return. The stewardess brought me filet mignon, a quiche, a croissant and pastries—a veritable feast. I wanted so much to be able to eat them all, but I settled for sampling a little bit of each. My mind was in a whirl. All of this food, attractively presented, fit for a king. Next they brought caviar and champagne. I thought, From an IV to this in just a few hours—I've got to be cautious, but I sipped a little champagne anyway. They came around with a trayful of cheeses. I didn't have any. In a while there were tarts, then cordials. I thought, Don't go too far. You're really pressing your luck as it is. I said no.

It was overcast and cool when we landed in Zurich and two Swiss medics came aboard with a stretcher. I had spent most of the flight talking to Mr. Kaufman, relating my experiences in Teheran—in fact, I had a case of diarrhea of the mouth. I learned later this happens to people who have been in captivity, but whatever it was from, I couldn't stop myself. I talked Mr. Kaufman's ears off, while, the blind pulled down, we passed out of Iranian airspace without my knowing it.

Now, six hours later, I walked down the plane's ramp and saw cameramen standing on top of buildings all around. "There he is," someone shouted. Were all these newsmen here for me?

"Just relax," said one of the medics, straightening his bright red overcoat for the camera. I looked a shambles, but I didn't care. I got on the stretcher and they belted me in.

"Let me know if the ride's too rough," said the medic behind me.

"So far it's wonderful," I said, looking in amazement at all the cameras focused on me. I was in Switzerland, I kept telling myself. A free country.

They carried me down the ramp and onto the ambulance and it pulled away through the streets of Zurich. No siren. Just flashing lights. My most recent ride through a city was still so fresh in my mind, I almost expected to see women in chadors, cars plummeting suicidally toward one another, revolutionary guards careering toward their next shoot-out. Instead all was quiet. We drove through the city to the University Hospital of Zurich. A wheelchair was waiting for me at the door, and we went onto an elevator and up several floors to a large room.

The nurses popped me into bed immediately. I wanted to take a shower; I hadn't showered in two weeks. The orderly helped me to the bathroom and asked me if I could manage. I said, sure, because even though it was still difficult to walk, just being able to do a little and to eat, too, made a big difference. But no, the hot water in the shower made me weak. I had to hold onto the handles to stand up, and I couldn't wash my hair. Still, I felt wonderful when I finished, and by the time I got into bed in my first clean pajamas in seven months, my freedom was starting to sink in.

Then in walked the doctor—the first free American I had met since the Easter service in Teheran. He examined me and asked to see the Swiss CAT scan, which had been done with a red dye that hadn't been used in Teheran. The whole process took forty-five minutes. Then back to bed to eat more food—with no nausea—and the telephone rang. A voice said, "This is Jimmy Carter."

I thought, My God, it's the President of the United States on the end of the line. He asked me how I was doing, and I said I was very honored to be speaking to him. I spoke to Mrs. Carter, too. Later Secretary of State Muskie called, wanting to know how I was and how I felt about the state of Maine, since he knew my parents were now local residents. I hung up, flushed with excitement. It was an incredible day.

The drugs they gave me in Teheran were affecting me now, and I must have dozed off, almost in a fantasy state. I remember being dimly aware of something familiar. Something very pleasant—a perfume from long ago. I should know that scent, I thought. My mother? I was afraid to open my eyes in case I was wrong. Could it be possible my mother was here?

"Oh, my precious son," she said, covering my face with kisses and tears. I looked up and smiled. I was so grateful to be in her arms. I felt like a child again returned to his parents after being lost and frightened for a very long time.

My father held me close and cried. I could smell his after-shave—a clean, cool, American smell. "I love you," he said. "I was so afraid I'd never get the chance to tell you that."

"I love you too, Dad," I said, holding him close. "I love you too."

My mother bowed her head and we all held hands; then I said the Lord's Prayer with a heart full of gratitude and love. I'm not a poet, I can't express what I experienced, but I knew then for sure that I was really out of the compound, really out of the Mushroom, really out of Teheran.

Chapter 8

The next morning the nurses brought in a big Swiss breakfast of meats and cheese, rolls and coffee. I saw my parents again, and Dr. Paul Eggertsen and Sheldon Krys, a calm, urbane man in his forties who was Executive Director for Near Eastern Affairs from the State Department. Krys was in charge of all State Department logistical planning for the return of the hostages from Teheran. He had met the thirteen blacks and women who were released after two weeks' captivity and the six who came out with the Canadians, and now he was in charge of me.

"Richard," said my mother, taking my hand. "We have so many questions. But they can wait. I just want to sit here all day and look at you."

I felt the same way and touched her cheek, wet with tears.

"You've got to stop crying. I'm home now. Everything is okay."

"She didn't cry when you were gone," said my father, "but now . . ." He turned away quickly and walked over to the window; in his conservatively tailored suit, he looked much younger than his sixty years. My mother—well, my mother was beautiful, but I could see concern and worry in her eyes, and her hair, once a deep, rich auburn, seemed to have much more gray in it than I remembered.

My father turned around, his eyes shining. "We love you, Richard," he said. "We're very proud of you."

Harold and Jeanne, the dynamic duo. A crazy mixture of Brooklyn, New York, and Rome–Paris–Bulgaria(!) that somehow worked.

They met and married during World War II. My mother was born in Bulgaria to a wealthy family from the landed gentry; she was raised in Rome and Paris. My father, born in Brooklyn, used to joke that *he* came from the aristocracy, because he once shook hands with Jackie Robinson. "In Brooklyn, that's enough to make you royalty."

We talked about our new home in Maine, and my brother Alex, who wasn't able to come to Zurich. My parents brought me some flowers that the owner of their hotel had given them, but a cloud hung over their joy because they were worried about my diagnosis. I wasn't ready to think about it, partly because I was still in a state of euphoria, but I certainly knew I was sick and that soon I'd have to face it.

We left Zurich that afternoon, going by ambulance to the airport with my parents, Sheldon Krys and Dr. Eggertsen.

We flew on an air force evacuation plane, from Zurich to Rhein-Main Air Base. They took me off the plane on a stretcher, and we rode in an army ambulance along the autobahn to the American Air Force Hospital in Wiesbaden with a twelve-car convoy of German and American military police, a limousine full of officials and a backup ambulance. It just didn't seem possible that all of this was happening to me. When we entered the hospital grounds, people were clapping and cheering and waving American flags. I sat, stunned, in a wheelchair as we rolled past the staff to a VIP room in one wing of the hospital, where two air force police were on guard outside. The whole hospital was off limits, and even my parents had to show passes, while air police, doing extra shifts, surrounded the whole air base. Inside the hospital I tried to come to grips with being the center of all this attention.

My mother came in my room laughing, "We were told to show our passes, but I couldn't find mine."

"So," says my father, interrupting, "she says to the policemen guarding the door, 'We're Richard Queen's parents—we'd like to see him.' The guard says, 'I'm very sorry but I can't let you in without a pass.'"

"Well," says my mother, continuing, "I said, 'but you can see the strong family resemblance. Isn't that enough identification?' Luckily, I found my pass, and the guard smiled. He knew who I was."

"You're really special to everyone now, Richard," my father said, "and they're not taking any chances."

The remarkable reception pointed up, as no one's telling me could, how strongly the taking of the hostages had affected the United States and what it meant to Americans that one of us, even a sick one, was out of Iran. I was a tangible link to the others, and already, along with my joy and relief, I knew it was important to show people that I was alright, that I had survived and that the other fifty-two could survive, too.

First, I had a pressing problem. I had to find out what my medical situation was, face it squarely, and get back into the real world as fast as I could. The hospital director had planned a six-day decompression period with batteries of tests and careful evaluations, and I was anxious to get on with it.

Reporters stood outside the hospital, but I didn't see them. I didn't even have time to look outside at the pleasant view. The minute I could use a phone I called Don Hohman's and Bob Ode's wives and, of course, Joe Hall's wife, Cherlynn.

The first home I reached was Bob Ode's.

"Hello," I said, "is this Rita Ode?"

"Yes?" she said, waiting.

"This is Richard Queen—I've been rooming with your husband . . ."

"Wait, what are you saying? You've seen Bob? My Bob?"

"Mrs. Ode, he's fine, he's not sick, he's really well. That's why I'm calling—just to talk to you. Nothing has happened to him," I reassured her as quickly as possible.

A long silence followed. Then I heard her crying softly.

"Mrs. Ode?"

"Yes, I'm fine. I am just so relieved. Bob has a heart condition, and I've been so worried about him."

I told her that Bob and I were rooming with Don Hohman, a top-notch medic who looked after both of us.

"Don saved my life—he'll know what to do for Bob if the need arises—but I'm sure it won't."

"You see, Bob and I haven't any children; he's really my

whole life. Until you called I've been sick with worry, thinking "If something happened to his heart, who would know what to do?" Then when I heard you were being released, I didn't know what to think. Had you been tortured? Were they all being tortured? Were you all going insane? We just didn't know."

I told her we'd talk again when I got back to the States. She thanked me so much, over and over, for calling her so soon. When we said goodbye, I lay back on my pillow suddenly aware of what anguish these wives and parents were going through. It was one thing to assume they were all "worried" but quite another to hear the torment in their voices. As Francis Bacon said, "He that hath wife and children hath given hostages to fortune." I thought that must be true as well when you loved someone very much— your heart and mind went wherever they did.

Next, I called Don Hohman's wife, a native of West Germany who was living in Frankfurt—a stone's throw away, comparatively speaking.

"You are calling me? But you are in hospital," she said, excitedly. "Is something wrong with Don?"

"Oh, no. Don is very well and just the best in my book. A number one medic. He knew how ill I was and insisted they get a doctor for me."

"Thank God, what good news—he's alright. My heart is so full. Don is so dedicated to medicine I thought maybe God would not let anything bad happen to him; but you worry anyway. Now I feel maybe the horror is coming to an end."

"I hope so, too," I said. "You can be very proud of Don. I know he is proud of you."

"Oh, you wonderful man," she sobbed. "Forgive me, it's

just such good news I can let go a little bit now."

I knew what she meant. But I also knew that until they were all home, none of us would be able to let go completely.

When I called Cherlynn Hall she yelled joyfully, "Richard! The Man from Sheboygan! You've seen Joe! Richard, just tell me everything, no matter how unimportant it seems. I just miss him so."

I told her about our lives in the Mushroom and the chancery and then the move. "I did get word from a guard that Joe said 'hello' and was doing fine. Really, Cherlynn, I do believe the worst was the Mushroom, and we got through that. When Joe feels down he just thinks about you and that cheers him right away."

"It's so good to hear that. I don't want him worrying about me. One of us worrying twenty-four hours a day is enough," she laughed. "Oh, Richard, I feel so hopeful now. I'm going to write and tell him Sheboygan is home and . . . Are you really okay?"

"I sure am," I told her. "Tell him the U.S. is the best medicine in the world." We both laughed long and hard.

When I hung up I just shook my head in amazement. These women were incredible people—I felt very proud to know them.

I couldn't reach Charlie Jones's wife, Mattie, but I would try again later. I knew it meant so much to hear, firsthand, that their husbands were surviving.

Next there were the debriefings—hours and hours of talking into a tape recorder with the two State Department psychiatrists. I kept talking straight into the night, wearing down the doctors and feeling better and better. I had to release something—all of my stored-up experiences and my frustration, probably—and I wanted to spill it out as fast as possible. I felt very coherent, and my mind was functioning easily; when they gave me a whole set of psychological tests, they found I was in excellent psychological shape.

After that I began on the physical tests, and in between I rested and I ate. The first day they brought my dinner, I asked for a beer, but they didn't have any. Sheldon Krys brought in a six-pack of double Bock beer, which is potent stuff, and later the State Department doctors brought me beer, too. I had gone eight-and-a-half months without any alcohol, and when I had a couple of bottles I nearly fell over. That night I went to bed very early!

I ate in the hospital mess with my parents, Sheldon Krys and Major Cuervo, the neurologist in charge of my tests. Then I would be wheeled back to my room. After one of these trips, I got up out of the wheelchair and was suddenly overcome with a strong feeling of claustrophobia; I felt dizzy and reached out to support myself against the wall. The room seemed to be getting smaller, the walls closing in. I was back in the Mushroom, the tomb. I could smell the dank air, see the stained mattresses on the floor, hear the guard pacing outside my door. I wiped my face; it was wet with perspiration. I felt as if I couldn't breathe. "Wait, hold on," I told myself, and tried to calm down. "You're safe. This is a nice, clean room. The guard outside is friendly. There are nice people here—your friends and family." The pounding of my heart subsided and the room retreated. I walked over to my bed and lay down, forcing the terrifying images of darkness and captivity out of my head.

I needed clothes—all I had was hospital pajamas and a

robe, so they gave me a five-hundred dollar advance against my pay and opened up the PX on Sunday. My parents and Sheldon Krys came along to help me find underwear, shoes and other basics. I began searching through the racks and racks of suits but found nothing to fit my six-foot-three, 180-pound frame. Just when I was about to give up, Sheldon Krys pulled a beautifully tailored pinstripe suit off a rack in the corner.

"How much is this?" he asked the store manager.

"Oh, those are all half price. That suit was custom-made for someone in the State Department who never picked it up."

"I vowed I'd never wear one of those things," I laughed, holding it up against me.

"Get it," said Krys. "You've earned the right to look like a diplomat."

"Besides," said my mother, "it's half price."

Except for a few tucks required here and there, it fit perfectly.

The captain who had flown me from Zurich had given me a T-shirt from the medevac unit; the hospital staff gave me and my parents spring jackets, and the American consul general in Zurich gave me a sweater. Pretty soon I was starting to build up my wardrobe again.

On the third day, I was given an unpleasant test called a lumbar tap that required a long needle injected into my spine. I knew they were zeroing in on a diagnosis, and I expected to hear something—good or bad—very soon. I had undergone an extraordinary battery of tests. It was clear that Wiesbaden was equipped with the best medicine had to offer—men and machines—and all of Wiesbaden's resources were ready to help us hostages when we came out of captivity. In my case the doctors wanted to be absolutely certain of their diagnosis.

Earlier in the day Dr. Cuervo said he wanted to talk to me and my parents that afternoon. My parents were very apprehensive, especially my mother. I knew what they were going through, waiting and imagining the worst. I felt differently. No matter what the doctors had to tell me, I knew I'd be able to deal with it. Not in the old fatalistic way but with a feeling of confidence that I could now handle what life had in store for me.

I was resting in my bed, really luxuriating in the snowy-white clean sheets and soft, fresh-smelling pillow, when my mother came over and began to plump the pillow for me.

"Let her spoil you a little, Richard," my father said, laughing.

"You better," she said. "It gives me so much pleasure to be able to fuss over you a bit. To know you're comfortable and taken care of. When I think . . ."

"Now, Jeanne," interrupted my father, "all that's over. Just look at these." My father was sorting through a stack of telegrams sent to me at the hospital from well-wishers in Germany and all over the world. "It's so amazing," he said, "to find out how much people can care."

I felt so good, so safe, surrounded by my family. At that moment, the door opened and a nurse asked if we were ready. The time had come.

We exchanged a last little burst of nervous chatter as Dr. Cuervo and Dr. Korcak came in and pulled a couple of chairs into place. Sheldon Krys sat near the door. I sat a little straighter in my bed. I looked at my parents, who at that moment seemed a bit older than they had just a few seconds before. I was amazed at how detached I felt. I knew that what was about to unfold might have the profoundest effect on all that I hoped for in the immediate future.

Major Cuervo sat back in his chair and smiled. That's an encouraging sign, I thought. "We do have a diagnosis, Richard, Mr. and Mrs. Queen. The lumbar tap was the final test we needed to determine specifically the nature of your disease."

"What does Richard have?" asked my mother quietly.

"Before we give it a label let me say right away it's not as bad as it might have been. Because of all those tests, we were able to eliminate several diseases with similar symptoms. The doctors in Iran thought you had encephalitis of the brain, which can be fatal. Well, you should be relieved to hear that that is not the case. What you do have is a disease of the central nervous system called multiple sclerosis.

My mother inhaled sharply and repeated the words to herself very slowly, "Multiple sclerosis." My father cleared his throat several times as if he were trying to swallow a large pill. I tried to attach an image to the doctor's words but none came forth. I couldn't quite separate multiple sclerosis from muscular dystrophy from cerebral palsy. Would I be crippled? Would I be able to provide for myself? Or would I be a burden to my parents?

"What exactly is multiple sclerosis?" asked my father. His voice was calm and even but sounded as if it were coming from a point far away.

Major Cuervo came from around his desk, sat on the corner and looked at all of us. "Before I get technical I want to assure you, Richard, that this is a disease you can live with. You can have a full, productive, independent life. Please believe that."

We all wanted to very much. My mother quickly dabbed the corner of her eye with a tissue and smiled shakily. "Well, that's good news right there . . . isn't it?"

"Very good news," said Major Cuervo. "Now, I'll try to explain as clearly as possible. Please feel free to interrupt me as I go along if you have any questions.

"MS is a neurological problem. Think of the nerves in your body as a series of telephone wires—and like telephone wires, coated with a protective material. This material is called the myelin coating. If the myelin coating wears away, then the nerves, or wires, are exposed. When this happens, messages are short-circuited. Impulses are transmitted erratically to various parts of the body, which explains why 'jerky' or rapid responses follow. Other messages just don't get through at all.

"Sclerosis means scarring. This is what happens along the central nervous system—multiple scarring in multiple places. This scar tissue can also block messages."

"But Richard seems fine now. He recovered almost as soon as he left Iran. Maybe a little numbness, but really he's so much better," said my mother. Her voice was hopeful, as if by pointing out this information she might get the doctor to retract his diagnosis.

"Richard is better and he will continue to improve. This is because his disease is in remission right now. We don't know why this happens, but it means that the myelin sheath has repaired itself. This remission could last for years or for the rest of his life. It's hard to say.

"MS is a very individual disease that ranges from mild to severe. Most people are somewhere in the middle. A series of attacks and remissions."

"Will I be worse after every attack?" I asked. My father

shot me a look as if to say: That is the question I was afraid to ask.

"No," said Major Cuervo. "Not necessarily. You could have an attack and at first seem worse than before but eventually have a remission that would take you back to square one. Like a roller coaster—peaks and valleys followed by more peaks and valleys. But as I say, you will not necessarily have another attack. If you do have one, it does not have to mean you will automatically be worse off than before.

"MS is not curable. You will always have it, but you should be able to live a very normal life with no severe problems."

"I feel as if I'm improving every day. Most of my symptoms are clearing up quickly," I replied, trying to reassure my parents.

My mother nodded almost imperceptibly. "He is doing well, isn't he, doctor?"

"Yes, he is. The important thing is not to worry. One's mental state has a lot to do with the rate of improvement. I'll be by tomorrow to talk with you some more."

"Thank you," said my mother. "You and everyone here at the hospital have been so kind to us."

It was my father's turn to startle me by asking a question that I did not at that moment have the courage to articulate. Quietly, hesitantly, he asked whether I would be able to continue as a Foreign Service officer. Sheldon Krys immediately replied that there was every reason for me to continue with my career, and Dr. Korcak added his assurances on medical grounds.

So there it was. It was good to have the answer at last, and I felt far more concerned for my parents' worry than for anything else. I knew for myself that I was improving so much every day. I could walk now. I used the wheelchair less. As the doctor said, the remission could last thirty or forty years, for my lifetime—or I could have another attack and maybe get worse. Maybe not.

I was alive. I was feeling better. I decided not to worry.

My father put his arm around my mother and tried to soothe her, but I could tell he was upset as well. My mother took my face in her hands and kissed me. "I wish there were some way for you not to have this; some way I could rescue you from this disease. I wouldn't care if I had it—but not you. Not now."

"We'll deal with it, Richard," said my father. "And we'll help you deal with it. It just takes a little getting used to. We both feel you've been through so much—and now this. We wanted good times for you."

"There's going to be great times ahead for me. I know it. Now you two have to know it, too."

The next morning Sheldon Krys, my mother, father and I were eating breakfast in my room when we heard a knock on the door. "Come in," I said. The door opened and a young man wearing medical whites poked his head in.

"Excuse me for interrupting," he said. "I'll come back later."

"No, come on in," I insisted. "We're just finishing up. Would you like some coffee?"

"Actually, no. I came to say something to you, and it's a little difficult."

After I introduced him to Sheldon Krys and my parents, he began to tell us his story. "I'm in my last year of interning; next year I'll get a residency . . . that is, if no one finds out."

"Finds out what?" I asked.

"I have what you have, multiple sclerosis. No one knows, and I hope no one finds out. It could affect my chances of becoming a doctor. Not the disease; just people's attitudes toward the disease."

"No one in this room will ever mention what you're telling us," said my father. "You can count on it."

"Thank you. I thought it would help if you could see me, how healthy I appear. I work very hard and have as active a social life as possible, considering my work load. And I have MS. None of my friends know. None of my co-workers know. They probably wouldn't believe it if I told them.

"I know what you're all going through. I felt the same way when I learned four years ago why my body was acting so crazy. Like you, Richard, my disease is in remission. I thought if I 'blew my cover' long enough to tell you that having MS is really not the worst thing in the world, it might help. As a matter of fact, it doesn't even come close to second place." He laughed.

My mother smiled. The first real smile since we heard the news about my disease.

"You're very kind to make this gesture to our son, to us. I'm so touched. You're very special to know how much it would mean to all of us to hear what you had to say. To see you."

We all felt much better after that, and I faced my medical treatment with renewed optimism.

I went across the street to the dental clinic and had my teeth cleaned by an extremely attractive hygienist with dark brown curly hair and freckles. And, of course, straight, gleaming white teeth. She really had a million-dollar smile.

A graduate of Ohio State, a rival of the University of Michigan, she threatened several times to stencil OSU on my teeth. Little, cheerful things like that brought me back to the real world again, and talking with all the people in the hospital did too.

I couldn't have visitors in my room because I was supposed to rest, but people called my name when I was wheeled down the hallways to the cafeteria, and we would stop and talk. Some of them brought me little things that touched me very much; on one day I received a cross, a Star of David and a rosary from three different people who wanted me to know how much they cared. I just couldn't get over all the love, warmth and generosity. America and Americans—I began to see for the first time what those words really meant.

The media were desperate to get in and get some information. My mother was reluctant to speak to the press because of her accent. "They keep misunderstanding me," she said. "And I don't want to say anything that will hurt the other hostages, or embarrass you."

"Talk to them in Bulgarian," I told her. She laughed and said she might be forced to. My father enjoyed talking to the press, and in one of his early statements he had said that I really liked the Chicago White Sox team. So I got a call from the owner of the White Sox, Bill Veeck, inviting me to a game at Comisky Park. We talked about the team— they had just lost a three- or four-game series, and when he caught me up on the baseball world, I suddenly thought about summer at home. I could almost taste the hot dogs, see the crowds, hear the "thwack" of the bat. When I hung up, a wonderful rush of energy flooded me with the realization that I was truly free, and I was going home.

Bill Veeck called me and reported our conversation to

Sporting News magazine, which then ran an article entitled "A White Sox Fan Comes Home." My mind flashed back to the chancery and the day we learned that the *Sporting News* publishers were going to send us six copies of the magazine every week. After a steady diet of women's magazines, this was fantastic news. The joy that magazine brought us! In addition to following the standings, sometimes we'd be able to pick up bits of information about what was happening in the States. The militants never read it. They thought it was totally about sports and weren't interested in our "corrupt American pastime."

Now I was going to be in the magazine. Now the others would know what had happened to me and realize that I would be able to get information to their families.

My uncle called and wanted to know if it was all right if NBC monitored conversations between my aunt and me. My father hit the roof. "Absolutely not," he said. "We will not accept any phone call like that."

In the end the media were allowed to film me but with no sound. They set up a pool crew and filmed me with my parents in my hospital room in my bathrobe and hospital pajamas. Of course I had a TV so I saw myself, and I didn't like it. Maybe it was vanity because I'd be thinking: God, do I look like that? Did I say that?

In addition to the film crews, I had all sorts of special visitors: Walter Stoessel, the American ambassador to the Federal Republic of Germany; General Pauley, in charge of the U.S.A.F. European Command; a representative of the foreign ministry of the Federal Republic of Germany; and a representative of the Governor General of Hesse. The Governor General of Hesse sent several bottles of their great wine.

People couldn't phone me directly—they had to leave

their names and numbers, but my friends called, including Pete Brown. I told him how much I liked his postcards and about my Alaska poster. "Okay," he said, "now you've got to come up for a holiday and see the real thing."

I laughed. The idea seemed marvelous. To think that I was free and I could do it. "You're on," I said. "Pete, I want to tell you . . . I want to tell you how I feel about you being willing to go to Teheran last fall and find me."

He interrupted me. "Don't even think about that," he said, dismissing the whole thing. "I know you would have done the same for me."

"Thanks, Pete," I said. I guess that was all I could say, but I knew how I felt: very lucky to have such a good friend.

On my last night in Germany, the hospital staff threw a surprise party for me, a buffet, and a longtime German employee who had been taken prisoner during World War II and was now working for the American army as a medic played the accordion. People danced and gave me plaques, beer mugs and coffee cups. It was a simple but very touching farewell.

The next morning I showered, dressed and watched my mother pack my few possessions and gifts. When it was time to leave, I walked part of the way and then slid into a wheelchair so that a nurse could take me outside. I waved goodbye to the hospital staff and patients, who stood on the balconies waving flags. The press, across the way, waved too.

My ambulance joined an eleven-vehicle convoy of police, a car for my parents and State Department officials, and a backup ambulance. We sped to the Rhein-Main Air Base half-an-hour's drive away and boarded a regularly scheduled medevac flight that would make a special stop for us at Andrews Air Force Base, outside Washington, DC. We had a reserve unit crew from the 732nd Air Medical Evacuation Squadron, and the plane was crowded with patients, some of them lying in the stretchers that filled, in triple tiers, the rear of the plane. One of the men asked me to sign his cast, and I shook as many hands as I could reach. Most of the time I sat with Sheldon Krys and three State Department doctors while my father sat at a typewriter in the cockpit, writing a story for *Newsweek*. I sat up there for a while too. The crew flew over land as much as possible for security reasons, and I enjoyed seeing the tip of Greenland slip by.

We tried to contact my brother, who is an artist and lives in Chicago, but all we could learn was that he had picked up his ticket at the Chicago airport and left for Washington, and though the plane had landed, no one knew where he was.

"That's your brother," said my dad. "He'll be late."

We had found out there was going to be a welcoming ceremony, and my father was worried about what my brother would be wearing—like sandals instead of regular shoes and a tie.

At noon they passed out box lunches. We couldn't talk because we all wore earplugs—it was a long, noisy flight—but I didn't care; I was going home. As we crossed into American airspace the crew gave me a T-shirt and coasters and flight charts marked with the date and the time.

In fact everything was perfectly timed. The big moment when the plane landed—2:00—and taxied to a stop; the ramp coming down—2:10. As the air force captain helped me down the ramp, the hot July air startled me. We had

had cool and rainy weather in Germany, and my suit felt inappropriately heavy. I spotted my brother, who was wearing a tie and standing next to the Secretary of State, and I waved weakly. I greeted Muskie and Deputy Secretary Warren Christopher, and Muskie helped guide me—I didn't use a wheelchair—along the receiving line and to the podium. The assistant secretaries and the head of the State Department's medical services stood there, too.

There was a brief welcoming ceremony, and I said how wonderful it was to be back home and how much I wished the fifty-two other hostages were with me, and then Louisa Kennedy, spokeswoman for FLAG, the Family Liaison Action Group, presented me with a bouquet. Katherine Keough and Louisa Kennedy had founded FLAG so that the hostages' families would have a central place to call, receive help, or just talk about how they were or were not coping. FLAG held candlelight vigils during the bitter cold winter months so people would not forget us, and Katherine Keough, Bill Keough's attractive, hardworking wife, urged people to gather in their churches and synagogues to pray for our release. She and Dorothea Morefield must have spent a fortune on yellow ribbons to distribute to community groups for all those "old oak trees."

A group of several hundred well-wishers stood nearby, and I shook as many hands as I could before I climbed into my last ambulance, headed for the Georgetown University Hospital. I was tired but determined to sit up and talk to the State Department people who flew with me from Wiesbaden.

"Wait until you are able to get around and realize for yourself how the whole country feels about the hostages," said one of the doctors.

"We're Americans again," said another, "in a way we haven't been for a long time."

I tried to respond, but my eyes were closing, so I settled for what I hoped came across as a sagacious nod. A police motorcycle led the ambulance and limousines carried my parents and brother. Traffic parted as the ambulance, sirens wailing, sped down the streets, and a feeling of awe and responsibility swept over me. People waiting at the hospital entrance waved American flags as the staff took me to my room, where a Welcome Home sign cheered me, a basket of fruit sat on a table, and flowers—even some from an Iranian–American—filled the room.

I took off my suit, slipped into pajamas and crawled into bed. They worried about how the heat would affect me, but I was more upset about being in another small room. Again that unpleasant feeling came back. I felt confined. The walls stood too close. A guard stood outside my hospital door . . . I forced myself to relax and reminded myself that I was at home and people here were nice, but it was a relief when I fell asleep.

The next morning, Sheldon Krys and my parents ate lunch with me in my room. My parents had lost their worried look and now considered my disease something that was "inconvenient but not devastating." Mr. Krys had brought my parents several books on the subject. My mother said, "I'll be an expert soon. You won't need a doctor." Krys had been extremely generous and caring toward all of us and seemed to know exactly what we needed before we did.

Two days later I received an invitation to meet President Carter, and my father and brother spent the morning arguing about what my brother should wear.

"You can't wear those old tan slacks to see the President of the United States," my father said.

"Why not?" Alex said.

My father didn't answer and instead tossed Alex a pair of blue pants that he bought for him in Wiesbaden. Alex threw the pants on the bed. But then he looked at me, and he said he'd wear them. It was a big concession, but my father didn't stop there. "You can't wear those worn shoes with the new pants," he said.

This time Alex stormed out, but again he came back and jammed his feet into the new shoes my father had bought him in Wiesbaden. He insisted on wearing his white socks; my father gave up and just hoped they wouldn't show.

At 10:30, a shiny limousine pulled up to the hospital entrance. I leaned back inside it, wondering what it would be like meeting the President. I had on a jacket, and my father had on a jacket, too. Alex did not; he and my father weren't speaking. Warren Christopher and Sheldon Krys met us in the Rose Garden; when we approached the White House, President Carter bounded out, hand extended. He wasn't wearing a jacket. He looked at my father and me. Alex shot a triumphant glance at Dad.

"Excuse me, let me get my jacket," the President said as he led us inside. As he took us to the Oval Office he put on his jacket and my father smiled at Alex. I smiled, too, because I felt relaxed—like I was meeting an old friend. I was very grateful for Mr. Carter's informality and warmth.

Our fifteen-minute meeting stretched to forty-five. My father told me later I talked for forty-one of the forty-five minutes, and the pictures of the meeting do show my mouth open most of the time.

The President asked me about my experiences, and I told

him all sorts of things that had happened and he seemed
moved, especially when I described our life at the Mushroom Inn; the feeling of being lost to the world and the
world lost to us. The dank darkness of our captivity, the
terror of the Gestapo raid, the bravery in so many little
ways of Jim Lopez, Joe Hall, Charlie Jones, Don Hohman
and the rest; the brotherhood and feeling of fraternity we all
shared; and the strong love of our country that never
wavered.

I couldn't stop talking. I told him about the tape that
the student had played for me—the one that said the
United States should tell the Middle East to keep their oil
and go to hell. And what a boost it was for me and Joe to
know that Americans really cared about us. He laughed
when I told him how disappointed the militants were when
they tried to get the blacks to side with them. They didn't
know what mean was until they rubbed Dave Walker the
wrong way.

The President of the United States sat and listened
intently when I told him how much the Christmas service
had meant to me; how I had heard the words of the Lord's
Prayer in a new and more meaningful way. I don't know
why I told him—it just seemed like the right thing to do—
that every night I got down on my knees and prayed that
we'd be released. My father looked at me, surprised to hear
this. It was, after all, something I had not shared with
anyone. President Carter nodded. I think he had been
praying the same prayer every night too.

Rosalynn Carter asked me how it felt to be back home
again. I looked at her and thought, Here I am sitting in the
Oval Office with the President of the United States and his
wife; both of them are sincerely interested in what I have to

say, while matters of state are put aside. How does it feel to be home? "Fantastic," I said. "Just fantastic."

This was the part I'd never be able to explain to the Iranians about our country: how much the individual really matters. What a heady trip. From the Mushroom Inn to the Oval Office. It occurred to me that two years ago I would have faced a meeting like this with a stomach full of butterflies, instead of feeling tranquil and at ease. I guess I had changed a lot in the last several months.

When I got back to the hospital, I climbed into bed and tried to read back issues of *Time* and *Newsweek* that I received in Wiesbaden. I couldn't concentrate—too many things were happening—and I began to reflect, as I had been doing more and more, on the free, almost startling outpouring of affection and goodness that I had been experiencing for so many days now. True, I had been back such a short time compared to the three hundred plus days I had spent in Iran, but the power of these American days, as opposed to those, was extraordinary.

I received a call from a man who said he had gone to Canada to escape the draft but had vowed to enlist if anything happened to the hostages. A school bus parked in front of the hospital and the kids held up a big sign, "We love you, Richard." I had left one America and had come home to another one.

I just wished, as I had so often since I left Iran, there was some way I could tell Joe and Don and Bob and Charlie and all the others what it was like. They were constantly in my thoughts, almost as if I was communicating it all to them anyway. Of course, I had written to all of them immediately, even though I knew the guards would never let anything with my name on it get through.

Wonderful surprises from all sorts of people arrived steadily at the hospital. Quarts of maple walnut ice cream, cheese, bread and wine from a gourmet shop in Georgetown; cards, letters, flowers and all kinds of other signs that people from all over the world cared. One of the best presents was the arrival of Pete and Anne Brown from Alaska with a huge box of Alaska King Crab. How we gorged on that wonderful crab meat!

The State Department arranged a press conference, and an information officer told me to use my own discretion about what I said. He realized I didn't have to be reminded that anything I said might affect the hostages.

When my family entered the auditorium, everyone, including the press corps, gave them a standing ovation. I wasn't strong enough to stand, so they moved the mikes down to me. The reporters, some of whom I recognized from TV, asked me questions for an hour. It surprised me at first that I wasn't nervous, because just two years ago, when I was a teaching assistant at the University of Michigan, the thought of lecturing to 150 students made my mouth dry and my stomach tense. Now I could speak on live television at a packed press conference, without anxiety. As I answered their questions—"What did you eat? How did you communicate with one another? Did you lose hope? How are the others doing?"—images of my captivity shot through my mind. "No speak. No speak." The Gestapo raid. Breakfast bread thrown on the mud-caked floor. Towels on our heads as we went to the bathroom. Images I would never forget.

A lot of little thoughts I hadn't connected before were beginning to come together in my mind. Maybe, it occurred to me, my serenity came from more than having some facts and trying to help people understand the situation in the compound. Maybe I was holding together now because I had held together in Teheran. All those weeks when I had had to face terror, fight despair, deal with the silence and the boredom and the fear of falling apart, those weeks had given me something that was keeping me from railing now at having multiple sclerosis, that enabled me to speak calmly on national TV.

I wondered how I could share this new strength with all these people. When I met with the families after the press conference the answer was clear. Whatever strength I had gained was badly needed here.

Families who lived in the Washington area had come to the State Department so that I could talk to them about their loved ones in captivity. They had gathered in one of the conference rooms. Mothers, fathers, wives, children, sisters and brothers waited for the few words I could give them. I was tired after the press conference, but I vowed that I would spend as much time as possible with each family that had come to meet with me.

First I spoke to them as a group, telling them in a general way what our daily lives as hostages were like. I told them about the rooms we lived in, the mattresses we slept on, the food we were given to eat, the sanitary arrangements, the medical care. And I told them how we spent the hours and days and months of confinement. Then I was wheeled into a small office across the hall.

Each family in turn entered my room tentatively, as if not sure they wanted to deal with what I was going to say. I smiled to let them know immediately that there was hope; that their husbands, sons and daughters were alive and would return.

I wanted so much to be standing for this moment, not confined to the chair, but my spirit was standing and I think they saw that.

"Please, come on in," I said. "We've got a lot of good things to talk about."

I thought my heart would burst when I saw their open American faces beaming at me, the strain suffered through all the months of gallant waiting visible beneath the smiles.

An attractive woman, about forty-five, with luminous brown eyes walked toward me; her trim figure shown to advantage in a soft, pale blue suit. She took my hand and placed it in both of hers.

"I'm Anita Schaefer," she said. "Welcome home, Richard. We're all so grateful you're okay." Her eyes filled with tears but she blinked them back. "How is Tom doing?"

Col. Schaefer had been put in solitary confinement by the Iranians early on in our captivity—but I wasn't going to tell that to Anita Schaefer. I told her instead how he hummed American patriotic songs to keep everyone's spirits up and that his spirit was by no means broken.

"Thank God," she said softly. "That sounds just like him."

Don Cooke's brother and sister introduced themselves and hugged me at the same time. The scene of Don and me tied to chairs in the ambassador's residence while Don sang "The Battle Hymn of the Republic" flashed through my mind and I told them about it.

"Well, I'll be," laughed his brother. "How about him. I didn't know he even knew the words."

"What about now, Richard? How is Don now?" asked his sister, a blond feminine version of Don. "Is he depressed? Is he eating? Does he have enough . . ."

"Whoa," I smiled. "Don is fine. He misses his beer and he hates Iranian sandals, but he's really fine."

Just outside the door in the corridor, I saw a fashionably dressed couple in their early sixties. They waited patiently while I finished talking to Lisa Moeller, Staff Sergeant Mike Moeller's wife. I had learned from the press that Mike might be tried, and I wanted very much to lend as much comfort as I could. I tried to put her mind at ease by telling her that he had not been hurt.

"Of all of us," I said honestly, "he has the most nonchalant attitude. When things get under his skin he sings 'The Marine Corps Hymn' at the top of his lungs."

As the older couple approached, they exchanged smiles with Lisa, the mutual smiles of those who share a common worry. This was John Limbert Senior and his wife. The Limberts were concerned that John, the best Farsi speaker at the Embassy, might be singled out for special treatment—none of it good—because his wife came from a prominent Iranian family. I assured the Limberts that I thought John's wife's identification was not known to the Iranian militants, and I told them what I could about John's circumstances. I had heard of John's ability to gather news of the outside world and pass it on to his fellow hostages. In fact, for a while John had managed to keep a radio hidden among his effects and therefore could at least get the Iranian version of world events.

"Here, take these," said Mr. Limbert, handing me a bouquet of yellow roses. "You're going to be our surrogate son until John comes home."

The day went on without a break between families. The mood in the room changed slowly from fearful hesitancy to an enormous uplifting as we talked, hugged and cried together. I had thought I might not be able to satisfy these people because of how relatively little I knew about some of the hostages after April 26, but even the few specific details seemed to help and comfort them. My being there with them meant as much to me as it did to them, and our thoughts were full of those who remained in Iran.

I was dimly aware that the chair I was sitting in was cutting into my back, but the joy of the day was giving me a new energy. Then, across the room, I saw her. A young woman in a pastel flowered dress; a cap of auburn hair framing a face aglow with happiness. She looked just like her picture.

"Cherlynn," I yelled. "You're Cherlynn Hall."

"Richard, the man from Sheboygan!" She ran toward me. We hugged and laughed simultaneously. I felt as if I had known her for a very long time.

"He's probably still trying to get those vacuum cleaners to work," I said. "I bet Joe was given at least four that whined to a halt as soon as they were plugged in. Then an Iranian would try to fix it by jumping up and down on the machine or cutting the cord in half. For engineering students, they didn't know a heck of a lot about the way things work."

Cherlynn laughed. "When Joe comes home I'll let him vacuum to his heart's content."

After six hours of talking to the families, I felt linked in an indescribable way to all of them. I had already felt this connection with all the hostages, even the ones I rarely or never saw. Now the circle was complete. I gave them all my phone number and urged them to call me at any time, for any reason, if they had a question I had not answered or if they just wanted to talk. It was an extraordinary meeting, and once it was over I knew without a doubt that as long as the others were still hostage, I was a hostage too, to my feelings of guilt, to my feelings of bridging the gap, to my determination to see this nightmare all the way through.

Even though I walked unsteadily, my multiple sclerosis had improved from the moment I stepped on board the Swiss airplane, and now the hospital staff cut my stay from seven to five days and suggested I finish decompressing at my parents' home in Maine. My brother flew back to Chicago leaving his new blue pants and shoes behind; a government plane flew Pete and Anne Brown and me to Owl's Head Airport in nearby Lincolnville, which they renamed Owl's Head International Airport in my honor.

A small crowd waved American flags while Governor Brennan greeted me and made a welcoming speech, in which he asked the community to respect our privacy. State troopers drove the limousines to town, past trees with yellow ribbons, street signs with yellow ribbons, children with yellow ribbons, and a big yellow ribbon tied around the oak tree standing in my parents' front yard.

The house, built just after the Revolutionary War, was beautiful, even more beautiful than the pictures my parents had sent to Teheran. A river runs nearby, and I could see the sea from most of the windows. But my parents had moved here while I was away, and for an instant, when I saw my room I longed for the stability and solace old furniture, books and mementoes bring. At first I walked around the house feeling cheated and a little out of place, and everything seemed unfamiliar. But as the days passed, I felt more comfortable, enjoying the quiet and wandering around. (In fact, I fell in love with the house.)

Every day I called three hostage families. Some conversations lasted an hour, and often, the wives or the parents cried. "Please tell me," pleaded one wife, "what I should do to help him?"

"Letters," I told her. "Keep writing—even if only one gets through, it's the most important thing you can do. It may even save his life."

The hardest part was talking to the children who wanted to know when Daddy was coming home. One little boy asked, "Why didn't you bring him home with you?"

The calls drained me, but they were something I wanted to do and terribly important to all of us; and in between, the lovely, quiet town restored me. The peace was easy. I took walks and ate dinner with my parents' friends or shopped in Camden, a seacoast town nearby, where I bought jeans and informal shirts to add to my meager wardrobe. I was recognized constantly, and the people told me how glad they were about my release and that I was a resident of Maine and that, to them, I represented all the hostages.

Every day gifts and letters arrived. Tony Orlando, who sang "Tie a Yellow Ribbon Round the Old Oak Tree," sent a ficus tree with a hundred yellow ribbons on it. Pete Brown's mother bought homemade ice cream in Cincinnati and Delta Airlines volunteered to fly it to Bangor where two college students drove it to me. How could people *be* so wonderful?

My mother continued to worry, and she wanted me with her, which was understandable but not always possible, because there were times when I had a great need to be alone.

251

"Don't smoke anymore, Richard. It's not good for your health," she'd say.

"It's just my pipe, Mom. It relaxes me."

"Don't stay up too late—you need your rest."

Images of my "rest" in the Mushroom Inn sprang to my mind and I answered gently, "I've had enough rest; it's time for me to start living now."

I wanted her to understand that I didn't survive captivity so I could come back and live in a cocoon. Ironic as it sounds, I was a stronger person now than ever before in my life—disease or no disease. I didn't want to hurt her, but sometimes I walked out of the house and took a long stroll, or went to drink beer with Pete and Anne. I had to do some network interviews, and just before I left I held an informal press conference in the backyard with the Maine press because I didn't want to leave them out. I mentioned that Pete and Anne had brought Alaska King Crab—we all joked that Pete and Anne might be ridden out of town on a rail if word got around. Word got around. The next day the lobsters started arriving. Some containers held as many as fifteen lobsters, so of course, we invited as many people as we could find to share them, including a seventy-five-year-old retired school teacher who lived across the street.

The Family Liaison Action Group had been meeting so its members could offer support to one another, and some weeks before I was released, they had planned a meeting in San Francisco. While I was in Georgetown Hospital, they asked me to attend.

I left for this meeting on August fifth, making a stopover for an important chore on the way—getting presents for the hostages wrapped and delivered to the Swiss embassy in Washington. I stayed overnight with the Kryses. The next day Doris Krys and I went shopping, filling carts with puzzles, models, games, and anything else I could think of to pass the time.

"Someone's birthday?" asked the saleslady, curious about the pile I was accumulating on the counter.

"Soon, I hope," I said.

Joe's pipes and tobacco went to his wife to send because I thought my name on the package would be the kiss of death. The rest of the gift would go by pouch to Switzerland and from there to the Swiss embassy in Teheran, which now represented American interests in Iran. Then I flew to San Francisco. It was the first time I'd been west of Fort Riley, Kansas.

All the hotels in San Francisco were having strike problems so the meeting with the families was moved to the airport hotel. The driver who took me there gave me a T-shirt with an American flag on it.

"Aw-right!" said the desk clerk, giving me a clenched fist salute when we checked in. "Welcome back! Welcome to San Francisco! There's champagne and cheese, and a whole bunch of stuff in your room. But if there's anything you want, and I mean *any*thing," he winked, "just give me a call."

August seventh was my twenty-ninth birthday. I celebrated quietly with the families, who gave me a little birthday cake and sang choruses of "Happy Birthday."

On the eighth, the meetings opened officially. About forty-five families came, including almost all who hadn't been in Washington. It is hard for me to describe their incredible hope and anticipation, their desperate need for any bits of information.

They wanted me to sit at their tables for meals. They

asked me to read and interpret their letters. They cornered me in the halls to question me. Many of the marine families told me I would just have to accept all this love and attention because "we've all been through so much together," and I was part of their family now. They felt guilty, because they knew about my MS and that I tired by evening, but they couldn't help themselves. I didn't blame them.

"Richard, Richard, sit here," called Mrs. Lopez, her warm friendly face beaming at me. "So you think my son Jimmy is a good artist?" She had laughed so hard when I told her about Jim's depiction in living color of the Ayatollah on the chancery's walls.

"Jimmy was always a smart boy. Do you know that in high school he won scholarship awards, plus being a great football player? Girls calling him all the time. But he always knew he wanted to be a marine. 'Mom,' he'd say, 'the marines are the best.'" She looked at me and shrugged, "So I knew when they got him he was not going to have an easy time. If they say something bad about America or the marines, I think Jimmy will say something about that crazy man in the robe—then Jimmy gets hurt.

"I pray every night to the Blessed Virgin, 'Don't let Jimmy get mad.'"

"He's doing really fine," I told her. "He was cool as a cucumber when the takeover occurred. No one lost his temper. He gets even with them through his drawings. They have no idea what he's writing in Spanish," I laughed.

Dorothea Morefield had made the trip to San Francisco from Houston and arrived that morning. She was dressed very smartly in a gray silk suit and matching blouse. I told her how attractive she looked.

"Oh, Richard, I haven't thought about things like that in so long." She introduced herself to Mrs. Lopez. "I feel so much better knowing Dick is surrounded by our marines— even if they are all hostages."

I told her about the fatal walk from the compound that Dick, Jim and the rest of us took that day. How we were headed for a few hours of beer and cards when things took a nasty turn. "Dick was so calm, even when the militants were screaming in our faces. He's a real pro."

"I know he is," she said, smiling. "I just want him out of there and home."

John McKeel's parents were eager to hear anything I had to say about their son. "The letters are so erratic," said his mother, anxiously twisting her wedding ring.

"We're not getting the whole picture, Rich," said his father, an older version of John's blond good looks. "What's going on over there?"

I told them that I had seen John frequently, and he was healthy, mentally and physically; "he's exercising and staying in shape. His spirits are good. For a while there I was wearing the pants he left behind when he was moved."

"He never did pick up after himself," his mother said, smiling as she remembered. She turned quickly and put her head on her husband's chest; he held her close.

"She's okay," he said. "This is all just a little rough."

They asked about beatings. During my debriefing, I told the story of the mock-firing squad; that story had leaked to the press. So now I tried to tell the incident as un-dramatically as I could. I told everyone that I had not been beaten.

The thought that their husbands and sons were being tortured or beaten was enough to undermine the strongest wife and mother; and, for the most part, these were strong people who had been through a lot without cracking. I wanted to give them some relief, some hope. They deserved it more than I can say.

It helped them, I think, to see me in the flesh, looking and sounding perfectly normal. They had worried about earlier newspaper stories, interviews with psychiatrists and speculative articles that said we'd all be psychological basket cases when we got out. Unable to adjust to society—maybe even psychotic. Partly this came from earlier rumors, circulated when I was released, that I was a psychological mess and had broken down.

There had been a lot of rumors about me, mostly from the Iranians' despicable press releases that said things like I was sick before I became a hostage and that I was such good friends with the militants I was inviting them all to my wedding.

Now I could stand here—back to my normal weight of 190 pounds—and state that though I had come out with a medical problem, it was a disease that was not contagious, so I hadn't "caught" it there. I had been in perfect health in Teheran, playing softball and volleyball and a lot of other sports until the day I was taken hostage. I could also state that although some of the militants were compassionate and friendly, especially toward the end, clearly no one was coming to my wedding since I didn't have a fiancée or even a regular girl friend. The appreciative laughter was good medicine for us all.

I didn't see much of San Francisco—the meetings went on for four days and we stayed closeted in the hotel—but then it was time to say goodbye to all these desperate, hopeful people and do one final thing for myself.

All through my captivity I had looked at my beautiful

Alaskan poster and fantasized going there. I used to imagine unfettered stretches of wilderness or high mountain slopes and deep forests, or see in my mind's eye the caribou herds that flowed across endless wildflower-covered tundra.

Some of the times I had been most despondent, I had looked at that poster and pictured fish leaping in silvery rivers and eagles wheeling high in the sky, their wild distant screams harsh on my ears. I could see myself hiking, camping, lying out under the stars.

I "escaped" to Alaska so well, I almost forgot that I was lying on a dirty, stained mattress. I forgot the militants, the gunfire, the captivity and thought instead of Mount McKinley and the limitless sky of a cold Alaska night. I remembered Hamid the Liar looking at the poster once and asking me, "Where is that mountain? Do you live there?" I wanted to tell him I was living there almost every day—in my mind; but I was afraid he'd take the poster down if he knew how much it meant to me.

Now I had two more weeks of vacation coming. I knew I needed that time away from everything, really on my own, for renewal and reorganization and I knew where I wanted to spend it.

Tomorrow I was going to Alaska!

Chapter 9

The hotel security guard drove me to the airport. "So how did you like San Francisco?" he asked.

I looked at him and laughed. It suddenly hit me that I had never left the hotel. I had started to once but then remembered I hadn't talked to Charlie Jones's wife, Mattie. I wanted to tell her what an amazing person I thought Charlie was. So I called her on the phone.

"Charlie's tough," she had agreed, "but I want him out of that hellhole now. You can stay tough for only so long."

Now the guard pulled up to the departure area, shook my hand and said, "Wherever you're going, have a great time. Enjoy yourself—you deserve it." As he drove away, a strange sensation swept over me. I was facing the world alone for the first time in a very long while. When I was a hostage, in hotel rooms, at home with my parents, even in San Francisco, everything had been taken care of for me, including travel arrangements. It was embarrassing to feel unsure of myself, but I did. I told myself all I had to do was board the plane; I had the ticket in my hand, and my baggage was checked. You've been waiting for this a long time, I said to myself, but no one's going to lead you on the plane by the hand. Do you need Hamid to put a towel over your head before you can move? This last did the trick. I started forward.

I walked up the ramp, and the disoriented feeling faded. It disappeared when the stewardess, tall, blond and beautiful, came along and smiled at me. She did a double take and returned. "Aren't you Richard Queen?" she asked, sitting down in the empty seat next to me.

At that moment I was certainly glad I could answer yes. We talked for the entire flight, and this time I did get the telephone number. By the time we reached Alaska, being Richard Queen, private (well, almost) citizen, again felt easy to do.

When I arrived in Anchorage, Pete and Anne Brown were there to meet me. There was no formal welcome—no one expected a hostage recently released from Teheran to show up suddenly in Alaska. We exchanged hugs for a long time. I was so happy to see these two very good friends, for a change I was almost speechless with joy. In Anchorage, Pete and Anne and I walked around the city. I was so excited about being in Alaska I just wanted to be able to get my breath and take it all in. Pete and Anne had moved here because they both loved the outdoor life. Pete was also a mountain climber, but he joked that he wasn't ready for Mount McKinley just yet.

Anne worked as a lab technician for an oil company on the North Slope, so the next morning I flew up with her in the company plane to Prudhoe Bay to see the pipeline. How can I express the freedom I felt, gazing out at the vast Alaskan tundra? The eagle on my postcard in the Mushroom Inn and in my heart was finally free to fly. The tundra was alive with pipeline construction as well as the caribou of my fantasies, but somehow it released me to see it.

Pete worked for the National Bank of Alaska, and one of his friends at the bank arranged to take us fishing. We flew to Dillingham, a village on a peninsula heading the Aleutian Island chain, where we landed on a gravel airstrip. We boarded a boat and chugged all day up the Nushagak, a very large river with spectacular scenery, and that night we camped out.

We sat around the crackling fire and I started to thank Pete and Anne again, not only for trying to find me and for giving moral support to my family, but for giving me a picture of hope I could concentrate on—Alaska.

"We were all so worried about you," said Pete, brushing a piece of soot from Anne's face. "But I began to feel a little better when I realized you were smart enough to keep your mind occupied. I suppose now I don't stand a chance of winning 'War Between the States.'"

"At this point," I laughed, "I don't care if I never play it again."

Anne crouched by the fire and turned a log over; she was wearing a red plaid shirt and jeans and looked very pretty and very young to me. "You know, Richard," she said, "until this happened, I didn't really realize what freedom meant. The thought of a good, dear, kind friend of ours being imprisoned just like that . . . Well, it made me so mad. We've all gotten very patriotic. The whole country has; and not in a bad, unthinking sort of way, but more like a family upset because some of its members are being hurt and . . . Oh, you know what I mean." She put down the stick and gave me a hug. "We want you to know you've made us all think about being American; about caring for our country and all the precious freedom we really have."

I couldn't believe that Anne was saying all of this. That what had happened to me and the others had stirred the hearts of everyone, not just our immediate families and our friends. That it was a permanent feeling—not just a front-page item for a few days.

"But why are you surprised?" asked Pete. "The crowds, the letters, all those phone calls?"

"It's just something so overwhelming I guess I don't trust it yet. And I want the others here to see and feel it too. I want it to last for them, not just for me."

"Oh, Richard," Anne replied, "it will, just wait and see."

Here I was at last, doing something I had been dreaming of for months, away from all the hubbub and hurly-burly. But even here, halfway around the world, experiences I had shared with Joe or Bob or snatches of conversation I had had with Don and Charlie popped into my head, and as usual I found myself wondering how they were doing. Then I had to laugh. If I'd thought that I was going to get my mind away even for a few days I was wrong. I was as busy as ever remembering little things to tell the families when I got back. It seemed very important to tell Colonel Scott's wife, Betty, that he liked *The Merchant of Venice* better than *Julius Caesar;* to mention to Regis Ragan's mother that he was the world's best checker player, Hamid the Liar notwithstanding. Then I wanted to call Katherine Keough to let her know I was available for any help with FLAG that was needed.

Before I left the airport at Anchorage, I had called Colonel Scott's home. The Colonel's daughter answered the phone, and then Mrs. Scott, who had been out, came home and got on the line. I told them both that the Iranians had a real respect for Colonel Scott's military bearing. Once a militant was in my room, I recalled, and Colonel Scott walked by on his way to the bathroom. The militant turned to me and said, "Now *that* is a soldier." We talked, too, about Scott's terrific sense of humor. Then, still at the airport, I had called my mother in Maine to tell her to give Pete and Anne's phone number to any of the families who might want to talk to me.

"But Richard," she said, "you've already told us that. We'll be sure to put them in touch with you. Now just relax and have a good time." There was a slight pause and then, "Richard, if it's really cold up there maybe you should buy yourself another sweater."

"Mom," I said, "you promised."

"You're right," she agreed, laughing. "But it's abnormal for me not to worry when I've been practicing all these years."

The next day we kept on up the river, stopping only to fish. I caught some grayling, which look like trout, and some pike. It was very cold even with sweaters (my mother, it turned out, was right—I should have picked up an extra one) and jackets, so we went ashore to an island and built another campfire.

We slept in sleeping bags, and the next morning I got up before the others. When I walked down to the water I really did smile, for here was my Alaskan fantasy. Fish *were* leaping all around me in the sparkling water, sunlight glanced gold off the rocks and trees, and the sky was just as blue as in my poster. I simply stood there for a few minutes, taking it all in; my country was so beautiful and big and clean and, well, just wonderful. I wanted so much not to be the only one enjoying this and prayed with all my heart that the rest would be out soon. That's all I wanted now. Then I waded into the water and hooked a beautiful silver salmon that battled me for twenty minutes before I got it ashore. A good omen, I thought, and one more thing I can tick off my list about coming home.

That night the weather got rough and windy, and we moved down river to a friend's summer cabin to ride out the storm. We were talking and yelling so loudly to be heard above the gale—the worst to hit Alaska in decades— that I almost expected to hear someone say, "No speak. No speak." Two words that seemed to be ingrained in my head. More talking, more sleeping and eating. The clean, fresh air driving out most of the goblins of Mushroom and the militants from my dreams. There was no point, if I could help it, ruining my freedom by dreaming about captivity. I would not allow what had happened or what had happened to me to mar the joy and happiness of coming home. Wilderness solitude is not really silence. Not the oppressive silence I knew as a hostage. To me it's a kind of alive, restorative force that I need periodically to touch, to hear my own voice more clearly. Somehow I could find out how I really feel, who I really am, what my condition really is, in this lovely, breathtaking silence. On this beautiful river my mind and my body gained a strength I had needed, and I realized that when I left

Alaska I would be ready to go back to work. I left a week later, stopping overnight at Ann Arbor. I knew I was indulging in nostalgia but it was an exercise I had to complete. Most of my daydreaming as a hostage revolved around my school days. In a way the memory of my good friends and those happy days helped me keep faith in captivity with what looked like a very shaky future.

I wanted to visit with my friends and say in person, thank you for being my friend, thank you for not forgetting about me. In Ann Arbor, I visited friends from graduate school. We did nothing special, visited bookstores, drank beer in the pub, visited some of my old professors—but oh, how special it was to me. In Ann Arbor I had friends everywhere I went. It became impossible to pay for a drink or a meal, taxicab drivers would shut the meter off when I got in the cab, and people were constantly shaking my hand or patting me on the back. I felt then as I do now, that the love and generosity shown to me by American "strangers" more than made up for anything I went through.

Before I left Ann Arbor I was approached by a naturalized Iranian who wanted to apologize on behalf of his former country. He said what had happened was "barbaric"; that his pain was very great because for the first time he was ashamed to say what his heritage was. "I pray daily for their release. Like you I will not be free until they all come back—alive," he said.

I left Ann Arbor and headed for Washington and the State Department.

When I reported for work, my first task was filling out an array of forms that officially transferred me from Teheran to Washington. I had volunteered to do my two-week army reserve duty and was assigned to the Pentagon. The army wanted recommendations on treating their six people still held in Iran, so I wrote up a report on my experiences in Wiesbaden and suggested some changes. (Just minor things like having their driver's licenses, their passports and identification papers ready for them—all the vital papers that were confiscated when we were taken hostage.)

The following week I was debriefed by the Defense Intelligence Agency. I found an apartment in Arlington, just across the Potomac river, and checked in with the doctor. I was concerned about what they would tell me: would I be able to work long hours, full steam ahead? Would my disease interfere with my work? I realized that I was asking myself the same questions over and over. Would I be able to work? I could walk reasonably well now, but I had problems with balance if I walked fast. My left hand was still numb but that only affected more delicate tasks, and I tended to use my right hand for those anyway.

The doctor was reassuring. He said I didn't need any medicine or special treatments and there was nothing to worry about so long as my symptoms stayed stabilized. I would be well enough to go on with my career as a Foreign Service officer. I felt so grateful I would not be prevented from working in my chosen career. That's all I needed to hear. It didn't matter to me that I had MS as long as I could stay in the Foreign Service. This meant everything to me. The events of the past year only increased my desire to serve my country in any way I could. "Thank you, doctor," I said, overcome. "Thank you."

I was assigned as junior Iran analyst in the Bureau of Intelligence and Research. The job was checking out raw data coming into the State Department about Iran and trying to piece it together into some kind of coherent picture of what was happening there. The reports had a special meaning for me, now that I was on the other side of the hostage crisis. The work was fascinating and demanding, but almost immediately I developed a worrisome problem—I'd get incredibly drowsy. By two o'clock in the afternoon I could barely keep my eyes open, and by five I could just about make it to my apartment. I decided not to panic and think my disease was affecting me this way, but I couldn't figure it out. I didn't say anything to anyone. I just kept going to work and going home, feeling exhausted and crashing in bed. As the days went by, the fatigue slowly lessened, and I realized what the problem was: I wasn't used to a sustained work period after so many months of enforced rest.

And more work was piling up. Letters were still streaming into the State Department as well as to my parents' home in Maine, and although I answered as many as I could, the numbers were overwhelming. My parents and friends helped, but we never seemed to catch up.

The packages addressed to me arrived daily; cans of peaches with yellow ribbons on the label, a certificate for a lifetime of free pizzas, movies, tune-ups, hair styling, spa membership, dance lessons, scuba lessons, roller-skating lessons, French lessons; even a free chance at a computer that would match me up with ten to twenty women just perfect for me.

Letters and pictures from grade school children crayoned to the nth degree arrived in cartons every day. One little boy drew a picture of the American flag with fifty-two hostages' faces where the stars should have been. He said his name was Richard, too, but his friends called him "Ritchie" and would I mind if he called me Ritchie.

Ritchie expressed the hope that the "Uraniums" wouldn't come over to this country and get me while I was sleeping. I shared Ritchie's hopes.

Then there were the things we were sending to Iran. Bruce Laingen, Victor Tomseth and Michael Howland, who were held in the Foreign Ministry, wrote several times to say that they were working hard to get the packages through. Sometimes I would leave my name in, other times not. I don't think—at this point—it really made much difference. The militants, as whimsical as ever, did not make these decisions in a very straightforward way.

I still had not accepted the fact that I was recognized almost everywhere I went. I was always appreciative because I realized I represented more than just myself—I was a symbol of all the hostages; in a way I was a symbol for those who wanted to express their new-found patriotism. But it took me a while to get used to it because I felt I had not done anything special. In a way, I wanted to tell everyone to please wait until the others returned so we could all appreciate the love and warmth together. I was in constant touch with the hostage families and heard over and over again from them how important it was for me to keep in the public eye so people could have a way of displaying a sincere emotional tie to the hostage issue.

How I wished so many times that I could call Joe Hall and the others and say, "Just wait until you get home and see what America has waiting for you. Please hang on because the good is coming."

I talked to one of the thirteen who had been released earlier. He said he had gone through some of the same feelings I had of guilt and loneliness. The close ties still bound him to those in Teheran as they did me. We both had this feeling—we won't be free until the rest come home. In the meantime my first concern, outside of my job, were the families. Talking to them, exchanging views, remembering what I could to tell them about their husbands and sons. I think we gave each other a strength that may have been passed on through letters to the ones in Iran.

I prayed daily that their families would stay strong and healthy; that no one would crack on this end. That was the thing that could break anyone in captivity—the thought that their families were in trouble—because there was absolutely nothing they could do about it. I know all the letters the wives and parents wrote were affirming ones. They were certainly a smart, loving bunch of people. There was no way any depressing information would be sent to their husbands and sons and daughters.

In addition to people wanting to express good wishes and shake my hand, there were those who needed to express something else: their hatred for Iran. A lot of it was directed at Khomeini, of course. You couldn't ask for anyone who *looked* more like a villain. His dark, unsmiling expression, that piercing demonic gaze, made his obsession with the satanic evil of United States ways very ironic. If Hollywood ever created such a figure, people would have said he was a cardboard character, but a lot of the hatred for him unquestionably spilled out into hatred for all Iran, which I felt was very unfortunate.

I thought when Iraq invaded Iran in September it might break the hostage logjam. It was pointless now for Iran to continue holding hostages when it brought her so little in return. No other nation was condemning Iraq for her aggression, and Iran was unable to get spare parts for her arms. I also thought that the militants themselves—at least those who did believe in the revolution—would not view guarding hostages as the best way to serve while their country was at war. It was very possible that the militants might be ready to give up the hostages to the Iranian government at this point. I had my own prejudices and feelings, too. It was hard especially to come back and find the Iranians protesting in the streets. I wanted to run out and yell, "Hypocrites! Why are you here instead of following your fourteenth-century Ayatollah?" Then later I wondered why they were still here when their country was at war. Why weren't they fighting instead of living in the "satanic" United States? The answer was obvious to everyone: they were here because this was where freedom was, and they knew it. We had one great reason to feel proud as Americans. Despite all our emotions, America kept to its laws. Even those demonstrating Iranians who were spitting on the United States were allowed to remain here and receive the benefits of our constitutionally guaranteed free speech. Ours was a more mature patriotism. A lesser benefit of the war was that it eventually shut up the Iranian demonstrators and proved them to be frauds. They protested for their country until she really needed them. Then they stopped protesting and refused to go back to fight. So many times I thought of those long lines at our nonimmigrant visa windows: all the people trying to come to America—still the land of the free and the home of the brave, and they knew it.

The crisis stayed constantly on my mind. I dealt with it in my job, during the regular family meetings arranged by the State Department, and when I visited the hostage families who lived in the Washington area. We all felt some satisfaction in seeing the Khomeini regime in the victim role, even though I had no bitter feelings toward the Iranian people or the nondemonstrating Iranians in the United States. Some Iranians here seemed to expect bitterness from me. They would avoid looking me in the face, or they would say how sorry they were that all this happened and I should not blame their country. Others would shout in Farsi, "Down with Khomeini!" By and large, I guess it did make them feel guilty.

We discussed the effect the Iraq war would have on the hostage release constantly.

"I just feel this war is going to help them," said one of the wives at a FLAG meeting. "It just has to . . ."

"But the problem," said another, "is that the Iranians are not going to have time to discuss the hostage issue. They have to use what little brainpower they have to fight Iraq."

"Maybe they'll wake up and realize that what little support they might have received is all being blown away by what they've done to our embassy people."

"I'd like to blow away that madman Khomeini—human life is just, is just . . . cowflop to him."

"Cowflop?" we all exclaimed at once. The laughter that followed helped break the tension, the constant wondering and rehashing, with very little resolved.

But as the war dragged on and the hostages were not released, my life remained involved with crisis-related activities. I had increasing responsibilities in my job, I was giving interviews arranged by the State Department press office, and my evenings were filled with answering mail and speaking engagements. In many ways my public speaking interfered with my new job, and I'd have to catch up on my work on the weekends. Then on Monday it would begin again; continuous reading and writing. It was fascinating work, and we were given a lot of latitude as long as we produced.

The result was that I was so close to the hostage issue at work and in my "spare time" that I rarely thought of anything else; I became totally with them in spirit, if not in person.

In October I went to a reunion at my college, Hamilton, in upstate New York; it was my final fantasy trip. The college is small but the campus is large, sitting on top of a tree-covered hill, with rolling farmland all around. A winding road, occasionally dotted with large, gingerbread Victorian houses, links the campus to the town of Clinton, below. Its old stone buildings circle around a shaded quadrangle; the grounds are peaceful and simple, much like the pocket of upstate New York in which they lie.

I flew up on a Friday afternoon and stayed at a professor's house. I took a walk around the campus, and suddenly my captivity, the ambassador's residence, the Mushroom, the chancery, came flooding back to my mind. I had thought about Hamilton so much—the friends, the water fights, the silly things college kids do—or used to do. Hamilton seemed to me like something off a Norman Rockwell *Saturday Evening Post* cover when I thought about it in Teheran. Now, looking at it, I realized my daydreams had not been exaggerated; it did look like a Norman Rockwell painting—sincere, poignant and very, very strong. Enduring.

On Sunday I spoke at the chapel, a white clapboard building in the center of the campus. It was packed. I felt strange standing at the podium rather than sitting in a pew, but it was a fantastic experience. Somehow it all seemed to connect; my college years, the strength remembering them had given me throughout my captivity, and the love and welcome I was receiving now.

After the service, many of the students wanted to talk to me to ask what it was like being a hostage. I was answering as best I could—always aware that the others were still captive and my remarks needed to be guarded. One girl, tall and thin, who carried herself like a model, wanted to know if I thought Hamilton College really prepared me for the real world—or did my years here just make the real world harder to take.

"Well," I said, trying to give her an honest answer, "I certainly don't think a prison in Iran is the real world. Not the world I want to adapt to permanently anyway. Hamilton prepared me for a good world—a world of literature, music, art; it also emphasized the importance of values. It's important to develop these values before you get 'taken hostage.' It is important to know yourself, to be able to be alone with your thoughts and to be able to laugh at yourself—even when someone gives you the worst looking haircut in the world. Hamilton and what I learned here helped me survive in Teheran."

After the Sunday talk, I was ready to let go. I talked with a number of professors, but not many students from my class were there, and, of course, I was no longer there either. I couldn't turn back the clock—and I didn't want to. It was time to move on. I went to the college store and bought all the things I had had to leave in Teheran—class mugs and a shirt. The thought crossed my mind that somewhere in that city was a militant running around in my Hamilton College shirt probably shouting, "Death to the Carter." I left that day for Washington.

In late October the left half of my face, including my tongue, started to grow numb, and for a while I lost my sense of taste. One of my doctors suspected the autumn weather had caused it. Washington had just begun to turn cold, and the doctor said that weather changes sometimes affect people with multiple sclerosis. The numbness eventually let up a little but never actually went away. I was able to ignore it after a while. I no longer had a fear of getting really ill, mainly because I was back in civilization again and not far from some of the best doctors in the world.

I did make some changes, though, based on common sense decisions. My apartment in Arlington was too far from the State Department; if I moved closer I could avoid a daily commute to work and walk instead. I found a little unfurnished efficiency just a few blocks away, with lots of sunlight pouring through big windows. After all those months in the Mushroom, sunlight had become very important to me. I suspect it always will be.

I bought a new bed, a desk, a dining room set, a side table and a nice rug, and it looked very cozy when I finished. I didn't mind how small it was as long as it had all that sunlight. Being right in the center of Washington, too, boosted my spirits. I can't describe the feeling I had when I spent the first night in my apartment—a free person living as I chose to live. No chanting mobs outside my window, no stained mattress on the floor. Why, I could get up and walk around at 2 A.M. if I wanted to. I could have two cups of tea instead of one; I could go to the bathroom all night if that's what I wanted to do. Freedom, still so precious to me, made life wonderful.

Better yet, my balance was improving. By Christmas it

was almost perfect, and I was ecstatic that I could run again. I knew the remission could end at any time and that each attack could be more serious than the last, but living day to day seemed the best way to handle multiple sclerosis.

At Christmas I went up to Maine and waited for the televised services from Iran. It was a very empty feeling to be sitting at home watching while the others were still held hostage. Last year I had been there doing exactly the same thing they were doing now.

I recognized Joe Hall immediately; he looked thinner, and the lines around his mouth appeared more deeply etched. And, of course, I'll never forget Kate Koob singing her mournful Christmas song to her family. I couldn't contain my emotion any longer, and I cried for them and, I guess, for me as well. It moved all of us who were watching it. Nobody said a thing, but we could feel the compassion we were all sharing for Kate and the others there. My father put his hand on my shoulder. "It's rough," he said, his voice breaking, "but they're going to make it. They'll be coming home soon." Almost the same words I had spoken so many times to the families. Let them be true soon, I prayed.

I imagined this scene was being repeated in almost every home in America—an entire country focused on fifty-two individuals and what their future held. I knew that most Americans were feeling blind hatred for the Iranians and the militants. We certainly were. You could have cut our hatred with a knife. "The American people are not going to take much more of this," said my father. "The Iranians would be well advised to get the hostage issue off their hands while they still can."

I was sure the militants expected these films to ease the fears and worries in the United States, which was just another indication of their total misunderstanding of America.

In the past our family had given out our presents after the Christmas Eve service at the church, but this time we waited until the morning. There was just no enthusiasm. We were happy to be together, but the ordeal wasn't over yet.

When I returned to Washington, I couldn't help noticing that the televised Christmas service had stirred Americans' hatred for Iran even further. Bumper stickers that said "Nuke Iran" and "Ayatollah Assa hola" proliferated. I agreed wholeheartedly with the sentiments of the last one. More and more, people would call me, write to me, talk to me on the streets and even approach me in restaurants.

The theme expressed over and over was one of acute frustration. "We've got to get them out now." "Not another Christmas, not another day." One letter I received summed it up for me. It was from a grandmother in Oregon, Joe Hall's home state.

Dear Richard Queen,

I know you are working at the State Department, and I would appreciate it if you could tell them a few things for me.

I am going to be eighty-eight on February 20th so you can imagine I've seen a lot in my lifetime—good and bad. Both my boys fought in World War II and my grandson was in Vietnam. There were many Christmases that were just too sad to celebrate. This

Christmas I sat with my great grandson and watched the hostages have their Christmas. My great grandson wanted to know why they couldn't come home—they don't look very happy, he said. I tried to tell him why they were there but I don't think I did a very good job.

He wanted to know why we didn't "go get them away from the bad men." How, I asked him, should we do this? Well, he said, if all of us go then it will be easy. I think my great grandson is right. We all want our people back and if we have to go over and get them to do it, then I'm ready. Maybe if those Iranians knew how an old lady and a little boy feel, they'd realize a whole lot of people in between feel the same way.

I believe strongly in good manners and giving the other fellow the benefit of the doubt, but don't you think we've been polite long enough?

Toward mid-January there seemed to be a ray of light coming through the wall around the hostages; news of release was getting stronger. It was different this time from the flurry of activity that led most Americans to hope release was imminent in November. Then Iran's internal politics were so chaotic that no one group had the power to make the hostage release decision; until that happened, the militants would hang onto their prize. Now it looked as if even the fundamentalists were in favor of release. In fact, Ayatollah Khoeini, the students' mentor had come around to that position as well.

I was following it all very carefully, of course, and my access to material that was not being made public helped. I wasn't sure what was going to happen though; there had been too many ups and downs already, but this time it looked better than before. In fact, it looked so good that none of us—families or friends—dared to talk about it. It was better to treat each new development on a one-day-at-a-time basis. As inauguration day drew closer, the rumors really began to fly. The person to watch was Sheldon Krys.

Sheldon had become like my second father. He made sure that my reentry into the civilized world went as smoothly as possible. Whatever it took to make me comfortable and at ease, he managed to do. Both he and Doris Krys insisted that I consider their beautiful Potomac, Maryland, home my own; I spent many wonderful weekends there away from the hubbub and turmoil of Washington, DC, enjoying the Kryses' hospitality. I watched as he worked tirelessly for the hostages and their families. He knew each one of us by first, middle and last names; could recite all our bios; and identify us all just by looking at a small newspaper photo. To me, he will always be one of the unsung heroes of the crisis.

In November, unbeknownst to the press, Sheldon Krys left for Wiesbaden.

This was the most important sign so far, I thought. Still I tempered my rising hopes with the knowledge that the Iranians were experts at bargaining. This could be still another ploy to get the "buyer" eager to pay the "seller's" full price. This time the "bazaar" had been set up on a grand scale—I only hoped we had better bargainers on our side than I.

Several months earlier, I had agreed to do a special with Walter Cronkite at CBS when the hostages got out. By that time, I had stopped giving interviews. They were too tiring, and they always gave me a horrible fear that I was going to say something that would hurt the negotiations. On the morning of January 19, the shrill insistent ring of my telephone woke me up. It was CBS. "It looks like today's the day. Can you come up?"

"Yes," I said. I dressed immediately, my heart pounding. Please, dear God, let them all get out. Let them be alright. I threw some clothes in a bag and went downstairs to the lobby to call for a cab. Waiting for me, TV cameras ready, microphones in hand, were about thirty people from all the networks.

"Oh, no," I said, out loud. "Not now."

"Looks like they're waiting for you." I turned around and saw Jerry, a boy in his late teens who picked up and delivered dry cleaning to the building.

"I've got to get to the airport," I said, "but I don't want to go out there."

"Follow me. We'll go down through the laundry room, and I'll back my van up to the delivery entrance. You can walk right into it without anyone seeing you."

"Great," I said, and we took off down the steps to the basement. I watched through the window as he backed up the van, and then I opened the door and got in.

"To the airport, right?" he asked, driving out into the street.

"I need to get to the airport, but if you get me to a cab . . ."

"Are you kidding? This is the best part." He stepped on the gas, and we took off like a shot. It was amazing how fast that van could go. I laughed to myself—Teheran traffic, Zurich traffic and now a maniacal ride through

Washington traffic. I seemed to be doing a lot of this.

Jerry made it to National Airport without anyone spotting me. If they had, I'm sure I would have looked like a big blur. I caught the next shuttle to New York.

I had gotten leave from the State Department to go to New York City both for the CBS broadcast and to attend a special Mass that Cardinal Cooke was saying at St. Patrick's Cathedral for the return of the hostages. I was planning to stay with my aunt and uncle while I was in the city. On my way up the steps of the cathedral, I was stopped by Randy Daniels of CBS, who hurried up and asked, "What do you think of the news?"

"What news?"

"The agreement to release the hostages."

I was thrilled. I went to the Mass, then rushed over to CBS for the broadcast.

At CBS, I paced up and down the studio. Nothing had happened so far. An agreement had been announced, but the hostages were not released. Damn those bastards, I thought, they're deliberately denying Carter his victory. In order to be closer to the studio I spent the night in a hotel room near CBS. Unable to sleep, I spent hours trying to outguess the Iranians, trying to visualize, almost will, the event I had been waiting for so long.

The next morning, January 20, I walked to the studio. I was very tired and tense. We all sat drinking coffee, waiting for word to come through. At 12:23 we had the word. *"The planes are out of Iran air,"* shouted a staffer from the newsroom. The studio went wild, people hugging, yelling, crying. I bowed my head and prayed: "Let them all be on that plane. Let them be alright."

I watched as the plane touched down in Algiers. This

was the moment I had been waiting and praying for. I was so afraid, now that it was here. The doors of the plane opened and we watched. And watched. Nothing. Then, finally, they began to file off. It was overwhelming.

My job for CBS was to identify each hostage and fill in with some background on each one. I began naming them as they got off: Bruce Laingen, Steve Lauterbach, Gary Lee, Fred Kupke, Kathryn Koob, Steve Kirtley, Bill Keough. My heart felt so full. They all looked great—a little tired and confused but great. Malcolm Kalp, Charlie Jones, Mike Howland, Leland Holland, Don Hohman, Kevin Hermening, Joe Hall, John Graves, Al Golacinski, Duane Gillette, William Gallegos, Robert Engelmann, William Daugherty, Don Cooke, Robert Blucker, William Belk, Corty Barnes, Tom Ahern, Mike Kennedy, Bruce German, Paul E. Lewis, John Limbert, Jim Lopez, John McKeel, Michael Metrinko, Jerry Miele, Mike Moeller, Bert Moore, Dick Morefield, Paul Needham, Robert Ode, Gregory Persinger, Jerry Plotkin, Regis Ragan, David Roeder, Barry Rosen, William Royer, Thomas Schaefer, Charles Scott, Don Sharer, Rodney Sickmann, Joe Subic, Ann Swift, Vic Tomseth, Phillip Ward.

I know my eyes were shining when I finished identifying all of them, but I didn't care. I think all of America was crying with joy, too.

"It's over, the nightmare is over," I said. "They're home free." My friends—my brothers and sisters had come back.

Someone opened a bottle of champagne, then another. It was New Year's Eve, Christmas, Thanksgiving and everyone's birthday all at once. I drank my champagne and laughed a lot. I knew now that I could go back to being completely normal again, to living a normal, everyday life.

I returned to Washington on the twenty-first of January. The city had been transformed into a yellow-ribboned fantasy land. Yellow banners hung everywhere, staid government buildings were festooned from top to bottom; ribbons were tied around construction equipment and trucks. Burly truck drivers sported the yellow badges on their T-shirts; women had them in their hair or pinned to their pocketbooks; babies oblivious to the whole thing slept in yellow-ribboned carriages. Even dogs and cats got the yellow ribbon treatment.

People would come up to me, tears streaming down their faces to say, "God bless," "Congratulations," or just, "Yahoo, they're home." I just walked around like the Alfred E. Neuman character in *Mad* magazine, with a perpetual ear-to-ear grin on my face. Life was suddenly, totally wonderful, with no reservations.

I decided not to go to Wiesbaden. Some of the families had asked me to, but I thought it better to wait until the ex-hostages arrived in Washington. Now that I knew they were truly free, I could wait without worrying.

That evening my phone rang and I picked it up to hear, "Hey, Sheboygan, how's it goin'?"

"Joe? Joe Hall? Are you in Wiesbaden?" I asked inanely.

He laughed, "I sure as hell ain't having tea and barbari bread in the Ayatollah's parlor."

He knew via Cherlynn and *Sporting News* that I had been released and also had heard that I had multiple sclerosis. He told me that Don Hohman was very relieved when he found out about me because he thought I was a dead man. Since we had separated, Joe had been moved all over Iran as the militants tried to keep the hiding places a secret.

"It got very grim," he said, quietly. "I think they were

afraid we'd be rescued, so they stuck us in every dump they could find. We knew they were at war with Iraq and were sort of losing interest in us. Akbar especially just wanted to send us home so he could go kill the Iraqis."

He told me that the pipes I sent him were waiting for him in Wiesbaden but he never got the other stuff.

"I began to think those jokers were holding us just so they'd keep getting all those good presents the Americans were sending. When I last saw Weasel he had on a T-shirt that said, 'Divers do it deeper,' so I knew I was right."

I knew that some of the militants had used the publicity from the embassy takeover to get cushy jobs in the Iranian government, but a few among them went off to fight. A good many of these were killed, including Akbar.

Joe and I talked for a long time, and then Joe said goodbye. I almost didn't say anything. It was all too much for words. That night I had the best sleep since coming home. It was as if an incredible weight was lifting slowly but surely from my heart and mind.

When the group flew to West Point, they were still pretty much incommunicado. Finally the day arrived.

I woke up in the morning to see the sun pouring in my window almost as if it were heralding the day's wonderful news. All fifty-two Americans were going to land at Andrews Air Force Base. The State Department had arranged for all the families to be taken by bus to the base—nine buses in all—and I went with them. On the trip to Andrews we could see the crowds forming, banners already waving, homemade and professionally printed signs proclaiming America's euphoria. "Welcome Home, Welcome Home," they said. We pulled into the airport and saw a huge crowd of orderly people waiting for the plane.

If anyone wanted a good idea of what Americans looked like, a perfect picture was here for the taking. There were businessmen in three-piece suits, carrying their attaché cases; dressed-for-success women in similar suits with similar attaché cases; preppie-outfitted teenagers hopping up and down on Bass-loafered feet; young couples holding babies in one arm while trying to control toddlers with the other; old people, small and frail in the crowd but with a happy look on their faces; black teenagers with huge stereo radios playing full blast, dancing with one another and laughing, freedom-filled laughs; youths in long hair and torn jeans tapping sandaled feet to the music.

And still the crowds grew. Blacks, whites, Vietnamese, Chinese, Japanese, Spanish, Polish, Italian, Protestants, Catholics, Jews, rednecks, blue-collar workers—all held signs proclaiming their identity and their allegiance.

ITALIAN-AMERICANS WELCOME YOU HOME
TO THE GREATEST COUNTRY IN THE WORLD

That sign struck such a positive note that our whole bus cheered when we read it. We got off the bus and walked into the tarmac to wait for the planes. Suddenly the crowd cheered—a sound I will never forget—a cheer that finally erased the memory of those crowds chanting maniacally outside the chancery windows, "Death to the Carter," "Death to the spies." They had spotted the first plane, barely visible in the distance. After an eternity passed, it landed and taxied up. Then everybody started pushing toward the plane.

The first one off was Bruce Laingen, his boyish face beaming with triumph and happiness, then the two women came out. The excitement was incredible, people were hugging and crying. Joe Hall spotted me on the tarmac and waved, "I'm home? Richard, am I really home?" I hugged him and Cherlynn and we grinned. We were both remembering the same thing: when we were back at the chancery and pretended to introduce ourselves. I stuck out my hand now. "Allow me to introduce myself," I said. "A slight oversight these many months." He made a formal bow. "Likewise I'm sure—Joe Hall here."

One after the other the fifty-three of us and our families came out. We all got back on the buses. The ride back to Washington was the most incredible experience in my life. Starting from Andrews Air Force Base, the crowds were lining the roads and waving flags and shouting. People were standing on the roofs of their cars giving us the V-sign, the clenched fist salute; others were honking their horns and throwing confetti. We passed fire trucks. Some of the ladder companies had their ladders up and people were standing on them.

Sanitation workers raised their brooms in salute as we passed. Our spirits and the spirit of the crowd joined in one overwhelming feeling—we were all crackling with love and exhilaration. As we crossed the bridge, fire boats let loose a spray of water that arced a salute; sailboats, power boats, barges formed a flotilla of well-wishers; motorcyclists in black leather jackets, their motorcycles decorated with red, white and blue streamers, held up their fists as we passed. Everyone in America, it seemed, was there that day. I hung out of the bus as far as I dared and waved until I thought my arm would fall off—a price I would have been happy to pay.

All over, everywhere the bus went, there was just a mob of people, shouting and cheering and waving flags. In the bus, too, people were doing the same. It was so spontaneous and enthusiastic. I came out with the feeling, my God, what more can I see of life? This is the culmination. You really had this enormous pride in the United States that day. You could feel the country was a unified nation again.

I looked out over the sea of faces at all the smiles. My God, what a good-looking bunch of people, I thought, and my heart filled with pride to see them all. They stood so tall and straight that day. And I knew we were all what we had always been—the people with the biggest hearts in the whole world.

"Oh, man," said Charlie Jones, his voice cracking with emotion, "this is just . . ." He didn't finish his sentence. He didn't have to. We all felt the same way.

"What a country," someone on the bus yelled. "Just look out there. Nobody's ever going to beat that. Not the Iranians, the Russians or the Martians."

The bus made its way slowly through the celebrating crowds and turned up Pennsylvania Avenue through the White House gates. So much had happened to all of us that it was hard to realize we were here—at the White House, to meet the new President of our country and his wife. Just as President Carter had greeted me warmly and sincerely, President Reagan did the same. His face radiated joy as he greeted us as a group, then talked a few minutes with each of us.

Late that afternoon we boarded the buses again for a welcome-home party at the Crystal City Marriott. I was exhausted, but I was at peace. I could finally say, unequivocally now, that I was free. Richard Queen was no longer a hostage.

For the rest of my life I will be able to replay that glorious ride from Andrews to the White House, happy that the role the other hostages and I played in this drama served to unite the country as it has not been united in a long time. What happened to me, at least—what I went through in Iran and the disease I developed there—was more than worth it for me to see how much this crisis helped America by renewing our pride and national spirit. This unity, and the overwhelming love we felt, gave meaning to what happened to us. For this I will be forever grateful.